Dangerous Alliances

Dangerous Alliances

Proponents of Peace,
Weapons of War

PATRICIA A. WEITSMAN

Stanford University Press
Stanford, California

Stanford University Press
Stanford, California
© 2004 by the Board of Trustees of the
Leland Stanford Junior University.

Printed in the United States of America
On acid-free, archival-quality paper

Library of Congress Cataloging-in-Publication Data

Weitsman, Patricia A.
  Dangerous alliances : proponents of peace, weapons of war / Patricia A. Weitsman.
       p.   cm.
Includes bibliographical references and index.
ISBN 0-8047-4866-7 (alk. paper)
    1. Alliances.   2. World politics—19th century.   3. Balance of power.
4. World politics—20th century.   5. International relations.   6. Diplomacy.
7. Europe—Politics and government—19th century.   8. Europe—Politics and
government—20th century.   9. World War, 1914–1918—Diplomatic history.
I. Title.
D397.W35 2004
327.1′16—dc21

                                                                    2003013394

Typeset by G&S Typesetters in 10.5/12.5 Bembo

Original Printing 2004
Last figure below indicates year of this printing:
13   12   11   10   09   08   07   06   05   04

For David

Contents

List of Figures and Tables *ix*

Acknowledgments *xi*

1. Introduction *1*

2. Theory of Alliance Formation and Cohesion *11*

3. The Two Leagues of the Three Emperors *39*

4. The Dual and Triple Alliances *65*

5. The Franco-Russian Alliance and the Triple Entente *99*

6. Alliances and the Great War: The Central Powers and the Triple Entente *137*

7. Conclusion *165*

Appendix. Great Power Capabilities and Proximity Data *179*

Notes *187*

Bibliography *217*

Index *235*

Figures and Tables

Figure 2.1 Curvilinear Relationship between Threat and Propensity
to Ally   20

Table 2.1 Threats and Cohesion   26

Table 2.2 Possible Dyadic Alliance Motivations under Conditions
of Threat   29

Table 3.1 Member States' Motivations for Joining the Three Emperors'
League, 1873   45

Table 3.2 Threat to Member States of the Three Emperors' League,
1873–78   47

Table 3.3 Member States' Motivations for Joining the Three Emperors'
League, 1881   57

Table 3.4 Threat to Member States of the Three Emperors' League,
1881–87   59

Table 3.5 Chapter Summary: Alliances, Threat, and Cohesion   63

Table 4.1 Member States' Motivations for Joining the Dual Alliance,
1879   74

Table 4.2 Threats to Member States of the Dual Alliance, 1879   76

Table 4.3 Member States' Motivations for Joining the Triple Alliance,
1882   87

Table 4.4 Threats to Member States of the Triple Alliance, 1882   91

Table 4.5 Chapter Summary: Alliances, Threat, and Cohesion   97

Table 5.1 Member States' Motivations for Joining the Franco-Russian
Alliance, 1891/94   111

Table 5.2 Threats to Member States of the Franco-Russian Alliance,
1891/94   114

Table 5.3 Member States' Motivations for Joining the Entente Cordiale, 1904   *124*

Table 5.4 Member States' Motivations for Joining the Anglo-Russian Convention, 1907   *130*

Table 5.5 Threats to Member States of the Triple Entente, 1904/7–14   *132*

Table 5.6 Chapter Summary: Alliances, Threat, and Cohesion   *135*

Table 7.1 Summary of Findings: Threat and Alliance Characteristics   *167*

Acknowledgments

I AM GRATEFUL to a number of institutions and individuals for their indispensable support in seeing this project through to fruition. I would first like to express my eternal appreciation to my mentors at Columbia University, especially David A. Baldwin and Warner R. Schilling. Support at the Graduate Institute for International Studies (IUHEI) in Geneva, Switzerland, enabled me to begin the process of developing the argument contained within these pages. I am especially grateful to David Sylvan and Urs Luterbacher at the IUHEI for their support and hospitality. I would also like to express my gratitude to Allen Lynch and the Albert Gallatin Foundation for presenting me with the initial opportunity to do research and study at the IUHEI. Tom Henrikson at the Hoover Institution, Stanford University, deserves thanks for providing the ideal environment for me to complete the manuscript.

I appreciate the feedback I received while presenting portions of the book at the Center for International Affairs, Harvard University; the Mershon Center, Ohio State University; and the Hoover Institution, Stanford University. My thanks to Celeste Wallander and Robert Keohane formerly of Harvard University, Brian Pollins and Donald Sylvan at Ohio State University, and Larry Diamond at Stanford University for arranging those talks. I am also grateful to Frank Cass Publishers and *Security Studies* for allowing me to reuse portions of my articles, "Intimate Enemies: The Politics of Peacetime Alliances," 7, no. 1 (autumn 1997), and "Alliance Cohesion and Coalition Warfare: The Central Powers and Triple Entente," 12, no. 3 (spring 2003).

I am deeply grateful to my home institution, Ohio University, for supporting the research for the book in a multitude of ways: a Baker Award and two International Travel Fund awards funded the archival research at the Archives du Ministère des Affaires Étrangères, Paris; the Public Record Office in London; and the Archivio Storico Diplomatico del Ministero degli Affari Esteri, in Rome. The Dean of the College of Arts and Sciences, Leslie

Flemming, and the Chair of the Department of Political Science, Michael Mumper, have been tremendous throughout the process of completing this project. It is hard to express how much I appreciate the myriad ways they facilitated the research and writing of this book.

I am fortunate to have close friends and colleagues who engaged in numerous conversations regarding the book as it unfolded over the years and who have read various versions and portions of the manuscript. I am especially grateful to J. Samuel Barkin and George E. Shambaugh for their unwavering friendship and their excellent feedback. I would also like to thank Alessandro Brogi, Victor Cha, Lisa Conant, Maria Fanis, Ted Hopf, Ed Mansfield, Jay Parker, Susan Peterson, Tom Schaller, Susan Varisco, and Michael Young for their support and guidance, as well as my colleagues in the Department of Political Science at Ohio University, particularly DeLysa Burnier, Ron Hunt, Judith Miller, Harold Molineu, Sung Ho Kim, Takaaki Suzuki, and Julie White. Susan Abbott, Rhea Douglas, and Anita Mondo provided administrative aid; Rixa Spencer Freeze and Tom Bruscino helped with research assistance. Vivian Heater provided invaluable support for which I cannot thank her enough. Carol Franco and Kent Linebacker talked with me at length about the book and gave me excellent advice.

The staff at Stanford University Press has been wonderful. I am especially grateful to Amanda Moran, who saw the book through the review and approval process. It has been such a pleasure to work with her, and I know the book is better for her efforts. I would also like to thank Muriel Bell for her interest in the project and Kate Wahl for helping to bring the project through to publication. Anna Eberhard Friedlander and Robert Burchfield not only made the production process easy, they even made it enjoyable. I am also deeply indebted to Timothy Lomperis and Glenn Snyder who very carefully and thoughtfully read the entire manuscript and provided numerous insights and critiques. The book is much improved because of them.

By far the biggest debt of gratitude I owe is to my family. I want to thank my parents, Allen Weitsman and Judith Rogers, as well as their spouses, Wei Cui and Jim Rogers, respectively, for the love, guidance, and wisdom they have provided over the years. My sisters, Stacy Young, Deborah Ogawa, and Susan Huter, have been the best siblings anyone could ever hope to have. I appreciate their unfailing support more than words can say. I would also like to thank my daughter, Sarah Evelyn Hoffmann-Weitsman, who unknowingly provided me with the best incentive of all to finish this book. And finally, I want to thank my husband, David L. Hoffmann, for reading the manuscript numerous times, for listening to me talk about it ceaselessly, for giving me invaluable advice and insights, and for so often providing me with the strength to soldier on. This book is dedicated to him.

Dangerous Alliances

CHAPTER 1

Introduction

MILITARY ALLIANCES shape worlds. They embody the patterns of conflict and cooperation in international politics; they drive those constellations as well. The North Atlantic Treaty Organization's (NATO) decision, for example, to alter the mission of the alliance and expand its membership after the end of the Cold War has had an important effect on the relationships of amity and enmity in the system. A different set of invitations to join NATO, a dissolution of the alliance after the end of the Cold War, or a continuance of the status quo all would have led to very different futures for the members of the international system. Yet despite the central importance of alliances in shaping the international system, a number of key dimensions of alliance behavior have not been fully explained.

Alliances have traditionally been considered principally as tools in a state's arsenal to augment its power capabilities. States, according to this view, form alliances to add the power of their allies to their own. A straightforward example of this thinking is the way that NATO calculates member states' contributions to the alliance. It does so by tabulating states' spending on defense. For decades, the goal of the United States was to get each signatory to the alliance to spend a minimum of 3 percent of its gross domestic product (GDP) on defense. Only two NATO member states (in addition to the United States) had defense spending above that level from 1975 to 1999. Ironically, the countries in question, Greece and Turkey, were arming against each other.[1] Their behavior highlights the problems associated with viewing alliances as mere tools to augment member states' power capabilities. It additionally illustrates that analyzing the external mission or goals of alliances should not come at the expense of examining the dynamics within military alliances. The internal dimension of alliances is a primary focus of this book.

The Greece-Turkey anecdote also demonstrates that the dichotomy between "enemy" and "ally" may be misleading. I argue that, under certain circumstances, adversaries may have incentives to form alliances with each other, either to react to other threats confronting them or to contain or manage the threat they face from each other. These latter alliances are actually used by states to keep the peace among the signatories.[2]

While the argument is counterintuitive, it does clear up a central empirical puzzle of the field—why it is that allies are not only unreliable but frequently fight each other.[3] Further, as I discuss below, it brings to the fore an important dynamic—what I call the "alliance paradox." The more effective alliances are at keeping the peace among their signatories, the more threatening they appear to nonmembers. This dynamic triggers a spiral of insecurity that heightens the prospect of war between alliance members and nonsignatories.

A broader view of alliances is dictated by the theoretical gaps in our understanding of the workings of alliances, as well as by the empirical realities of the contemporary world. NATO was formed to counter the Soviet Union but also to consolidate and solidify democracy in Western Europe, to reconstruct peaceful relations with Germany, and to ensure continued American involvement in Europe. As NATO's first secretary general, Lord Ismay, once said, the Atlantic Alliance was a program for keeping the Russians out, the Americans in, and the Germans down. In other words, NATO from its inception had key internal missions in addition to its external one. These internal missions sustained the alliance in the immediate aftermath of the Cold War.

Highlighting the internal dimension of alliances raises the importance of alliance cohesion—a topic of exceptional importance yet one that has generated few detailed studies. This is especially surprising given that studies of alliance formation have straightforward implications for cohesion. In this book, I develop a theory that explains both alliance formation and cohesion from one theoretical vantage point. I elaborate more fully than has been done elsewhere on the factors affecting alliance cohesion—in peacetime and in wartime.

Insights regarding alliance dynamics are generally unspecified in regard to the environment of state interaction. Scholars are more likely to identify the polarity of the system under which their arguments hold than they are to discuss whether their insights are relevant to peacetime alliances, wartime alliances, or both. There is an assumption that the contentions are universally valid, regardless of peacetime or wartime, although nearly all theoretical studies of alliances refer implicitly to peacetime situations. In order to make explicit the similarities and differences, I contrast peacetime and wartime alliance dynamics. This analysis also fills an important void in the study of alliance politics. Such considerations are especially important in an era in which coalitions are frequently constructed to prosecute wars.

Alliance decisions have grave consequences for their signatories and for the international order. A state's decision regarding when to ally and with whom shapes the system and dynamics of interaction for all. Miscalculations and uncertainty regarding alliance commitments can be catastrophic — be they miscalculations about one's own or one's enemy's allies. Failing to consider another state's intervention in a conflict or misreading one's ally's commitment to intervene can be disastrous to a state's welfare.

Our understanding of alliances has been greatly enhanced by a number of important contributions to the literature, which will be discussed in detail in the next chapter. What we still lack, however, is a sense of how the insights of the literature tie together. This book seeks to synthesize these contributions into one theoretical framework that can help us arrive at a better understanding of the internal and external dimensions of alliances. By exploring the conditions under which certain insights hold, I generate a theoretical apparatus that differentiates alliance types. The framework informs us when alliances serve as devices for capability aggregation as opposed to when they act as vehicles to manage and constrain partners. Such a theory unifies previously competing ideas regarding alliance behavior. It helps us capture the essence of alliances in a more comprehensive way.

The Argument, Part One: Alliance Formation

The principal building block for the argument I put forward and test in this book is Stephen Walt's seminal work, *The Origins of Alliances*. His insight, that states balance against threats rather than power, offers an important explanation for a plethora of alliance behaviors. His conclusion that balancing is far more frequent than bandwagoning behavior also motivates this project. I couple Walt's findings with the compelling observation by Paul Schroeder that alliances, in addition to their capability aggregation purpose, serve as tools to manage allies.[4] This argument, too, is central to this book. It reminds us that we should not examine alliances in a unidimensional way.

In thinking about the fundamental issues of alliances — their capability aggregation purpose, balancing and bandwagoning behaviors, and management functions — it becomes clear that these different behaviors emerge under different conditions. Threat does generate each of these responses, and, more precisely, different levels of threat will result in different alliance behaviors. In other words, it is not enough to assess whether a state is threatened to predict its alliance behavior. We need to look at just how threatened that state is. Low levels of threat will produce certain alliance patterns, while {moderate and high levels will yield different results. By examining the actual level of threat from one state to another we can forecast the types of alliances that will materialize.

In contrast to Schroeder, who views the management function of alliances as coexisting with the capability aggregation purpose, I posit that alliances are not always tools for capability aggregation. Under certain circumstances alliances are formed for the sole purpose of keeping the peace among adversaries. Alliances, under these conditions, may offer important opportunities for states to improve their relationships by facilitating transparency, providing a forum for communication, and serving as mechanisms to manage partners. States may form alliances to reduce conflicts with their adversaries and to prevent the deployment of their enemies' capabilities against them.

I argue that the relationship between threat and the propensity for states to form an alliance together is actually curvilinear. At low levels of threat, states have incentives to hedge their bets by forging low commitment level agreements with potential friends and enemies. States hedge with an eye to consolidating their power and blocking off avenues of expansion for their potential rivals, while simultaneously seeking to curry favor to ensure their actions are not overly provocative. As the level of threat from one state to another grows, states have incentives to come together in an alliance in order to manage or constrain their alliance partners. This behavior, tethering, entails reciprocal or symmetrical threats—it does not represent the capitulation of one state to another, as does bandwagoning behavior. Yet if a threat from one state to another continues to grow, states will seek to secure themselves elsewhere, that is, they will balance against threats. If the level of threat grows to such an extent that a state's survival is on the line, the state will indeed capitulate to the greater threat and ally with the source of danger, that is, it will bandwagon.

This framework, as will be discussed in greater detail in the next chapter, revises the way we traditionally think about alliances. In so doing, it synthesizes a number of key strands of thought regarding alliances. For example, balancing and bandwagoning behavior have traditionally been viewed as competing dynamics. From the argument presented here, we can see the conditions under which they may emerge from one theoretical vantage point.[5] No longer are the two behaviors in opposition to each other theoretically. Further, we see that bandwagoning may be rarer than balancing because threat levels to states do not usually reach those very highest points. Additional alliance behaviors, hedging and tethering, are brought to the fore in this framework as well. Both of these behaviors, at the lower end of the threat level spectrum, are more consistent with institutionalist thinking about alliances than realist. Thus, by proposing that all of these behaviors emerge at different threat levels, a simple idea yields a fairly powerful theoretical innovation. A central implication of the argument is that we should not focus exclusively on the external role alliances play at the expense of their internal dimensions.

The Argument, Part Two: Alliance Cohesion

Alliance cohesion is an extremely important dimension of alliance behavior, yet we still have a lot to learn about its causes and effects. Since a better understanding of alliance cohesion could ultimately lead to more effective military alliances, it is certainly useful to improve our knowledge of the factors that contribute to or undermine cohesion. Furthermore, the theoretical dimension is significant, as the reasons why states ally should have a considerable effect on the cohesion of alliances. In other words, if states are hedging, tethering, balancing, or bandwagoning, there are clear predictions we can make about how cohesive the alliance will be. For example, if an alliance is concluded to challenge a common threat, the states naturally have a meaningful purpose around which to rally. Cohesion will flow from the raison d'être of the alliance. If, however, internal dynamics are driving the alliance, when states ally to manage their conflicts of interest, the very factors or issues that bring them together may be the same ones that contribute to a low level of cohesion within the alliance. This is so not simply because of the absence of an external threat but because the threat level within the alliance is so high.

Thus, threats emanate from within alliances as well as from outside them. Tethering alliances highlight how even states that form alliances may be threatened by each other. This insight helps us understand the empirical puzzle mentioned at the start of the chapter, the finding by Bueno de Mesquita and subsequent scholars that not only are allies often unreliable, but they also frequently fight each other. In fact, the puzzle regarding alliance behavior becomes not why allies are undependable and fight each other but why enemies ally in the first place. The answer to this puzzle reveals a great deal about the dynamics of alliances, their formation, and their cohesion.

By drawing out the implications of alliance formation for cohesion, we can also begin to understand another important dimension of alliances—their functioning during and after wars. Some alliances collapse in the aftermath of war, while others endure. The argument presented here suggests that this is so because of variation in the level of external threat, which plummets in the aftermath of war, and also in the level of threat internal to the alliance. In wartime situations in which alliances are formed for expedient purposes and the level of threat within the alliance is high, once the level of external threat recedes, the alliance may very well disintegrate. If, however, the level of threat internal to an alliance is low, even if the level of external threat diminishes, the alliance may very well endure. This may explain, for example, why NATO endured after the end of the Cold War but the Allied Powers after World War II did not. The external threat diminished in both cases after the end of conflict, but the level of internal threat was low in the first case and high in the second. In other words, variation in the level of internal, not external, threat determined the outcome.

Thus, a final point that begs examination is how alliances function once wars begin. How do the conditions of wartime alter the dynamics of alliances that exist during peacetime? Since this book assesses alliance formation and cohesion under conditions of threat, the question regarding wartime is a natural one. Are the factors that facilitate cohesion in peacetime the same ones that affect cohesion in wartime? Most studies on alliances focus on alliance formation and peacetime maintenance. Less attention has been paid to how alliances actually function during wars. This is a significant gap in our understanding of both alliances and war, one that is becoming pointedly clear as states increasingly set about building coalitions before undertaking military action.[6]

This book provides a bridge between the study of peacetime and wartime alliances by addressing some of the similarities and differences between them. During wartime, the level of threat to states is even higher than it is during peacetime. This would suggest, in theory, that wartime alliances are more cohesive than are peacetime alliances. Moreover, we would expect wartime alliances to be even more cohesive when they are losing than when they are winning. Yet, empirically, the story is very different. The dynamics of wartime place additional strain on the alliances involved—cohesion becomes more difficult to attain and maintain. Understanding these complexities and detailing why wartime alliances function so differently from peacetime ones require that I extend the analysis of case studies from the pre–World War I period through the war.

The argument that emerges is that while similarities do exist, the cohesion of peacetime and wartime alliances derives from different sources. Further, wartime alliances require as a baseline a high degree of integration in strategy. The needs of maintaining a wartime coalition are greater than they are during peacetime. Thus, wartime alliances struggle more with cohesion than do their peacetime counterparts. In addition, the level of external threat is generally higher during wartime than it is during peacetime. As such, states may make additional efforts to maintain the cohesion of their alliances. This process has consequences as well: the need to maintain effective and cohesive alliances during the First World War made any possibility for an early compromise or negotiated end to the war unrealizable. The states' efforts, particularly in the Triple Entente, to maintain the cohesion of their alliances frustrated attempts for a separate peace. Because the states continuously expanded their own war aims in order to accommodate the aims of their allies, compromise with the adversarial coalition became exceedingly difficult. This was true despite the fact that traditional allies were fighting in opposing coalitions and that traditional adversaries were allied. This finding runs counter to the realist idea that great power coalitional warfare should be relatively easy to end in an international system with more than two great powers. One's adversary is a potential ally, and one's ally is a potential adversary. Gains that may be reaped in a favorable separate peace offered by the adversarial coalition should induce cooperation. Instead, flexibility in alignment manifests itself in increased intra-alliance bargaining to ensure the solidarity of the alliance, not realignment.[7]

Dangerous Alliances and Keepers of the Peace

The paradox that underscores this work is that although alliances are not all formed for capability aggregation purposes—and in fact are frequently forged to keep the peace among the signatories—the way they are perceived may have nothing to do with the motivation that brings them to life. Though alliances are sometimes formed to keep the peace, they may actually wind up increasing uncertainty in the international system and the prospects of war. The alliance paradox arises from the anarchic environment of international politics and the centrality of perceptions as a consequence.[8] Since states must rely on themselves, they will engage in worst-case analysis. The uncertainty and insecurity this generates may trigger a reaction in kind. The alliance paradox—an attempt to keep the peace culminates in drawing the system closer to war—is a consequence of the security dilemma.[9]

The cases that will be explored in the subsequent chapters of the book are the European alliances of 1873–1918. They include the two Leagues of the Three Emperors between Germany, Austria-Hungary, and Russia; the Dual Alliance between Austria-Hungary and Germany; the Triple Alliance between Germany, Austria-Hungary, and Italy; the Franco-Russian Alliance; and the Triple Entente between France, Russia, and Great Britain. The alliances are all among the major powers of Europe between 1873 and 1914. I then examine the wartime alliances, the Central Powers and the Triple Entente from 1914 to 1918.

These cases are ideal for the study of alliances for several reasons. First, six alliances form in this rather contained period of time, which gives me a number of cases to examine and compare. Since several of the alliances in-

clude the same states in different combinations, the comparisons are somewhat easier to control than if I had to address huge variations over time and
space. Second, the alliances endure for long periods of time with varying de-
grees of cohesion. This allows me to determine whether there are similar
changes in the level of threat, internal and external, to the alliances in order
to assess the relationship between the independent and dependent variables.
Further, these are cases that have traditionally been understood from a balance of power perspective, providing an important testing ground for the
theory presented here. While it seems intuitive that the analytical framework has currency for today's alliances—contemporary NATO enlargement
cannot easily be understood from a realpolitik perspective—the pre–World
War I alliances have been used as the classic examples of balance of power
politics.[10] Applying the framework to these cases thus offers a difficult test
case for the theory. In addition, the alliances offer an important opportunity to observe the transition from peacetime to wartime. This will allow me
to glean insights about the workings of peacetime versus wartime alliances
while holding as many other explanatory variables constant as possible.

The alliances formed prior to the First World War have been cited as an
important cause of that war—the bloodiest, most violent war the world had
seen to that point in history. Yet the majority of these alliances were formed
among adversaries to keep the peace. The two Leagues of the Three Emperors, the Triple Alliance, and the Triple Entente were all forged to manage intra-alliance relations. The process of forming these alliances, however,
had the unintended consequence of making the world a far more dangerous
place. The spiral of insecurity touched all of the great powers. War, ultimately, was the result, despite the fact that traditional friends were in opposing camps and traditional enemies were allied.

What Lies Ahead

By relaxing the capability aggregation assumption, a different picture of alliance politics develops. Solely focusing on the idea that states ally to add the
power of others to their own obscures the reality that military alliances serve
numerous functions and that a range of incentives underpin alliance decisions. In addition, the reasons that states form alliances affect how well they
coordinate their external policy and strategies to attain their goals. This idea
will be explored comprehensively in the chapters ahead. In the next chapter, I describe in more detail the theoretical argument of the book. I review
the literature, develop and elaborate the concepts used throughout the book,
and provide an overview of the propositions and the cases. In Chapter 3, I
examine the first two alliances of the period under review, the two Leagues

of the Three Emperors. A qualitative examination of the Dual and Triple Alliances follows in Chapter 4. Chapter 5 then examines the extent to which the Franco-Russian Alliance and the Triple Entente can be predicated on the same theoretical framework to understand both the formation of the alliances as well as their levels of cohesion. These case studies of the pre–World War I period are important in order to test the central arguments of the book. They illustrate the significance of taking a broader theoretical view of alliances and demonstrate how alliances under some instances serve to manage intra-alliance relations, while in others they are tools for capability aggregation. They reveal the nuances of alliance behavior that emerge under conditions of threat. Chapter 6 analyzes the wartime cases, the Dual Alliance and the Triple Entente, in order to establish whether a similar relationship between threat and cohesion holds during wartime as well as to contrast the experiences of these alliances during peacetime with their wartime operation. Chapter 7 offers conclusions and speculations regarding the support for the theory and with respect to the generalizability of the findings. I also, in the concluding chapter, address policy implications for alliances in the contemporary system in light of lessons from the past.

This book explores broad ideas about the purposes of alliances—why they are formed, how cohesion is attained and sustained, the contrasts between alliance dynamics during peacetime and wartime—and uses the case studies to assess the arguments. I take on the crucial question of the causes and consequences of alliance behavior in the international system. The alliance behaviors in which states engage and the conditions under which they emerge are fundamental to our understanding of the workings of the international system. Having a better sense of the complexities of alliance behavior will inform our policy making as well as our interpretations of state behavior in the system. Developing a sense of the factors that enhance and diminish alliance cohesion will similarly inform our theory and practice in important ways. Alliances have frequently been used as important mechanisms to keep the peace, yet the consequences for systemic stability are sometimes very dangerous. In order to escape the alliance paradox, it is imperative that we enrich our theoretical and practical understandings of those dynamics.

CHAPTER 2

Theory of Alliance Formation and Cohesion

DESPITE THE central importance of military alliances in shaping the constellation of states in the international system, our comprehensive understanding of the underlying sources of their formation, their continuance, and their cohesion is still somewhat limited. While numerous scholars have provided insightful analyses of the reasons why states seek to ally, very few have sought to address the fundamental questions of alliance dynamics—formation, cohesion, and endurance—within a single analytical framework.

The different theoretical perspectives that dominate the study of alliance politics may be combined to push our understanding of alliance dynamics further. Instead of applying these different perspectives piecemeal, it is possible to explore the connections among them to better understand the conditions under which the divergent theoretical arguments inform us about the dynamics of alliances. While one theoretical orientation might not be better than the others overall, there are conditions under which one may better explain the patterns of alliance than others. For example, realism, focusing as it does on power politics, threats, and conflict, may have a lot to say about wartime, or near wartime, alliances. Liberalism, with its emphasis on cooperative endeavors, harmonies of interest, and similar state structures and ideologies, may generate a number of insights concerning the operation of peacetime alliances.

It is not surprising that realist theory dominated the field of international relations following World War II and throughout the Cold War, while liberalism challenged that predominance in the aftermath of the Cold War, with the "triumph" of democracy and the durability of NATO—the alliance of liberal democracies. Yet each school of thought has important insights to contribute to an understanding of alliance formation, cohesion, and endurance. What we lack is a road map to help us navigate when and under what circumstances the insights hold. They are not necessarily competing explanations—they actually speak to each other in important ways.

While no one book could distill the alliance literature in its entirety and then specify the conditions under which each argument holds, the theoretical framework outlined in this book attempts to unify several of these divergent strands. More specifically, it addresses arguments about alliance formation and cohesion that deal with conditions of threat.[1] It incorporates realist arguments that focus principally on shared threats. It also incorporates institutionalist arguments that emphasize the ways in which alliances enhance cooperation among their signatories.

I posit that a variety of alliance behaviors emerge depending on the level of threat. I argue that the specific level of threat emanating from one state to another will drive state preferences regarding alliance partners. In other words, instead of seeing a linear relationship between threat and allying, as both balancing and bandwagoning arguments do, I propose that there is a curvilinear relationship between threat and alliance formation. At low levels of threat, states mix their strategies, or hedge. They seek to consolidate and project their own influence, closing off avenues of expansion of potential rivals while simultaneously seeking to curry favor with those potential rivals. That is, states "bet a little each way." As the level of threat from one state to another increases, the threatened state has growing incentives to form an alliance with its adversary, to resolve their conflicts of interest. States seek to tether threats. Yet if the threat continues to grow, states will choose to balance against the threatening state. If the threat becomes so grave that a state's very survival is at stake, the threatened state may again opt to ally with its enemy, that is, bandwagon, to save itself.

There are consequences that flow from this argument for the cohesion of alliances. One primary implication is that we need to look not only at the level of external threat to anticipate the level of cohesion but also at the level of threat internal to the alliance. In balancing alliances where the internal threat is low, one generally finds a high level of cohesion. But tethering alliances, formed between states seeking to manage their conflicts of interest, are not usually terribly cohesive—it is difficult for them to coordinate their goals and strategies for attaining those goals.[2]

For an alliance to emerge, two states need compatible, not identical, motivations. In other words, an alliance may have balancing appeal to one state, while hedging motivations may underlie another state's decision to come to agreement. Since alliances are at a minimum dyadic, they may incorporate more than one motivation. Certain motivations—such as tethering ones—are more likely to be reciprocal than others that, by definition, are not, such as bandwagoning. When a state seeks to bandwagon with an overwhelmingly threatening state, the threatening state is not bandwagoning with its weaker partner. It may be balancing or, more likely, hedging. It is important to draw out these distinctions; otherwise, important dynamics of alliances become hidden. For example, NATO was certainly forged by the United States as a balancing alliance. However, not every signatory in the alliance had the same motivations. I elaborate on the possible alliance outcomes under conditions of threat later in the chapter.

The theoretical framework I present builds on insights from realism, liberalism, and rationalist approaches to the study of alliance politics. In order to make the most of the scholarship that has been done, I detail the ways in which the arguments speak to each other rather than presenting them as competing explanations. This serves as a positive heuristic, in the Lakatosian sense. The positive heuristic allows for added explanatory power via change or modification of a theoretical enterprise. It is a "strategy for both predicting (producing) and digesting [refutations]."[3]

In addition to unifying different approaches, the argument helps us understand certain important puzzles that have plagued theorists and practitioners alike concerning alliance behavior. As mentioned in the introduction, Bueno de Mesquita and others have observed that allies are not only often unreliable, they actually frequently fight each other.[4] We may better understand why this is so if we expand our understanding of the reasons why states ally and the consequences of those choices for durability and cohesion.

Literature: Questions Unanswered and Puzzles Unsolved

The alliance literature can be broadly categorized into three different groups —realist approaches, formal and rationalist approaches, and liberalist approaches. While drawing these lines is somewhat artificial—a number of works do not lend themselves well to classification—it is useful to try to construct certain analytical boundaries in order to optimize and pool insights. The purpose of this section is not to review exhaustively the entire alliance literature—it is voluminous. The point is to draw out some of the themes that have played an important role in advancing our understanding of alliances.

REALISM AND RATIONALISM

For a very long time, balance of power has provided the conventional wisdom concerning alliance formation as well as cohesion. The tradition of proclaiming power as the central driving aim of political units predates the state system. Thucydides himself described the conflict between Sparta and Athens as emanating from the growth of Athenian power—that is, the structure of the system and balancing of power. In contemporary times, the theme still pervades the international relations and, particularly, the alliance literature. There are strands within this school of thought—structural arguments that focus exclusively on power capabilities and perceptual arguments that emphasize threats.[5] I address these separately in the next two subsections.

Balance of Power and the Distribution of Capabilities

Structural realists write that much of international relations can be explained and predicted based on the distribution of power capabilities across states in the international system.[6] According to this view, state behavior is a consequence of states' drives to maximize their security in an anarchic world.[7] The quest for power, and therefore alliances, becomes central to this end. Alliances are formed because they function as security-maximizing tools. States ally either to enhance their power position relative to other states or to enhance their absolute power position.[8]

Alliance politics are determined by the distribution of capabilities. According to Kenneth Waltz, when the potential for military power is distributed relatively equally among more than two states, that is, when the international system is multipolar, "relationships of friendship and enmity [are] fluid."[9] When the largest share of power capabilities is distributed relatively equally between two states, that is, when the system is bipolar, there are few potential alliance partners that can alter the balance of power. Clear identification of the adversary—the only other state in the system that has sufficient capabilities to pose a military threat—fosters hostility between the two great powers. Cohesion within blocs, as a consequence, is enhanced.[10]

While alliance decisions are subsidiary in structural realism—the main purpose is to explain the larger patterns of interstate actions and reactions—insights regarding alliance behavior may be generated. States will form alliances when there are imbalances of power, particularly in multipolar worlds. The distribution of capabilities across states in the international system affects both the formation and cohesion of alliances.[11]

Threats and Extensions to Balance of Power Theory

Structural realism fosters the view that alliances will be used for capability aggregation purposes; alliances will form when states need to bolster their power vis à vis another state or set of states. Yet above all, structural realism is more concerned with stability of the international system than with the specific alliance decisions that inform policy. This has given rise to scholarship in which theoretical innovations have helped balance of power theory predict more specific foreign policies.[12]

Waltz's argument and its derivatives have two analytical strands in common. The first is that alliances are formed to balance against others—states balance against an external threat or a preponderance of power. The second theme that pervades both of these arguments, and the whole of the alliance literature, is that military alliances are formed for capability aggregation—to add others' power capabilities to their own. I will focus on the first theme, returning to the second later.

The predominant alliance behavior that realists describe is that of balancing—against threat or against power. Yet bandwagoning behavior occurs in the international system as well. This behavior is somewhat problematic for "balance" theorists. While some have argued that this behavior is rarer than balancing, it is the behavioral opposite;[13] states ally with, not against, their enemies.[14] It thus raises questions about realist arguments. Understanding that a key to advancing realist theory within the realm of alliance politics hinges on explaining bandwagoning behavior, arguments have been made that either dismiss bandwagoning behavior by positing that it is undertaken by small, weak states that are unable to secure themselves any other way[15] or explain it by suggesting that bandwagoning states are doing little different from balancing states—strategically maximizing the benefits reaped from alliance policy.[16]

Yet bandwagoning is problematic for realists, since the very core of bandwagoning behavior is distinct from the core of balancing—it is not driven by the desire of states to aggregate their capabilities. As much as realists have tried to escape the starkness of the capability aggregation assumption, it underpins the very heart of their school of thought.[17]

Rationalism

The assumption that states seek to ally with others in order to add others' power capabilities to their own in fact underlies nearly the whole of the alliance literature. This is true of the formal literature as well. The central questions addressed by formal theorists examining alliances focus on deterrence and signaling, the security versus autonomy trade-off, decisions regarding arming or allying, and the formation, frequency, and endurance of alliances.[18] Rationalist explanations have, in fact, emerged as powerful supplements to realist ideas. In some cases, works straddle the realist/rationalist divide. For example, Glenn Snyder has developed a more holistic model of alliance behavior.[19] Snyder also emphasizes the capability aggregation and "other" orientation of alliance politics. To Snyder, the central value of alliances results from the enhanced deterrent from external attack as well as the greater capability to defend oneself.[20] Randall Schweller's work on band-wagoning similarly contains components of realism and rationalism, by emphasizing the costs and benefits associated with a state's alliance choices.

Rationalist approaches offer room for theoretical innovations regarding alliance behavior and are largely responsible for bringing to the fore fundamental questions about the dynamics of alliances. With some significant and notable exceptions, much of the work shares important assumptions with realism, particularly with regard to the capability aggregation assumption.

INSTITUTIONALISM AND LESSONS FROM THE PAST

Although liberalism experienced an ascendancy in international relations theory after the end of the Cold War, it was slower to reach the topic of military alliances. There has, however, been some work that has explored the insights yielded by institutionalism in the area of alliance politics. Most of this work has sought to understand the longevity and durability of NATO after the fall of its principal enemy, the Soviet Union.[21]

Regime theory was used to explain NATO conventional force levels during the Cold War and the function NATO serves in the post–Cold War era.[22] NATO's persistence after the end of the Cold War has also been explained by institutionalist theory.[23] In addition, institutionalist theories have described some of the more general ways in which alliances as institutions affect interstate behavior. They influence cost-benefit calculations, shape strategies, induce convergence in policies, and alter societal views in important ways.[24]

The literature provides approaches that straddle realism and institutionalism as well. Ronald Krebs, for example, compellingly reasons that transparency in an institution, or alliance, may lead to competition and anxiety, not simply enhanced cooperation. He uses the Greek-Turkish conflict within NATO to test and illustrate his argument.[25] Christopher Gelpi describes a process through which alliances offer a framework for intra-allied control via mediation. In his study, he finds that the success of mediation efforts are a function both of the mediator's alliances and its military capabilities.[26]

These works have all advanced our understanding of how alliances represent institutions and function, therefore, as other institutions do.[27] This is an extremely important contribution to the literature, as it reminds us that alliances really are tools that extend beyond capability aggregation. Until recently, Paul Schroeder's call for additional exploration into this question went unheeded. Schroeder does maintain that the capability aggregation function and conceptualization of alliances is the most important aspect of alliances, but he also argues that the management function of alliances is essential to understanding their nature.[28] The contributions to the alliance literature that do advance our understanding of alliances as mechanisms that foster important intra-alliance dynamics are limited to NATO. While this is a significant first step, NATO is in so many ways a unique alliance, and the crucial test of the applicability of this school of thought to the study of alliances needs to extend beyond insights concerning it alone. To date, little work has developed along these lines.[29]

One reason the institutionalist literature has been so narrowly focused is that organizations such as the United Nations or NATO are unique to the twentieth and twenty-first centuries. Their intricate, formalized structures distinguish them from other international organizations of the past. This is not to say, however, that earlier institutions did not exist and were not influential in affecting state behavior. The Concert of Europe, for example, entailed codes of conduct that were observed by the great powers of Europe for nearly thirty-five years. States' expectations about the others were influenced and their own behavior constrained as well. There was a substantial change in the system as a consequence, one that marked a significant departure from the balance of power system that preceded and succeeded it.[30]

Similarly, long-lived alliances of the nineteenth century, though not as "global" or far-reaching as the Concert, may also be characterized as institutions, broadly conceived. If we adopt the prevalent definition of institution as a "persistent and interconnected sets of rules (formal or informal) that prescribe behavioral roles, constrain activity, and shape expectations," then the alliances under review in this book can be classified as such.[31] The Dreikaiserbund, the Dual Alliance, the Triple Alliance, the Franco-Russian Alliance, and the Triple Entente all had a set of rules regarding each state's behavior with respect to their allies and other states in the system; these rules prescribed certain behavioral roles, namely as allies and the scope of behavior that was expected as a consequence of signing the agreements. These rules constrained adhering states' activity and shaped the expectations in regard to those commitments. Certain of these alliances were more effective institutions, particularly the Dual Alliance and the Franco-Russian Alliance, but all meet the criteria at the most essential level. Defining institutions broadly reveals a multitude of ways in which they inform the study of alliances, those of the late nineteenth century and beyond.

A Unifying Theory—Alliance Formation

As we have seen, the existing alliance literature emphasizes external threats and the capability aggregation assumption. The only alternative logic, that embodied by institutionalist theory, is still nascent and linked specifically to arguments concerning NATO. Within the literature, balancing arguments are still the most pervasive. Yet bandwagoning arguments have also been made. Bandwagoning is at its core an alternative to capability aggregation. This is so because bandwagoning is undertaken to stave off threats to survival or to reap other profits from a successful alliance. States to which bandwagoners are capitulating do not need the aggregation of the smaller states' capabilities; nor are the bandwagoners likely to be interested in adding the power of their ally to their own. States bandwagon for many reasons but not for capability aggregation.[32] The fact that balancing theorists have recognized this behavior as recurrent, if not frequent, opens the door for relaxing the capability aggregation assumption of alliances.[33]

Further, the existence of bandwagoning behavior alerts us to the notion that while threat may be essential to governing alliance behavior, there may not be a linear relationship between threats and alliance decisions. Balancing states are not necessarily facing a threat to their statehood—these are states that can secure themselves by adding the power of others to their own. In other words, states engage in this behavior because the level of threat is not nearly so high as it is for bandwagoning states. Yet as the threat level grows, instead of additional balancing, states bandwagon. In contrast to Stephen Walt's argument, that bandwagoning is undertaken by small, weak states that fear being vanquished, I posit that these are states facing levels of extreme threat.[34] What becomes important here is not whether a state is big or small, strong or weak, but the level of threat it is facing from another. In other words, the essence of bandwagoning behavior concerns asymmetrical threats, not state size. Perhaps small states experience asymmetrical threats more often than big states, but there is nothing in the argument that analytically suggests that big states cannot be asymmetrically threatened.[35]

States that bandwagon are allying with their enemies under conditions of asymmetrical threat. But what about when the level of threat is symmetrical? These situations may still leave open the possibility of resolution through alliance. I argue that it is here that institutionalist arguments have insights to offer. Alliances between or among adversaries may be productive ("hold your friends close, but your enemies closer"). States can seek to control threats by tethering them.

Putting these arguments together, a comprehensive theory regarding alliance behavior under conditions of threat emerges. I suggest that states behave differently according to the specific level of threat they experience. At low levels of threat, states engage in hedging behavior. They desire to consolidate their power and project it further, to the extent that they can do so without being overly provocative to potential rivals. The alliance patterns we see emerging here are low commitment level agreements with states that will allow the hedging state to draw others into its sphere of influence as long as the course of action is not overly costly or too provocative to potential enemies. We will also see low-level commitment agreements established between the hedging state and states it deems potential rivals. Hedging states are simultaneously seeking to curry favor with potential adversaries and closing off their avenues of expansion.

China

At moderate levels of threat, when threats emanate reciprocally from one state to another, states have incentives to come together to manage those conflicts of interest, that is, tether. Military alliances offer excellent opportunities for states to facilitate transparency, contain hostility, and manage their partners. States may not form alliances to aggregate capabilities but to reduce conflicts and prevent the deployment of the enemy's capabilities against them. States thereby further their military security, yet not in the way traditionally conceived by alliance theorists.

In the event that the threat level between allied adversaries grows, however, or in the event that other temptations arise, a strategy of tethering threats will not succeed. While wars may be prevented by allying with adversarial states, once a war begins it is unlikely that states in a tethering alliance will actually fight on the same side. As threats increase, states may no longer be able to contain their adversaries. Tethering behavior can only be undertaken within a moderate range of threat. If the level of threat rises beyond that range, states will defect from these alliances and seek to balance against the threatening state. If the threat from one state to another continues to rise to a point that their very statehood is threatened, they may indeed, again, seek to ally with their adversaries, that is, bandwagon. Figure 2.1 illustrates the curvilinear relationship between the level of threat and the propensity for states to ally.

Because hedging and tethering are new concepts, the following sections elaborate on them further. In discussing these behaviors, it is important to remember that there are two central dimensions of alliance behavior, the substantive issues that drive states to ally and the tactical benefits that derive from the alliance.[36] These latter considerations may also play a role in driving states' alliance choices. With hedging alliances, the tactical side benefits dominate states' considerations; with tethering alliances, both the substantive issues (that is, the conflicts of interest that divide the allying states) as well as the tactical advantages of doing so (such as preventing your adversary from allying elsewhere, reducing your arms' burden, increasing the likelihood of long-term improvement of your relations) influence state decision

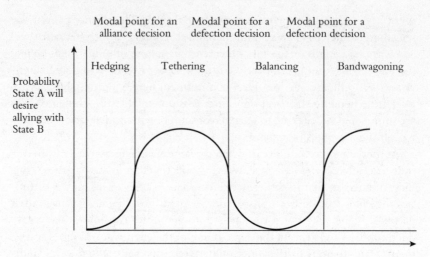

FIGURE 2.1. Curvilinear Relationship between Threat and Propensity to Ally

making. I will turn now to a discussion of hedging and tethering and the substantive issues and tactical benefits they entail.

HEDGING   Forging an alliance may be risky: tying oneself to another frequently means assuming one's allies' enemies as well as antagonizing one's own. Hedging entails a low commitment move toward a state that represents neither entirely friend nor foe—one with which there is little or no conflict, yet little or no amity either. Hedging is a tactic designed to reduce some of the risk inherent in more full-fledged alliances. States may hedge with potential rivals, thereby currying favor with them; they may simultaneously hedge with possible allies of their adversaries, shutting off possible avenues for their expansion. States may be able to keep a foot in more than one camp and in so doing can consolidate their power, even project it forward in a modest way.

Hedging occurs when states face more than one potential rival and do not want to choose sides. Since they may not know which would be the better camp to align with and since they may not want to align with one over the other, they hedge by forging an agreement with both. Germany's alliances with Austria-Hungary and Russia (archenemies of each other) in 1873 and again in 1881 are examples of this type of behavior.

The motivation behind hedging is flexibility, keeping one's options open. In hedging situations, states have a choice in alliance partners and may assume the role of "the pivot." This would give them significant bargaining

Don't forget China!

leverage with respect to their potential allies.[37] Additional tactical benefits of engaging in hedging behavior are numerous. Hedging could serve to keep a state in one's camp and simultaneously shut down avenues of expansion by a potential enemy; it could also serve to draw states into the hedging state's sphere of interest at a very low cost. Hedging works as insurance; states are seeking to guarantee their position in the system. These agreements are not overly provocative to others, though they may serve as preliminaries to tethering or balancing agreements as the level of threat confronting the hedging state grows.

TETHERING   Tethering is a strategy to manage relations with one's adversary by drawing closer to it via agreement. Its distinctive characteristic is that it is motivated, above all, by mutual antipathy. When states confront threats, one option is to conciliate them—not simply balance them or capitulate (bandwagon) to them. Tethering is a general tactic in international politics to accommodate adversaries; cooperation between enemies does occur fairly often. Tethering agreements will, at a minimum, stave off the immediate possibility of armed conflict between the rivals and at most will facilitate cooperation between them through heightened transparency and opportunities for trust to grow. States, in striving to tether, may not reach any long-term reconciliation or actual settlement of the conflicts that divide them. They are attempting to forge an agreement that will reduce the level of threat emanating from their enemy. They seek an understanding that will allow them to control the conflict and rein it in. Tethering is trying to hold animosities in check; it is an agreement of mutual restraint between adversaries.

Tethering agreements serve, at least temporarily, to improve relations between rivals. Hitler and Stalin tethered one another in the 1939 Nazi-Soviet Pact. Germany and France tethered in 1952 when they signed the Schuman Plan creating the European Coal and Steel Community. In some cases, as the latter example shows, the cooperation that emerges is enduring, while in other cases tethered allies may end up at war. The agreements adversaries make in order to control or contain their hostility is tethering behavior. It involves moves designed to lower the threat level states are experiencing.

Within the scope of alliance behavior, tethering takes the form of an attempt to conciliate an adversary through an alliance agreement. The idea is to draw close to one's rival by forging an alliance. States seeking to tether via alliance strive to reduce the level of threat and also garner important tactical side benefits. These include preempting one's ally from allying elsewhere, increasing the chance of deeper alignment and cooperation over time, reducing one's arms burden, and ensuring that an adversary's capabilities are not deployed against you.[38] In addition to reducing the likelihood of war, tethering agreements may appear less provocative than balancing arrangements because there is no state that is automatically put on the defensive by these moves.

One thing worth bearing in mind when examining alliance behavior in general is the fact that the world is one of many states; behavior toward one state may be driven in part by its relations with another.[39] With balancing, this dynamic is clear—states come together in the face of a common threat. With tethering, third parties may play a role as well. Here we see the dynamics of systems come into play—straightforward interests are not necessarily all that matter, and relations take on a more complex dimension.[40] When a state faces multiple threats, for example, it may feel all the more compelled to tether one. Although the agreement is not a balancing one— states are not being driven to their adversary to counter a common threat —multiple threats may make the incentives for tethering even greater.[41] Tethering may also appeal to a state to prevent two adversaries from allying against it. Tethering states seek to reduce conflict with one another; the benefits of doing so result because of the threat reduction vis à vis the adversary but also because of considerations arising from other states in the system.[42]

Tethering states may also serve to mediate disputes between their partners, as France did between Britain and Russia during the Russo-Japanese War. Britain and Russia very nearly came to war; without France—ally to both—they may very well have. Third parties to tethering agreements may play an important role, too, even if they have not acceded to an alliance for tethering purposes. They may help pacify adversaries, as the United States did between France and Germany in NATO or as Germany did in the Drei-kaiserbund, the alliance between it, Russia, and Austria-Hungary.

In sum, tethering is undertaken in order to reduce the level of threat states face from their adversaries by allying with them. The advantages of undertaking such a course of action are manifold: staving off the immediate possibility of armed conflict with the tethered ally; lowering the level of threat these states face and perhaps freeing a tethering state to deal with other hostile fronts; preventing the adversary from allying with another rival; and increasing the chance that cooperation will deepen over time.

The tethering dynamic is not unlike the binding mechanism described by Grieco and elaborated on by Deudney.[43] Binding is Grieco's realist answer to why certain forms of cooperation, such as regional integration, will occur. Why would, he asks, smaller states, such as Belgium or Luxembourg, or even France or Italy, agree to be dominated by larger states, such as Germany, in the context of European integration? The answer he gives is that for smaller states it is better to have at least some voice in creating the rules of interaction and the institutions. This say grants them more control over larger states in the long run than they would otherwise have. States that have a mutual interest in containing animosities and preventing the domination of the strong over the weak will bind, to have a voice in policy. Grieco explicitly writes that binding takes place for states that are weaker, even if they still have influence.[44] Once again, then, the emphasis is on small, weak states; the implication is that they cannot wholly fend for themselves. Similarly, John Ikenberry argues that binding institutions are those that incorporate power asymmetries; he focuses on the question of why powerful states would agree to limits on their power by adhering to binding international institutions.[45] He argues that newly powerful states, in the aftermath of major power war, are more inclined to use institutional strategies in order to reduce compliance costs, while weaker states want to decrease the costs of their security.[46] But these arguments focus on states that are of unequal power. The tethering dynamic focuses on situations of symmetrical threat.

Deudney's description of binding is somewhat closer to the idea of tethering. The emphasis he places is on the reciprocal reduction of autonomy of binding states via institutional connections. States establish "institutional links . . . that reduce their autonomy vis à vis one another."[47] There is nothing inherent in Deudney's analysis that suggests that states of symmetrical size and power are precluded from employing this mechanism to facilitate cooperation. This is important to my argument, since tethering works in this very way. Tethering states seek a particularly strong form of institutional commitment, a particularly intense form of binding, since they are containing one another, reducing each other's autonomy by joining an institution that is at the core of states' security interests. Combining institutionalist insights with those generated from realism allows a more comprehensive understanding of alliance politics to unfold.

Forming a tethering alliance may be a highly successful strategy of keeping the peace between or among adversarial states. This is precisely the reason for two states to form such alliances: there is no better means of transparency, no better guarantee of keeping the peace, no better way of facilitating trust. The resulting alliance may not be terribly cohesive, but the heightened transparency concerning military planning and increased frequency of consultations will reduce the likelihood of conflict between states. This was exactly the argument used behind the development of the Partnership for Peace program, as well as the joint exercises and consultations between NATO and Russia embodied in the Founding Act and the NATO-Russia Council.[48]

The fact that states form alliances in response to threats (and that the type of alliance depends upon the level of threats) suggests that alliances serve functions beyond bolstering power capabilities. Just because states are responding to threats does not mean that they are allying to augment their power capabilities. By adding this component to a theoretical framework that embraces and explains both balancing and bandwagoning, a complete picture of how states behave when confronted by threats emerges. What also emerges is a more comprehensive understanding of alliance cohesion. As important as alliance cohesion is—the very essence of how alliances perform—few works analyze it comprehensively.[49] The closest is Snyder's discussion of alliance management, though it focuses on the interactions and negotiations that take place among allies rather than on the forces that make for effective external policy planning and implementation.[50]

The Implications of Alliance Decisions: Alliance Cohesion

The phenomenon of group cohesion has attracted significant attention from scholars of sociology, anthropology, and psychology, as well as political science. Although each field has its own agenda, similar questions underlie all of these studies: what draws groups together, and what keeps the bond strong?

Despite the importance of these questions, the answer in the case of alliances is unclear. One problem is divergence among authors regarding the meaning of cohesion. Fred Chernoff, for example, implies that alliance cohesion refers to the distance between or among allies' goals.[51] Similarly, Louise Richardson's analysis of the relationship between the United States and Britain during the Suez crisis and the Falklands War implies that cohesion has to do with differences between or among allied states' objectives.[52] Stephen Walt indicates that cohesion is connected to alliance duration;[53] James O'Leary writes that cohesion is about agreement and shared goals, although in the same edited volume Earl Ravenal indicates that cohesion is about commitment.[54] In a comprehensive assessment of cohesion by Ole Holsti, P. Terrence Hopmann, and John D. Sullivan, the authors put forward the most useful definition. They offer a behavioral conceptualization of cohesion—the ability of states to agree on goals and strategies for attaining those goals. It is this definition that I adopt.[55]

The reason behind a state's decision to ally is essential to understanding how effective an alliance will be with respect to its external goals, that is, for alliance cohesion.[56] If states are coming together to counter a uniform external threat, it will certainly be relatively easy for them to coordinate their goals and strategies to attain those goals. Yet if states ally in order to reduce the conflict between them rather than to aggregate capabilities, then the very forces that lead states to ally will inhibit the cohesion of the resulting alliance. States will be, after all, allied with their adversaries. This suggests that peacetime alliances lack cohesion not simply because there is no common, external threat but rather because a high level of threat emanates from within the alliance. The implication here is that a deeper examination of the relationship between threat and cohesion is necessary.[57]

✳ Just as relaxing the capability aggregation assumption illuminates alternative driving forces for alliance formation, so, too, does it reveal insights regarding alliance cohesion. We see that an overemphasis on external threat diverts us from assessing threats internal to the alliance. Further, as with formation, the level and source of threat will affect the cohesion of an alliance. If cohesion were a constant function of external threat alone, we would never expect alliances to be cohesive in the absence of an external threat. Yet the security communities literature tells a different story.[58] This body of scholarship suggests that the relationships among the liberal democracies manifest in NATO transcend a mere military alliance. Instead, a "community of values [that] leads to mutual responsiveness" has evolved.[59] This community's existence is independent of external threat or may even create the external threat. As Risse-Kappen continues,

> One could then argue that the North Atlantic Alliance represents an institutionalization of the security community among democracies. While the perceived Soviet threat certainly strengthened the sense of common purpose among the allies, it did not create the community in the first place. . . . From a liberal and social constructivist perspective, one would argue that the sense of community, by delimiting the boundaries of who belonged to "us" also defined "them," that is, those outside the community who were then perceived as a threat to the common values. In other words, the collective identity led to the threat perception, not the other way round.[60]

While the presence of a security community embodied in an alliance does not necessarily imply that member states will easily agree on goals and strategies for attaining those goals, it is likely that with shared values, shared goals and strategies will emerge as well. What the security communities argument does imply is that in alliances where member states have mutual values and a sense of loyalty, the level of internal threat is low. The security communities literature would lead us to expect that it is possible to have alliances with relatively high levels of cohesion and low levels of external threat.

Combining the insights generated from the liberalist and institutionalist literatures with the insights yielded by realist arguments provides an enriched understanding of alliance cohesion as well as formation. Instead of seeking to understand alliance cohesion from the point of view of one of these perspectives alone, the combined framework unifies the ideas and helps us understand the conditions under which each argument will hold. The realist perspective on alliance cohesion suggests that it is important to look to

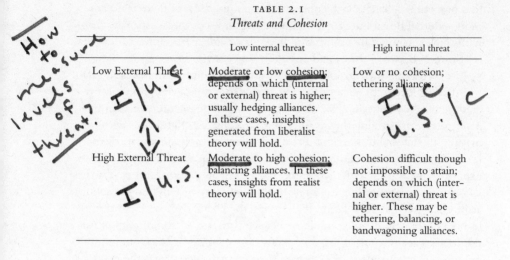

TABLE 2.1
Threats and Cohesion

	Low internal threat	High internal threat
Low External Threat	Moderate or low cohesion; depends on which (internal or external) threat is higher; usually hedging alliances. In these cases, insights generated from liberalist theory will hold.	Low or no cohesion; tethering alliances.
High External Threat	Moderate to high cohesion; balancing alliances. In these cases, insights from realist theory will hold.	Cohesion difficult though not impossible to attain; depends on which (internal or external) threat is higher. These may be tethering, balancing, or bandwagoning alliances.

the levels of external threat. The liberalist ideas imply that looking at the level of threat within an alliance is also important. Indeed, by looking at both, more nuanced propositions about alliance cohesion can be generated.

The most straightforward way to analyze the relationship between internal and external threats and alliance cohesion is to construct a two-by-two matrix. Additionally, the alliance types spelled out in the preceding section can be categorized accordingly. Table 2.1 illustrates the hypothesized relationships between threats and cohesion.

Alliances that confront a low level of internal threat combined with a high level of external threat are pure balancing alliances; cohesion will be relatively easy to achieve. External threats do, in these cases, provide member states with a reason for being and continuing. An example of a balancing alliance is the Franco-Russian Alliance, formed to counter the threat of Germany, Austria, and Great Britain.

In cases that have high levels of external threat as well as high levels of internal threat, states have combined to target a specific menace but are also threatened by each other. Cohesion will be difficult, although not impossible, to attain. These are alliances such as the Allied Powers during the Second World War. The threat of the opposing coalition eclipsed the threat within the alliance, but as soon as the Axis Powers were defeated, the wartime coalition fragmented. Indeed, this is precisely why wartime alliances often come to an end with the termination of a war—not simply because the external threat decreases but also because there are often internal conflicts that undermine the alliance. On the other hand, an alliance such as NATO could endure beyond the end of the Cold War because the low level of internal threat provided the necessary conditions for cooperation to continue.

Alliances that confront low levels of internal threat and low levels of external threat provide the necessary, though not sufficient, conditions for cohesion to burgeon. Insights from institutionalist theory are relevant here. In the absence of conflicts of interest, common values, institutions, and goals may flourish. Examples here include the Partnership for Peace initiatives, which were undertaken with an eye to heightening transparency and deepening cooperation between NATO and the Partnership for Peace signatories. ✱Alliances that have low levels of external threat and high levels of internal threat are <u>pure tethering alliances. States have combined in order to reduce conflict rather than to aggregate their capabilities.</u> Conflicts of interest among member states will inhibit them from effectively coordinating joint goals and strategies for attaining those goals. In these cases, since it is the competing interests that bring states together in the first place, cohesion will be difficult if not impossible to achieve. The two Leagues of the Three Emperors, concluded by Germany, Austria-Hungary, and Russia in 1873–78 and 1881–87, were alliances of this type. Austria-Hungary and Russia had intense rivalries in the Balkans, and the states formed these alliances in order to manage and contain those conflicts of interest. <u>The overriding objective of these alliances was to keep the peace</u> among the signatories. The level of internal threat was quite high. There were no common enemies, so a low level of external threat prevailed. The cohesion of both of these leagues was very low—throughout the duration of both leagues, the states were completely incapable of forming joint goals and strategies for attaining those goals. *In what sense, then, are these really alliances?*

Possible Alliance Combinations

Alliances are bilateral or multilateral agreements to provide some element of security to the signatories. States have different reasons to enter into them. Even when we restrict the examined motives to conditions of varying threat, we must still consider a range of alliance motivations. Some of the motives specified above are not compatible; others require reciprocity; still others may be paired with similar motives. Further, the commitment level of the agreements emerges from the motivations bringing states together in alliance.

In this section, I outline the possible alliance combinations—those motives that are compatible and likely to emerge. I do so for only dyadic relations, since any multilateral agreement can be reduced to the dyads of which it is composed. It is actually most useful to do so, since a state entering a multilateral alliance may have certain motives toward one state and different motives in regard to another. For example, Russia had balancing motives against Great Britain when it formed an alliance with France in 1891/94, but it had tethering motives toward Great Britain in 1907 when it signed the Anglo-Russian Convention. These two agreements, together with the Entente Cordiale between France and Great Britain, were the treaties that formed the Triple Entente. So within the Triple Entente, Russia had balancing motives toward one ally and tethering ones toward the other. I also offer predictions for the commitment levels that will be manifest in the agreements. Commitment levels are driven by states' motivations to join an alliance and then the bargaining that takes place between the signatories. States hedging will invariably seek low commitment level agreements; balancing states will generally prefer high commitment levels. Tethering and bandwagoning states will have variable preferences, depending on the threats they are attempting to contain.

Under conditions of threat, two states may form an alliance to hedge their bets, seeking low-level commitment agreements with potential friends and enemies. The mutual threat level will be low to both and result in an alliance that has a low level of internal threat. One state may seek to hedge while the other balances. These alliances will also have a low level of internal threat, but the states will have divergent goals, and cohesion will not flow automatically, although it should not be too difficult to attain and maintain. The states will not have opposing or conflicting or even incompatible aims.

One state may seek to hedge, while the other bandwagons. In these asymmetrical alliances, the latter power is threatened by its ally, while the former is not. Terms will be dictated by the hedging state, and cohesion will follow via coercion rather than cooperation. Similarly, in a balance/bandwagon alliance, the threat will emanate for one state from within the alliance, and terms will be dictated by the stronger power. The primary difference between a hedge/bandwagon and a hedge/balance alliance will be that the former agreement will have a lower commitment level than the latter.

Tether/tether relationships will have high levels of internal threat and very low cohesion. States form these alliances to manage their partners, not for coherent external purposes. These are alliances that serve to keep the peace among the signatories. Balance/balance alliances, in contrast, will have very high levels of external threat and very high cohesion. States form these alliances for clear external purposes. As long as the external threat remains, the alliance will endure as well. Alliances that have a low level of internal threat in addition to a high level of external threat may endure beyond their initial purpose, while those with a high level of internal threat as well as an even higher level of external threat may collapse once the external threat has receded. Again, this framework helps us understand why some wartime al-

Where to place U.S. : India?

TABLE 2.2
Possible Dyadic Alliance Motivations under Conditions of Threat

State A's motives	State B's motives	Characteristics of alliance
Hedge	Hedge	Low commitment level; modest cohesion; low internal threat
Hedge	Balance	Low to moderate commitment level; limited cohesion; low internal threat
Hedge	Bandwagon	Low to moderate commitment level; limited cohesion; threat within alliance to State B
Tether	Hedge	Low commitment level; moderate to intermediate internal threat; low cohesion
Tether	Tether	Variable commitment level; low or no cohesion; high internal threat
Tether	Balance	Variable commitment level, moderate internal threat, low to moderate cohesion
Balance	Balance	High commitment level; high cohesion; high external threat
Balance	Bandwagon	Variable commitment level, though probably high; moderate cohesion; internal threat to B is high, external threat to A is high

NOTE: For simplicity, duplicate outcomes have been dropped (e.g., Balance/Hedge and Hedge/Balance do not both appear). The Tether/Bandwagon combination drops out, since tethering is reciprocal —both sides need to be of the same approximate power level. Bandwagon/Bandwagon drops out, two states will not bandwagon with each other—bandwagoning requires capitulation of one to another. The latter state will therefore have other motives, i.e., hedging or balancing.

liances come to an end once the war is over and others endure. It illustrates why it is important to look within the alliance at the threat level and not just at the level of external threat. A summary of dyadic motives for alliance under conditions of threat is offered in Table 2.2.

Summary of Propositions: Alliance Formation and Alliance Cohesion

HEDGING

Formation At low levels of threat, states will mix their strategies by seeking low-level commitment agreements with potential friends and enemies. They will do so with an eye to consolidating their power, blocking off avenues of expansion for their potential rivals while simultaneously seeking to curry favor to ensure their actions are not overly provocative.

Cohesion Cohesion of hedging/hedging alliances will be modest, since there is no driving goal on which states can agree, let alone strategies for attaining those goals. Hedging/balancing and hedging/bandwagoning alliances will also have limited cohesion, since each state will enter the agreement with divergent objectives. The level of internal threat within the latter type of alliance may frustrate cohesion. The aims of the alliance will be dictated by the hedging state.

TETHERING

Formation   At relatively high levels of threat, states will seek to ally with their adversaries to manage their hostility and conflicts of interest.

Cohesion   The cohesion of tethering alliances will be very low. States will have entered these alliances as a consequence of their differences, and they will undermine the capacity of the members to agree on goals and strategies for attaining those goals. The level of threat internal to the alliance may be quite high, further undermining members' attempts to agree on goals and strategies.

BALANCING

Formation   At relatively high threat levels, states will seek to secure themselves by forming alliances to counter the state or states that most threaten them.

Cohesion   Balancing alliances will be quite cohesive as states enter these agreements with similar goals, although there may be differences over strategy for attaining these goals. In balancing/bandwagoning relationships, goals will be dictated by the balancing state. The threat to the bandwagoning state by its partner may frustrate cohesion, but the states may agree on goals and strategies to attain them as directed by the balancing state.

BANDWAGONING

Formation   At very high levels of threat, when states' survival is at stake, they will seek to ally with the most threatening state.

Cohesion   The goals and strategies of a bandwagoning alliance will be divergent. Because bandwagoning alliances represent the capitulation of one state to the other, cohesion may exist, yet it may also be coercive. This is true of hedging/bandwagoning and balancing/bandwagoning alliances.

Peacetime versus Wartime Alliance Dynamics

Although this book is principally concerned with the dynamics of alliances —formation and cohesion—during peacetime, it also seeks to answer a very important and all too often ignored question of how those dynamics are transformed during wartime. It is somewhat surprising how thin the literature is on the dynamics of alliances during wartime; scarcer still are the studies that contrast those dynamics with those at work during times of peace. Yet the complicating processes of military conflict inevitably alter the peacetime functioning of alliances in important ways. Further, no study of alliances is truly complete without attention to the ways in which wartime alters the theoretical relations that otherwise hold. This is especially true for this study, as the alliances of the period are frequently viewed as the cause of the war itself. I therefore extend the empirical analysis through the First World War in Chapter 6, assessing the ways in which threat affects the cohesion of the alliances during wartime.

The dynamics of peacetime and wartime alliances are quite different. Questions of burden sharing become far more intractable during wartime than peacetime, as the stakes are greater and the resources dearer. Division regarding resource allocation arises from the specificity and immediacy of the threats that states confront during wartime. During periods of peacetime, states can use promises for bargaining leverage with their partners; they can also use promises to enhance relationships with their partners. During wartime, however, action is what really matters. Once war comes, states may not make good on the promises they have made; commitments may become unrealistic or unfulfilled. It will thus be difficult to sustain cohesion under these circumstances.

Using the logic of the peacetime arguments in regard to external threats, we would anticipate alliances to be cohesive when they are losing—and threats are higher—and less cohesive when they are winning—and threats are lower. Empirically, the relationship between the cohesion of wartime alliances and the threat level states face is more complex. The symmetry of threats confronting alliance members, the clarity of the threats involved, and the commonality of threats facing the signatories will play an important role in determining wartime alliance cohesion. Threats that are complementary during peacetime—emanating from a rival coalition, for example—may be divisive during wartime as they culminate in different fronts and result in disagreement regarding resource distribution and allocation. Further, during peacetime, if one state in an alliance is threatened more than another, it might not affect cohesion at all. During wartime, however, it may once more lead to division over resource allocation and undermine the cohesion of the alliance. Finally, ambiguous threats during peacetime may actually serve to enhance alliance cohesion—they can be manipulated to serve the interests of the member states. During wartime, however, ambiguous threats are likely to culminate in disintegrative forces. Since states during wartime must agree on how to concentrate their war-fighting resources, ambiguity may give rise to friction. If states perceive or interpret threats differently, then they will not agree on necessary action to confront those threats. Hence the way threats are perceived—their symmetry, clarity, and commonality— will all affect alliance cohesion during wartime very differently than during peacetime.

Assessing wartime cohesion is also more complex than assessing peace-time cohesion. Employing a behavioral conceptualization of cohesion implies that alliance members fighting together during wartime must have some element of cohesion. In order to tailor the behavioral conceptualization of cohesion to periods of wartime, I focus in the wartime chapter on three central aspects of coordinated alliance behavior. First, I assess the level of cohesion according to the capacity of the member states of the alliances to coordinate their war-fighting strategy. This is a straightforward extension of the peacetime analysis. The second component of wartime alliance cohesion that I examine is the ability of member states to agree on war aims. This element, as with the first, is a straightforward extension of the analysis of cohesion during peacetime. In the peacetime cases, it is important to explore the states' abilities to agree on goals. In the context of war, those principal goals are allied war aims. Third, of fundamental importance to coalition warfare—and alliance cohesion—is the ability of a wartime alliance to prevent the conclusion of a separate peace. This is, therefore, the third element of cohesion I will investigate.

I have emphasized the importance of threat to explain peacetime alliance dynamics, and I maintain the same is true in wartime. Threats, however, are mediated by different forces during wartime than during peacetime. Once war comes, threats loom larger than ever for states, as states' territorial integrity and even survival are at risk. Yet we know that this high level of external threat does not automatically culminate in cohesion; if it did, all wartime alliances would be cohesive—something we know intuitively and empirically is not true. Part of the reason for this is that threats may still persist within an alliance. Although external threats generally loom larger, usually significantly larger, than the internal ones, we need nevertheless to attend to the question of whether the level of threat internal to an alliance during wartime frustrates cohesion as it does during peacetime.

The final case study chapter of the book thus explores the similarities and differences between peacetime and wartime alliances. In particular, I investigate the ways that the degree of symmetry, clarity, and commonality of threats to the alliance members affect cohesion during the alliances' wartime years. I also examine whether the level of threat internal to an alliance during wartime undermines cohesion in the same way it does during periods of peace. I do so by contrasting the experience of the peacetime alliances with their wartime counterparts.

Methodology: Concepts and Cases

It is important to strive for methodologically rigorous tests for the theories we propose. It is similarly essential that we not sacrifice the richness that the empirical world offers us.[61] Qualitative analysis facilitates our ability to yield effective insight into the power of our theories to explain the world. Using a straightforward case study approach to testing the theory I propose in this chapter, I provide a diplomatic and military history of each alliance and examine the theoretical linkages between the variables. I use process tracing in order to establish the causal relationships between the independent variable, threat level, and the dependent variable, alliance formation in the first place and alliance cohesion in the second. In order to provide both richness and rigor, I examine in depth the theoretical ideas in light of the empirical material for eight cases. I have conducted multicountry archival research in addition to mining the secondary literature in order to present thorough, structured, focused comparisons of all eight cases.[62]

CONCEPTS

THREAT   Threat is an inherently perceptual concept. While capabilities play an important role in determining what is deemed threatening, the other essential ingredient is intentions. A threatening state has both the capability and the will to do harm to some important interest. Gauging threat thus has to do with identifying those states that have the capacity to undermine one's interests and the perceived desire to do so as well.

While decision makers have a tendency to infer intentions from capabilities, it is clear that they do not do so uniformly. The degree of threat is nevertheless a function of capabilities most essentially. While it is critical that the intention to do harm exists, the level of damage that could be wrought is a function of capabilities. Capabilities concern not only military expenditures, technological prowess, industrial capacity, population, and size of the military but also proximity. During the period under review, proximity has to do with the closeness of the two countries and with their colonial holdings. Threat grows as military expenditures, military size, population, and industrial and technological prowess grow and/or as intentions become more belligerent. This threat is exacerbated when the state in question is very close or its colonial holdings are close to one's own. The power data for military expenditures, military personnel, iron and steel production, energy consumption, and urban and total populations are generated from J. David Singer and Melvin Small's study of National Military Capabilities from the Correlates of War project.[63] I also use their classifications to define the great powers of the era. The great powers' border data—both of their homelands and colonial holdings—I glean from Siverson and Starr.[64] I qualitatively assess the historical record as well to determine which states others found threatening and which states others considered to have hostile intentions.

The level of threat, therefore, is a function of the following:

- military expenditures
- military size
- industrial resources in terms of iron and steel production and in terms of urban population
- total population
- proximity of the homeland
- proximity of colonial holdings
- intentions

If there is growth in any one area, it is characterized as an increase in threat. A reduction in any of these categories is a decrease in threat. Fundamental to the analysis here will be the ratio of external threat to internal threat that a state is experiencing. The book's Appendix contains all of the above data for the six great powers of Europe in the period under review.

ALLIANCE FORMATION   An alliance is defined here as any formal or informal agreement between two or more states intended to further (militarily) the national security of the participating states. It is a continuing security association among member states with an element of forward planning and understanding to aid member states militarily or through benevolent neutrality. While there are a number of different commitment levels that can be identified, adopting as broad a definition of alliance as possible will be the most powerful conceptually and analytically. Thus, alliances are formed when two or more states conclude an agreement to advance their mutual security via an implicit or explicit agreement to come to the other's aid or to maintain benevolent neutrality in the event of war.[65] I identify six different security promise levels. Ranging from the least to the most committed, the categories are:[66]

- a promise to maintain benevolent neutrality in the event of war (1);   *low*
- a promise to consult in the event of military hostilities with an implication of aid (2);
- promises of military assistance and other aid in event of war, but unilateral and without pre-prepared or explicit conditions specified (3);   *mod*
- a promise to come to the active assistance of an ally under specific circumstances (4);
- an unconditional promise of mutual assistance, short of joint planning, with division of forces (5);   *high*
- an unconditional promise of mutual assistance in the event of attack with preplanned command and control and the integration of forces and strategy (6).

Each gradation represents an increase in the promised response of an ally in the event of war. Each cohesion section states what security level the alliance meets, according to the above criteria. The first two levels represent low commitment; the second two represent moderate commitment; the third two represent high commitment. States do not always make good on these promises. In fact, it is highly likely that, particularly in tethering alliances, the obligations will not be honored.[67]

ALLIANCE COHESION   I adopt a behavioral conceptualization of alliance cohesion rather than one that emphasizes social characteristics. Cohesion is the ability of member states "to agree on goals, strategy, and tactics, and coordinate activity directed toward those ends."[68] This is in contrast to Liska, who distinguishes between cohesion and efficacy.[69] In my view, cohesion is not analytically the same as duration. It might be preferable to discuss cohesion as a "we feeling," but assessing it as such would be inherently impressionistic. Adopting a behavioral conception is a suitable alternative.

Alliance cohesion has not received the same amount of attention as alliance formation, although most arguments concerning alliance formation speak to the issue of effectiveness by default. As described above, there are significant differences among the authors who do mention cohesion. I will assess alliance cohesion according to the extent to which the member states are in agreement over the overriding goals of the alliance and the ideas of how to attain those objectives. The level of cohesion, therefore, will be manifest in the degree to which the member states agree over how to proceed, particularly during moments of crisis. When states confront a policy decision and are able mutually to agree on how to approach the situation and coordinate accordingly, cohesion will be interpreted as high. In general terms, when states agree on mutual goals and strategies toward those ends, I will interpret cohesion as high. When states cannot come to any agreement over their goals and strategy, or if they undertake policies that undermine their allies, I will interpret cohesion as low. In the wartime cases, these assessments will be made in regard to the states' coordination of military strategy, their agreement on war aims, and their prevention of a separate peace.

CASES

The cases that I will examine in the next three chapters are the two Leagues of the Three Emperors, between Germany, Austria-Hungary, and Russia, formed in 1873 and again in 1881; the Dual Alliance between Austria-Hungary and Germany of 1879; the Triple Alliance between Germany, Austria-Hungary, and Italy of 1882; the Franco-Russian Alliance of 1891/94; and the Triple Entente between France, Russia, and Great Britain concluded in 1907. I then examine both the Central Powers and the Triple Entente from 1914 to 1918 in order to assess the validity of the propositions raised in this chapter as well as to contrast the dynamics of the alliances during their peacetime years with their experiences during wartime.

As mentioned in the previous chapter, I have elected to examine the alliances of the pre–World War I and World War I period for a variety of reasons. First, these are cases that have traditionally been understood as consistent with balance of power theory and are powerful examples of how alliances undermine international stability. Further, these are alliances of relatively long duration with variation in the level of cohesion over time. This will allow me to explore whether the level of threat also varied in conjunction with the level of cohesion, while holding constant as many other explanatory variables as possible. In addition, this is a period in which a number of alliances did emerge, which will allow me to examine the level of threat that emanated between the member states prior to the coming together of the states in question. Finally, the outbreak of war in 1914 allows me to contrast how the alliances functioned during peacetime with their wartime operations.

While the Europe of the past is dramatically different from the Europe of today, in the conclusion I will also assess the extent to which the insights hold in the contemporary era. I believe that the cases in some ways are representative of present-day alliance dynamics, although clearly there are profound differences as well. Those similarities and differences will be discussed in Chapter 7.

Conclusion

The theoretical framework that I propose is based on a number of important insights in the literature. Instead of viewing these propositions as competing, I have outlined an argument that allows us to see those insights as complementary. I examine alliance behavior under conditions of threat and propose a curvilinear relationship between threat and alliance formation. I present a unifying theoretical framework of alliance formation that incorporates the traditional view but also explains the anomalies that are ignored by that approach. I argue that different alliance behaviors emerge at varying levels of threat. Those behaviors include hedging, tethering, balancing, and bandwagoning.

One implication of the theory presented here is that states confront external threats, as the traditional view suggests, but they also confront threats internal to alliances. By examining both, a better understanding of alliance cohesion is achieved. The motivations that draw states together in the first place determine which of the following will be most pronounced: the level of threat within the alliance or the level of threat external to it. The level and source of the threat will have a profound effect on whether the signatories are able to agree on goals and strategies to attain those goals.

Further, by drawing out the implications of alliance formation for cohesion, we also begin to understand another important dimension of alliances—their functioning during wartime. An implicit assumption underpins much of the alliance literature—the assumption that its arguments and findings are universally valid. Yet we know intuitively that wartime dramatically transforms the context of state interaction, which most assuredly will have an effect on the dynamics of alliances that hold during peacetime. The prevailing conventional wisdom, that alliances are more cohesive the higher the external threat, implies that wartime alliances should always be cohesive—again, something we know is not true. I contrast the factors that facilitate cohesion in peacetime with those that affect cohesion in wartime in more depth, making explicit the similarities and differences that operate under these different contexts of interaction. This comparison of peacetime and wartime alliances provides a more comprehensive understanding of alliance dynamics. I turn now to the testing of the theory by analyzing eight cases in the next four chapters.

CHAPTER 3

The Two Leagues of the Three Emperors

THE LEAGUES of the Three Emperors are interesting cases for historical and analytical reasons. Historically, Europe of the early 1870s looked dramatically different than it had in the preceding decades. Germany was unified, Italy, too; Austria-Hungary and France were badly defeated in the process. The wars of unification ushered in a lengthy period of peace. From 1870 to 1914, the great powers of Europe were frequently in conflict but never at war with one another. During the Concert of Europe from 1815 to 1854, the great powers deliberately sought to keep the peace through consultation and compromise. From 1870 to 1914, the great powers of Europe were committed to keeping the peace among themselves, but the primary mechanism through which they chose to do so—forming alliances with their rivals—culminated in disaster.

The first alliance constructed to keep the peace in this period was the first Three Emperors' League, or Dreikaiserbund. Its analytical importance stems from the fact that it was an alliance formed among adversaries whose principal threats, for two of the members, came from each other. It was a mechanism through which Austria-Hungary and Russia tethered, and Germany hedged its bets between Austria and Russia at the same time that it balanced against France. Above all, the Three Emperors' Leagues manifest well the strategies of this period—ally with your enemies and keep the peace.

The Dreikaiserbund, 1873–78

The first League of the Three Emperors of Germany, Austria-Hungary, and Russia was created in 1873. This alliance heralded the era of Bismarckian diplomacy conducted by the newly unified Germany. The League was the first in a series of secret treaties between the great powers of Europe in the four decades prior to the outbreak of the First World War.

The Dreikaiserbund represented the coming together of the conservative elements of central and eastern Europe at a time when revolutionary socialism in western Europe threatened dynastic control.[1] It was an alliance forged among rivals in order to keep close watch on the other member states; it was an alliance designed to keep the peace among the signatories.

Austria

Austria's defeat by Germany in 1866 left a legacy of hostility, suspicion, and distrust. Austro-Prussian rivalry had dominated the states' relations since 1848. The Seven Weeks' War in 1866, ending in the Treaty of Prague, perpetuated Austrian animosity, as its defeat was absolute. Despite the fact that the peace terms embodied in the Treaty of Prague were not unduly severe, the humiliation of the defeat led Austria-Hungary to support France wholeheartedly in the Franco-Prussian War in 1870. The total defeat of France in the Battle of Sedan on September 1, 1870, however, prompted the Austrians to rethink the orientation of their policy and ultimately led them to alter it. When it became clear that France would lose its war with Germany, Austria no longer wished to tie its fate too closely to France, especially in light of repeated Prussian attempts to reconcile.

The threat posed to Austria by the newly united Germany ultimately made a tethering alliance appealing. The conflicts between them underpinned Austrian motives. As Austro-Hungarian foreign minister Friedrich Ferdinand Beust reported to the emperor regarding a Prussian offer of friendship:

> We must not forget that this offer is made at a time when our neighbor has increased in power to gigantic extent, when the only other European State that deserves to be powerful has shown itself friendly to Prussia and hostile to us, and that this offer of friendship comes at a time when our domestic affairs could easily offer the German government a pretext for hostile action.[2]

Beust continued, arguing that Austria-Hungary should "keep a sharp watch" but "conceal any mistrust."[3] By early 1871, the foreign minister believed that Austria needed to tether the German threat. Without an agreement, he feared that Bismarck would foment revolution among the Austro-Germans.[4] Austria was thus drawn into the Three Emperors' League in order to keep close watch on Germany. It was an effective tethering mechanism and offered the possibility of keeping the peace among them. The institutional incentives—the clarity of expectations regarding the member states' behavior that derived from the rules embodied in the agreement—made the alliance appealing.

The alliance also served to advance Austrian eastern interests vis à vis Russia. The Balkan question had been reopened, and with it the need to tether Russia as well. It would be easier within the context of the alliance "to repel Russian encroachments."[5] It was clear that Russia and Austria had conflicts of interest, but management of that threat provided the key incentive for the states to ally. The threat posed by Russia to Austria had several dimensions. First, Austria feared war with Russia in the Balkans because it would likely be devastating. Russia was very powerful—its share of total system capabilities was some 10 percent, and it possessed an army that could deal a severe blow to the Habsburg Empire. Second, a war with Russia would sorely tempt Italy. Italy had not relinquished hope of detaching Trento and Trieste from the Austro-Hungarian Empire; a war between Austria and Russia could easily provide an opportunity for Italy to try to satisfy its irredentist desires. The need to neutralize the threat of Italian intervention in the event of war with Russia was one factor that ultimately led to the conclusion of the Triple Alliance; the desire to neutralize the Russian threat in the event of war with Italy heightened the utility of the Three Emperors' League. As Peter Alexandrovitch Saburov, a special emissary to Berlin and subsequently (1880–84) Russian ambassador to Berlin, observed some years later in a letter to Nicholas Karlovitch de Giers, assistant minister of Foreign Affairs from 1875 to 1882 and thereafter minister of Foreign Affairs (until 1894), "For Austria, that Alliance has become a matter of safety, for could she be at rest a single day with on the one hand the Italian aspirations, and on the other those of the Slav populations, towards whom she has not the ability to know how to make herself sympathetic?"[6]

We may also identify the tactical side benefits accruing to Austria-Hungary for entering the Three Emperors' League. Tethering both Russia and Germany was essential so as to prevent a Russo-German coalition from forming against Austria. Russia and Germany were traditional friends; an alliance between them was easy for Austria to imagine. Such a combination would have been threatening to Austria-Hungary, given its antipathy toward Germany and its rivalry with Russia. Further, the threats Austria confronted resonated within the empire. The Dual Monarchy faced a plethora of challenges to its control. These came in the form of pan-Slavism and revolutionary liberalism. The commitment to monarchical solidarity offered by the League of the Three Emperors would provide a bulwark against the rising tide of domestic agitation.

In sum, the threats Austria faced emanated principally from Germany, Russia, and Italy. Austria entered the first League of the Three Emperors in order to tether Germany and Russia. The Schönbrunn Convention provided the formal rules designed to dictate behavior, activities, and expectations of the member states. It was designed to hold two of those threats at bay. The Italian threat was subsequently managed via the Triple Alliance, signed in May 1882. The first League, though informal and at a low commitment level, was the first alliance of this period to be used as a strategy of conflict management. The conflicts were not resolved, but they could, at least for some time, be tabled.

Russia

In 1872, Austro-Hungarian emperor Franz Joseph agreed to meet German kaiser Wilhelm in Berlin. The meeting of the two emperors would be a historic moment in improving relations between their respective countries. The news of this impending visit, when it reached Tsar Alexander II of Russia, was greeted with suspicion and apprehension. His immediate thought was that the emperors of Austria-Hungary and Germany would be coming to agreement on an alliance against Russia. The tsar's reaction to the news was what one might expect in the context of tethering alliances—he sought to invite himself to Berlin. He asked Prince Henry Reuss VII, the German ambassador at St. Petersburg, "Hasn't anyone in Berlin written to you that they wish to have me there at the same time as the Emperor of Austria? Do you think this would be agreeable to the king?"[7] A formal invitation followed shortly thereafter. Although the Three Emperors' League was not constituted until Franz Joseph reciprocated and invited both Alexander and Wilhelm to Vienna the following year, it does reveal how the League was born in enmity rather than amity, in suspicion and distrust rather than confidence and faith. Trusting neither Germany nor Austria, ultimately the best strategy for Russia was to stay close to them both.

One critical function the League served for Russia, and one of its principal motivations for acceding to the alliance, was to manage the threat to it that emanated from Austria. Russia sought a truce with Austria-Hungary in the west. While the alliance certainly did not dispel completely the suspicion and distrust upon which it was based, it did serve as a mechanism through which both states could keep close watch on the other, while tending to their respective domestic situations. It allowed for the preservation of the status quo in the east and ensured that war between the two adversaries would not result.[8] In the words of Tsar Alexander, "I do not wish to oppose the views of Austria. I will therefore go to the end in order to maintain intact the *entente à trois.*"[9]

Russia was motivated to ally for many of the same reasons as was Austria.

It was driven by the desire keep the peace between it and its adversary. The League would enable Russia to keep its eye on both Austria and Germany and to manage the Balkan question in a way that would avert war with another great power. The League, in sum, offered an institutional context in which Russia could keep watch over its allies. It served to reduce the conflicts Russia faced with Austria-Hungary by providing informal and formal rules that would alter the behavior of the member states.

Germany

For Germany, in contrast to Austria and Russia, the Three Emperors' League served as a hedging device. Above all, Germany wanted to preserve good relations with Russia and to improve its relations with Austria. Germany also was dedicated to improving Russo-Austrian relations. In order to generate cordiality, agreement among them all was necessary. Keeping both states on good terms—with Germany and each other—would eliminate them as possible alliance partners for France and would spare Germany from making a difficult and perhaps perilous choice between them. This approach thus allowed Germany to hedge its bets in two ways. First, the alliance guaranteed that Germany would not have to take sides between the two adversaries; second, the alliance ensured that neither would be free to ally with France. The alliance also allowed Germany to secure itself against France.[10] Hedging served to ensure Germany's position in the system.

The motives underlying the decision of Germany to forge the Dreikaiserbund were manifest in Bismarck's reasoning to Bernhard Heinrich von Bülow in a letter about holding a congress on the eastern question.

> I consider it dangerous to the Kaiserbundniss, to peace, and to Germany's relations towards her allies, for a Congress or a Conference to be held. . . . The danger to the Kaiserbundniss rests on the fact that Austria's interests lie much nearer to those of England than of Russia, and that a Congress will sharply accentuate this difference, seeing that Austria will be obliged to choose between the two absolutely opposed interests of England and Russia. Austria will be forced to declare herself for one or the other for the time being. Each Cabinet will have to negotiate not under the mediation of one equally friendly to both, and itself interested in keeping the peace, as is the German Cabinet, but will be hampered by the interference of other participants in the business, whose object will be to disturb the friendly relations between Russia and Austria. France, a competitor for Russia's friendship, will bid up the claims of Russia and the personal importance of Gortchakoff; England realising that her interests no longer coincide with those of Russia, will try to induce Austria to follow England's lead and Count Andrassy will find it extremely difficult to withstand the pressure of circumstances. Up to present the Drei-Kaiser-Bundniss has been the security for peace. If it is weakened and relaxed by the deliberate rapprochement to one another of Austria-

England and Russia-France respectively, the impossibility of reconciling Austrian, Russian and British interests in the East will lead to war. . . . Germany would be called upon day after day to act as umpire between the two hostile groups at the Congress; the most thankless task that could fall to us; and as we could never see our way from the outset to seize and bind fast either of the two parties, the most probable result for us would be that our three friends, Russia, Austria, and England, would leave the Congress in a state of annoyance against us.[11]

Bismarck thus sought to prevent such a situation from arising. Above all, he wanted to continue a policy of rapprochement between Russia and Austria, despite the attendant difficulties.[12] Germany needed to stand between Austria and Russia "like a man between two vicious dogs who would fly at each other as soon as they were unleashed."[13] If Austro-Russian antagonism were left unmanaged, Germany would ultimately have to choose between them, creating a situation in which a friendly power would necessarily become an adversary. To most German statesmen, not Bismarck alone, the idea of conflict between Russia and Austria-Hungary was intolerable. As Bülow argued, "The most unpleasant possibility of all,—which we happily consider unlikely—would be a war between Russia and Austria especially if the latter were invaded. . . . [S]ince a Russo-Austrian war involves danger for us, we are forced to do our utmost and foremost to stop it by one means or another."[14]

Germany sought to hedge its bets by securing an alliance with both Austria-Hungary and Russia. This strategy assured the peace between the two adversaries and precluded either from allying with France. This also manifested Germany's desire to balance France. In other words, the alliance for Germany embodied threat motivations toward Austria, Russia, and France. There were tactical side benefits accruing to Germany as well. The alliance further represented the conservative ideal; it embodied a commitment to the monarchical fraternity that would serve as a physical and psychological buffer to liberal threats emanating from the west.

Germany in the early 1870s sought to maintain its newfound dominance and unity. In seeking to secure that end, it hedged its bets by forging an alliance with both Austria and Russia. The alliance, however, was unable to withstand the centrifugal forces at work in the east, which ultimately led to the Dreikaiserbund's demise in 1878.

The motivations for Austria-Hungary, Russia, and Germany for joining the first League of the Three Emperors are summarized in Table 3.1.

EXTERNAL VERSUS INTERNAL THREAT

The level of threat within the Dreikaiserbund was greater than the level of external threat. Within the alliance, the principal threats to Austria-Hungary's

TABLE 3.1
Member States' Motivations for Joining the Three Emperors' League, 1873

Country	Motivation for allying
Austria-Hungary	Tether Russia
	Tether Germany
Russia	Tether Austria-Hungary
Germany	Hedge between Russia and Austria-Hungary
	Balance France

and Russia's interests derived primarily from each other. Germany was most threatened by the possibility of a Russian-French coalition. This was a threat not wholly dispelled by the alliance of the three emperors.

Each member state was a major power, and they all shared contiguous borders. Power and geographic proximity were certainly sufficient to be threatening. In 1873, France had over 10 percent of the share of system-wide capabilities; Germany had about the same, as did Russia. Austria-Hungary possessed about 5 percent and Italy about 3 percent.[15] Further, as discussed in the previous section, the Austro-Hungarians were wary of the intentions of both Germany and Russia, most particularly the latter. Russia, too, was leery of Austria, less so of Germany. Germany was not particularly threatened by either—its principal threat, France, emanated from outside the alliance.

The specific threats to the member states may be identified as follows. Austria-Hungary, as mentioned above, was vulnerable to Italian irredentism and Slavic nationalism. The combination was very threatening for a couple of reasons. First, Italian irredentism and Slavic nationalism offered challenges to the centralized authority of the empire. Once the empire's Slavic nationalities began voicing demands, political control over them would become more difficult. Moreover, other minorities would be encouraged to follow suit by making their own demands for autonomy and self-determination. This was true, too, of the irredentists in Trento and Trieste. Any development that opened the door to discontent with the central authority of the empire could be dangerous. Second, the domestic threat was matched by an international one coming from Italy and Russia. As these states nurtured rebellions against authority, they assumed threatening status themselves.[16] The fact that Russia supported the Slavs in attaining freedoms from the Ottoman Empire implicitly posed a grievous threat to Austria-Hungary's control over its Slavic minorities.

Relations between Austria-Hungary and Russia were further strained by the fact that any expansion by either power would be at the expense of the other. Russia, with its interest in protecting its trade route through the

Straits at Constantinople and the Dardanelles, threatened Austria-Hungary. The extension of Russian influence into Ottoman territory to protect those routes and attempts to facilitate the creation of states sympathetic to Russia in that area (such as Bulgaria) would result in the encirclement of Austria-Hungary with Russian satellites. Austria-Hungary considered the territory to its southeast its natural realm of expansion. It, too, relied on trade routes through the Danube, which would be endangered if relations between it and Russia deteriorated even further.

Russia was also threatened by tensions in the Balkans. Once Austria began to enlarge its sphere of influence in the Balkans and Russian influence began to wane, the threat to Russia grew. The other major threat to Russia at this time was posed by Great Britain.[17] The threat derived from British strength, the proximity of its colonial holdings in south Asia, and the perception that its intentions were adverse to Russian interests. In addition, Great Britain, as mentioned in the previous section, also had an interest in the Balkans. Its interests were more closely aligned with Austria's, in conflict with Russia's.

Germany, newly unified, having recently defeated both France and Austria-Hungary, was wary of those states maintaining hostility toward it. This was especially true of France, since Germany was aware France would never reconcile itself to the loss of Alsace and Lorraine. Throughout the decades following the Franco-Prussian War, Germany feared that France would launch a war of revenge to recover the territories annexed by Germany in 1871. Given warm relations between Russia and France, Germany wanted to prevent an alliance between the two, a partnership that might encourage France to initiate a war with Germany. As long as France could be isolated, no such threat was imminent. For Germany, then, the League represented an opportunity to avoid isolation and to drive a wedge between France and Russia.[18]

The situation with Austria-Hungary was not so grave. Because the Treaty of Prague had not imposed unduly harsh terms, Germany was more optimistic regarding its ability to improve relations with its southeastern neighbor. In short, a number of potential enemies faced Germany but, other than France, none that posed any serious threat to it.

In sum, the threats external to the alliance were not insignificant, but they were diffuse and not shared by alliance members. The internal threats, however, were quite vivid. The internal threats were what drove two of the member states to join the alliance and, as will be seen in the next section, were what inhibited the cohesion of the alliance. Austria-Hungary and Russia proved unable to better their relations with one another. Germany tried to nurture improvements between the two, but ultimately to no avail.

As it became clear that Germany's mediating role would not be sufficient

TABLE 3.2
Threat to Member States of the Three Emperors' League, 1873–78

Member state	Source of threat	Degree
Austria-Hungary	Russia	High
	Germany	Moderate
	Italy	High
Russia	Austria-Hungary	High
	Great Britain	Very high
Germany	France	Very high

to resolve the differences plaguing Russia and Austria-Hungary, it also became evident that Germany would have to choose between the two. An alliance of the three emperors could not withstand the differing threats facing each country. The best Germany could do was form an alliance with one or the other while trying to maintain cordial relations with the third. Relations between Germany and Russia became strained following the Congress of Berlin, and these tensions were exacerbated by new tariffs imposed by Germany on certain Russian goods. The Russian press, reflecting mounting hostility, became increasingly anti-German. Germany was further antagonized by Russian troop movements in Poland and the ever-increasing strength of the pan-Slav party. Consequently, in 1879 Germany decided to pursue a dual alliance with Austria-Hungary.[19] The threats to each member state are summarized in Table 3.2.

COHESION

The Schönbrunn Convention, initially signed by Russia and Austria-Hungary, provided the legal basis of the League. This convention was a pledge "to prevent any one from succeeding in separating them in the field of principles which they regard as alone capable of assuring, and, if necessary, of imposing the maintenance of the peace of Europe against all subversions, from whatever quarter they may come."[20]

The agreement also held that the signatories would consult and respond together in the event of an attack from another state. Five months after the convention was signed by Austria-Hungary and Russia, it was signed by the emperor of Germany.[21] The promise level of the convention was low, since it stipulated only the loosest of agreements in the event of war. It nevertheless specified the rules that would govern member states' behavior.

Because the League was an attempt to temper continued hostility between Russia and Austria-Hungary over their competing interests in the Balkans, its very raison d'être derived from conflicting rather than complementary interests. As it turned out, the League was not wholly able to survive the frictions that continually arose, particularly between Russia and Austria-Hungary. The reciprocal threats between Austria and Russia crippled the League from the start, which lasted only until approximately 1878. It was then reconstituted in 1881 for three years, renewed in 1884 for three more years, but expired for the last time in 1887.

The first serious strain to the alliance came with the war scare of 1875. At this time, Germany became convinced that France was drastically increasing its military strength—on the order of some 144,000 troops.[22] Although this belief was not entirely justified, many in diplomatic circles believed Germany was considering launching a preventive war. The new French military law also sparked a series of articles in German newspapers, the most famous of which was published in the *Berlin Post* and entitled "Is War in Sight?" This heightened fears of imminent war in France and Britain.

As the crisis escalated and French concerns over a possible German attack increased, France sought support from Russia and Britain. Although the Russians were somewhat restrained in their response, they did in fact lend moral support to France. This angered the Germans, who believed that the League of the Three Emperors should have bound the Russians to them or at least ensured Russian neutrality.[23]

The war scare of 1875 is significant in demonstrating the tenuousness of the League. Russia did not behave consistently with German interests; the alliance failed to operate in any unified fashion. The crisis represents the extent to which the member states of the League viewed it as an instrument to advance intra-alliance objectives, not as a force to guide external policy. The member states were simply unable to coordinate their goals and strategies for attaining them. In this case, Russian commitment to the League was insufficient for Russia to alter its history of relatively warm relations with France.

The competing interests of Austria-Hungary and Russia in the Balkans were even more problematic for the cohesion of the League. These tensions came to a head in 1877–78 with the Russo-Turkish War. In 1875, uprisings in Bosnia and Herzegovina against the Ottoman Empire brought to the fore latent competing interests of the great powers, Russia, Austria-Hungary, and England in particular. Russia, culturally bound to the Slavs, believed itself to be the natural "protector" of the provinces. In April 1877, Russia declared war on Turkey. Austria-Hungary, on the other hand, feared that its own Slavic minorities might be enticed and encouraged by Balkan nationalism and seek the same sorts of freedoms. As a multiethnic empire, Austria-Hungary found such rebellion threatening and thought it was necessary to resolve the conflict before its eastern boundaries disintegrated.[24]

The uprisings and Russian intervention served to exacerbate other geostrategic conflicts between the great powers. Russia coveted control of the Dardanelles and, as always, desired an ice-free port. Such control, however, would endanger Austro-Hungarian trade routes, particularly through the Danube. The Ottoman Empire's inability to suppress the rebellions caused consternation on the part of the European powers as a result of their significant interests in the area. This was true both because of the uncertainty engendered about the disposition of the territories and also because of the brutal methods being employed by the Turks to quell the uprisings. The Russians were particularly offended by Turkish methods, and when Serbia entered the war many Russian volunteers joined the cause even before Russia decided to intervene.[25] Bismarck, afraid that the revolts would disrupt the League of the Three Emperors, did his utmost diplomatically (in his role of the "honest broker") to produce a resolution acceptable to all involved parties.

Despite Bismarck's efforts and Austro-Hungarian and British objections, Russian troops continued to fight until they reached Constantinople. The great powers were disturbed by the fact that the Russians intervened in the conflict. The Turks assumed that British support against the Russians would be forthcoming. A British fleet was sent to Constantinople, yet the Turks received little other support. In particular, Austria-Hungary decided not to mobilize; war between the allies was averted. The Russians prevailed over the Turks. In March 1878, they dictated an agreement with the Ottoman Empire very favorable to their interests, the Treaty of San Stefano. The treaty's terms represented virtually complete Turkish capitulation to all of Russia's demands. Bulgaria was given independence and exceedingly generous borders, among other concessions.[26]

Although the League constrained Austrian behavior—it did not directly oppose Russia as it might have otherwise—the alliance strained under the weight of such asymmetrical gains to one member in an area of critical interest to others. In fact, both the British and Austro-Hungarians were dismayed by the gains incorporated in the Treaty of San Stefano. To resolve the disputes among Russia, Austria-Hungary, and Britain, Bismarck invited representatives from all of the major powers in Europe to a congress in Berlin. The outcome of this meeting, to the dismay of Russia, superseded the Treaty of San Stefano and modified Russian gains significantly. Bulgaria's borders were redrawn, and other European powers with interests in the area made significant gains (for example, an Austro-Hungarian occupation of Bosnia and Herzegovina was sanctioned). Moreover, the Russians were not assured free passage through the Dardanelles. This was an enormous diplomatic setback for the Russians. As Count Corti, the Italian minister of Foreign Affairs and representative at the Congress, recollected:

The Congress of Berlin resulted in a defeat for Russia all along the line. Her only territorial gain was in Asia. Bessarabia was restored to her. South of the Danube, however, everything happened as England and Austria wished. Bulgaria was not made into a large State; on the contrary, the territory inhabited by the Bulgarians was divided, and one—the southern—half was rechristened Eastern Rumelia, remaining a Turkish province, though an autonomous one. Russia was once again excluded from the Balkans and was caught in the mouse-trap of the Black Sea, for the exits by way of the Dardanelles and the Sea of Marmora were still barred to her. Her dream of reaching the Mediterranean had vanished.[27]

The uprisings of 1875 and their consequences demonstrate the impossibility of maintaining alliance cohesion in the face of highly conflicting central interests. In the case of the Dreikaiserbund, the rift generated by the uprisings and the settlement revisions proved to be insurmountable. In addition, it became clear that Germany would have to choose between its two allies; an alliance between the three powers was not viable. The Congress of Berlin was the final blow to the League. It was unable to survive the heightened threat within it. The increased discord among its signatories culminated in the end of the first League.

The one aspect of the League that should have allowed the member states to bolster cohesion of the alliance was the shared commitment to conservative monarchicalism. The League had been forged as a consolidation of the conservative, dynastic powers in Europe against the rising tide of revolutionary socialism and democracy. The three empires shared the same fundamental ideology, one that supported monarchical and dynastic political authority. Yet the conflicts of interest and variegated array of threats described earlier affected each member state differently and ultimately undermined cohesion. Those effects were too strong to be overridden by common ideological interests. In fact, the ideological component highlights the domestic aspects of the threats each state faced. Inherent in the efforts to bolster the great monarchies of Europe was a need for strong, centralized control to compensate for their questionable legitimacy in the face of democratic and socialist sentiments. As Saburov wrote in his memoirs, Bismarck thought that

there is no doubt that the republican spirit is astir in every part of Europe. In Italy, since the death of Victor-Emmanuel, there remains to their King only his title. France goes from bad to worse; that people imagine every day a regime more republican than that of the day before. And now, all the republican parties have their eyes turned towards England in the hope of finding encouragement there that the name of Gladstone promises them. I have said all this to the King, and I added that there was a good side to the matter; and that is that I shall now have the means of setting Haymerle's Austria in motion, and of removing the obstacle which stood in the way of the fulfilment of our programme. For Austria herself is not so safe as she supposes. It would be the height of imprudence for her to ignore the coming struggle between the monarchical and the republican principles. And if the three Emperors are slow to unite in view of this common danger, it is the most exposed of the three that will be the first to suffer from it.[28]

However, each monarchy faced different domestic threats, and their efforts to shore up internal control often led to conflict within the alliance.

German attacks on its Catholic population through the passing of the "May laws" (the first legislation of Kulturkampf) illustrates this dynamic. The new German state faced significant resistance to consolidation.[29] A major part of the resistance came from the Catholic populations of Alsace, Lorraine, and Bavaria and from the Poles who were now part of Germany. Germany, fearing that these elements would forge an alliance with the papacy in order to resist the central government, began to legislate increasingly strict laws against German Catholics.

It is not necessary to describe the specifics of these laws, the first of which were passed in May 1873. Important for this analysis is, however, that Germany's counter-Catholic measures served two purposes simultaneously. In addition to controlling its domestic opposition, the new laws reinforced German efforts to isolate France.[30] In France during these years (especially 1873–75), the Catholic Church had a great deal of influence. At the height of the papacy's influence in France, Germany was fighting the church via Kulturkampf. Hostility and suspicion between the two countries grew. France appealed to both Russia and Austria-Hungary, and while the former was lukewarm in its criticism of Germany and German endeavors to contain the Catholic Church's authority, the latter was more receptive. Austria-Hungary believed Germany was going too far in its quest to destroy Catholicism and gave tacit support to France, indicating that the Habsburg Empire would not follow Germany's lead. Russia was also in conflict with Germany's policies, and in 1875 it reached a negotiated agreement with the Vatican, resolving conflicts of interest between them.[31]

Although Kulturkampf was a domestic policy, it did have ramifications for German relations with France and, more important, with its alliance partners. As Germany pressed ahead with these policies, its relations with France grew ever more antagonistic. Ultimately, this suspicion and hostility culminated in the war scare of 1875 discussed earlier. One might expect that the ideological issue of containing the influence of the Catholic Church would have resulted in a manifestation of the member states' commitment to conservative dynastic control. It could thus have represented a shared threat and enhanced the cohesion of the Dreikaiserbund. Neither Austria-Hungary nor Russia, however, supported the extent of Germany's measures. Although both Austria and Russia faced turbulent domestic environments, they were not supportive of Germany's approach to its problems.

In sum, shared threats to dynastic control had a divisive effect on the alliance. This was true in the German case of Kulturkampf as well as in the urgent and direct threat facing Austrian political control from Russia in the form of pan-Slavism. These issues served to exacerbate the threats within the alliance, and, as a consequence, the cohesion of the alliance suffered. Even though all three states had a mutual desire to strengthen conservative elements within their states, in the end the domestic threats undermined the capacity of the states to act in a united way. The monarchical ideology was connected to threat and had a corrosive effect on alliance cohesion in another way as well. Dynastic interests brought the monarchs together, but such interests could not serve as a focal point around which domestic populations could rally. If anything, the very ideology upon which the alliance was predicated needed to be de-emphasized, given the liberal preferences and ethnic nationalism within and surrounding the empires. The threat of weakening domestic control fostered a united conservative front, but that front ultimately needed to be downplayed. Once more, a factor that drew the emperors together undermined the cohesion of the alliance.

Cohesion of the alliance was low. The members of the Dreikaiserbund had constant disagreements over their goals. Each individual state had separate aims. Further, these aims were in direct conflict with each other, as observed in the war scare of 1875, the uprisings in Bosnia and Herzegovina of 1876 and consequent Russian intervention, and the negotiations at the Congress of Berlin. If fundamental goals of the signatories are in conflict, cohesion is simply unattainable. In the case of the League, the desire to preserve the peace among the member states was about the only aim identifiable, and the League was barely successful in achieving it. Disagreement on how to maintain the peace was quite evident. To Austria, it meant that Russia should not intervene in the Balkans; to Russia, it meant Austrian restraint. The price to the Russians for Austrian restraint was the concessions granted to Austria in the Congress of Berlin. In short, the League did not embody common goals.

SUMMARY

The first Three Emperors' League was characterized by high levels of threat internal to the alliance and low levels of cohesion. The alliance was not exclusively designed to serve an external purpose—it was not designed simply to balance France, Britain, or Italy; it was not designed to provide a united front to attain shared goals. It was designed to manage the member states' relations with each other. The alliance lacked cohesion because the threat that drew them together in the first place emanated from each other.

The absence of a uniform external threat certainly mattered—the states never did develop any sense of common purpose. But this should not obscure the point that the alliance was not created or intended to be used to achieve shared external goals of its members. Intra-alliance dynamics were the focal point of the League.

The Three Emperors' League illustrates the importance of examining relations among states within an alliance. Because alliances are not solely formed to advance united goals of the signatories, it is important not to ignore their internal dynamics. Alliances, like other institutions, play an instrumental role in shaping the relationships of the states that join them. In the case of the League, there was a very high level of internal threat. The threat level within the alliance may have kept the peace among the signatories, but it paralyzed the alliance in every other way. It was the high level of threat within the alliance that undermined cohesion. The threat level within the alliance had a more significant effect on cohesion than did the level of external threat.

The Dreikaiserbund II, 1881–87

The second Dreikaiserbund shows the determination of the signatories to find a peaceful way to manage their difficulties. Virtually from the funeral of the first League, Bismarck tried to revive it. This alliance, too, is important analytically; it illuminates vividly the use of alliances to manage relations among signatories in the absence of a common external purpose.

As in the first Dreikaiserbund, the relationship between threat and cohesion was interesting and complex. Threat motivated the signatories to form the alliance—again, the threats from each to the other. The conflicts of interest embedded in the alliance, those that gave it impetus, were the very ones that rendered it discordant. The absence of a uniform external threat was only a small part of the story; the high internal threat was what prohibited the states from coordinating their goals and means to attain those goals.

FORMATION

Russia

Russia in the late 1870s and early 1880s was recovering from the military success of its war with the Ottoman Empire and its diplomatic failures at the Congress of Berlin. It was apparent that even a stunning military victory could not achieve its political objectives. The conversations between Saburov and Bismarck, and the negotiations that ultimately culminated in the reconstituted League, reveal the difficult position in which Russia found it-self.[32] Victory in war bred heightened threats from other quarters. Neutral-izing those threats via a tethering alliance, the second Dreikaiserbund, be-came the strategy Russia pursued. Allying with Germany and Austria was the best way to ensure that Russia need not fear the two forming an alliance against it.[33]

As it did earlier in the decade, the need to tether Austria came from the two states' conflicting policies in southeastern Europe. Events in the Balkans had heightened the antagonism between Russia and Austria. The second Three Emperors' League was formed and renewed to try to constrain that hostility, perhaps even diminish it.[34] The treaty was important to Russia to prevent the eastern crisis from overwhelming the two states, to prevent war from occurring between them. The Dreikaiserbund, to Russia, was to keep the peace between it and its ally, to manage the eastern situation. As Saburov wrote in 1880, "In the present situation, our best chance of stemming Aus-tria's action would be the way of the Triple Entente." These motives sus-tained the League as well. As Giers wrote in a letter in 1883, "It is in our in-terest to maintain it as long as possible. It guarantees us against Germany and saves us from a conflict in the immediate future with Austria."[35]

Russo-German relations deteriorated in the aftermath of the Congress of Berlin. Misunderstandings between the two states were threatening to dis-rupt completely their traditionally warm relationship. An additional worri-some development for Russia was the rapid economic and military growth that Germany was experiencing in this period. German military spending went up 902,000 1990 British pounds in 1880–81—a significant sum.[36] This heightened Russia's need for an alliance. The "mutual antipathy" that colored their relations at Berlin and after needed to be remedied.[37] These combined effects—the growth of German power and the perception of in-creasingly antagonistic intentions—created some urgency for the Russians.

It was the sharp increase in German threat that ultimately led Tsar Alex-ander II to view the Three Emperors' League as no longer viable or capable of preserving the peace by 1887. The threat levels precluded cooperation via alliance.[38] Before that point had been reached, however, "Giers, who was in effective control of Russian foreign policy by this stage, readily accepted Saburov's view that close treaty relations with Germany formed Russia's best defence against German hostility. . . . Russia's decision to enter the alliance . . . was due . . . to Russia's conviction that [Bismarck] would be less dan-gerous within alliance than outside."[39]

Russian motivations were unquestionably tethering ones. In Giers's memo to Baron von Mohrenheim, the ambassador in London, he wrote that the very hostility of Austro-German intimacy led him, the ambassadors, and the tsar to desire restoration of the Three Emperors' League.[40]

Austria

The Austrian motive for joining the reconstituted League was above all to tether the Russian threat. Austrian foreign minister Heinrich von Haymerlé made his views very clear to Bismarck when they met in Friedrichsruh in early 1880: he wanted a truce in the Balkans. "There is only one real influence in the East. We are conscious of it at every step. Whenever we wish to turn an Austrian interest to account, we clash with the hostile action of the Russian agents." He was, however, afraid that an alliance would make the Austrians "dupes of Russian diplomacy."[41] Austrian distrust and suspicion of Russia punctuated the negotiations that culminated in the agreement. Haymerlé sought to constrain Russian hostility and achieve sanction for eventual annexation of Bosnia, Herzegovina, and Noripazar. He sought, further, to enlarge Austrian influence in Serbia. The alliance offered a means to de-escalate the clash of interests in the Balkans.[42]

Haymerlé was ambivalent about the Three Emperors' League. He wanted to prevent the Germans from defecting from the Dual Alliance and to avert Russian encroachments and aggression.[43] Austria-Hungary appeared to be moving toward accession to the alliance, although it would not necessarily be a popular decision. As Bismarck remarked to Saburov: "[Austria] gains so much from being reassured with regard to you, and if the choice is between a treaty of alliance and the prospect of bloody conflicts, it is the first duty of governments to close their ears to the antipathies of public opinion, and save their people from their own impulses."[44]

There were important tactical side benefits motivating the Austrian decision as well. If left unchecked, a Russo-German agreement could come at the expense of Austria. For Austria-Hungary, facing problems of internal instability, Italian animosity on its southern border, and Russian hostility to the east, a strategy of neutralizing these threats via a tethering alliance made sense. As Bismarck suggested: "When Austria has worn that flannel for three years next [to] her skin, she will no longer be able to discard it without running the risk of catching cold."[45]

The advantages of constraining and managing the threat from Russia were apparent; the Three Emperors' League was useful to Austria until the point at which the threat exceeded a manageable level. As will be described in more detail below, the crisis in Bulgaria that started in 1885 and culminated in Austria sanctioning the exclusion of Russian influence in the area by 1887 led to an implosion of the alliance.

Germany

Germany's motives for joining the second League were the same as those for joining the first League. It sought to hedge its bets by maintaining cordial relations with both Russia and Austria-Hungary and to balance France. This strategy would deprive France of an ally and not require Germany to choose between Russia and Austria. Germany, as in the early 1870s, wanted to control Austro-Russian hostility. Reconciliation between Russia and Austria was crucial. As Bismarck wrote in his memoirs: "We could endure indeed that our friends should lose or win battles against each other, but not that one of the two should be so severely wounded and injured that its position as a Great Power taking its part in the council of Europe would be endangered."[46] Bismarck wanted to keep the peace; he believed that a war between Austria and Russia would potentially be devastating for Germany. Bismarck was also convinced that avoiding war was necessary so as to avoid taking sides between the two neighbors.[47] This would put Germany in a precarious position indeed.

The Austro-German alliance alone would not be enough to keep the peace between Austria and Russia, nor would it prevent a Franco-Russian combination from emerging. The Three Emperors' League thus allowed Germany to hedge its bets regarding those two possible outcomes. Germany had a significant stake in preventing France from finding allies and in securing Russian neutrality in the event of a Franco-German war.[48] The Three Emperors' League would also allow Germany to hedge its bets by guaranteeing it not become overly dependent on either Austria or Russia. Securing only one as a principal ally would restrict German policy; alliance with both would allow Germany to balance its interests and continue to be fairly independent in its selected policy course. The Dual Alliance allowed Germany to secure Austrian cooperation; Bismarck, however, did not want to become overly committed to or overly dependent on Austria. As Hans Lothal von Schweinitz, German ambassador to Vienna 1871–76 and ambassador to St. Petersburg thereafter, wrote, "Only mounted on horseback are we as tall as the Russian Giant, and Austria was supposed to be our horse. The Prince wanted to 'ride' Austria, not 'marry' her."[49]

In his memoirs, Bismarck reflects upon a conversation he had with Count Paul Shuvalov, Russian ambassador to Germany, regarding an alliance between their countries. It highlights the tactical side benefits Germany would reap from acceding to the alliance of the three emperors. Bismarck was swayed by the argument that alliance with Russia would guarantee no future alliance against Germany. He understood that alliance with Russia was key but regarded Austria as necessary in the equation so as to ensure that Ger-

TABLE 3.3
Member States' Motivations for Joining the Three Emperors' League, 1881

Country	Motivation
Austria-Hungary	Tether Russia Maintain close relations with Germany
Russia	Tether Austria-Hungary Keep close watch on Austro-German relations
Germany	Balance France and prevent it from finding allies in Austria or Russia Hedge Austria and Russia and prevent hostilities between them from escalating.

man influence would not be diluted by Russian power.[50] Interestingly, having both Austria and Russia as allies meant that Germany could play each off of the other, thereby granting it more flexibility in action. An alliance with either might eventually become a balancing alliance against the other; alliance with both served to hedge its bets.[51] In Bismarck's own words, "I declined at that time also the 'option' between Austria and Russia, and recommended the alliance of the three Emperors, or at least the preservation of peace between them." [52]

Domestic politics also played an important role in Germany's desire to forge the second Three Emperors' League. Germany's need to consolidate its power dictated caution in its foreign policy. Moreover, a shared commitment to monarchical conservatism in the face of seditious and contagious liberalism would shore up the power of the great monarchies. Russia appeared disturbingly close to revolution; Austria-Hungary's internal authority appeared to be eroding. An alliance of the three emperors, harking back to the great Holy Alliance of decades past, offered an avenue to consolidate monarchical authority in the face of a multitude of uncertainties.[53]

The reconstituted Three Emperors' League was highly appealing to Germany. It allowed the newly unified and powerful state to consolidate its power internally and externally. It served Germany well in hedging its bets against possible threats in the form of an adversarial neighbor or in the form of potential avenues of expansion for its principal rival, France. A summary of the member states' motivations for joining the reconstituted League is contained in Table 3.3.

EXTERNAL VERSUS INTERNAL THREAT

The absence of an overarching threat to the members of the Dreikaiserbund as a unit highlights the fact that it was principally a tethering alliance.

Similar to the first League, the alliance embodied deeply entrenched conflicting interests that emanated from within, particularly between Austria
and Russia. The threat facing Austria arose from Russia, and the threat to
Russia derived from Austria. The level of threat internal to the alliance was
overwhelmingly greater than any uniform external threat. Germany continued to hedge against a choice between Russia and Austria, preventing either
from allying with France. Even after the League's demise, Germany continued on this path by concluding the Reinsurance Treaty.[54]

The second Three Emperors' League, then, as with the first, was not a
product of a common enemy. It largely served to contain and manage the
animosity between Austria-Hungary and Russia by delineating the spheres
of influence in the Balkans. The same was true for Russian motives toward
Germany.[55] As Saburov wrote in his memoirs on March 29, 1880:

> Whatever the improvement in our relations with England, we shall always have
> near us a powerful Germany; we shall always have the difficulty of struggling
> against the two currents which manifest themselves only too clearly in the pub-
> lic opinion of the New Russia and the New Prussia, against that mutual antipa-
> thy arising from the too rapid growth of our neighbours. That is a situation
> which will always carry the risk of leading to catastrophes if the Governments re-
> main in tow to the popular impulse instead of restraining and guiding it. . . . As
> long as he [Bismarck] is there, our best security is to continue to be sincerely will-
> ing for an entente with him.[56]

Hence, threat did play a role in guiding the member states into signing
an alliance, yet not in a straightforward manner. In the case of Russia and
Austria-Hungary, deeply conflicting interests and therefore a very high level
of threat resulted in an alliance rather than opposition. There were important tactical side benefits accruing to the member states as well. As discussed
in the previous case, Austria-Hungary's authority over its multiethnic population was in jeopardy and would have been even more gravely threatened
if Russia continued to act with a free hand in support of the Slavs. In addition, both states depended on free access to the Straits of the Bosporus and
Dardanelles. In order to reap the gains of cooperation in the face of their divergent interests, the two states sought to ally.

Although conflicting interests may generate an alliance, its cohesion will
be very low. The forces that lead states to ally are not necessarily the same
ones that enhance their cohesion. In fact, if divergent interests bring states
together, these same interests may eventually drive them apart. Allied adversaries may ultimately resolve their differences, especially if a common threat
emerges, as will be seen in the peacetime case of the Triple Entente. Yet in
the absence of a common enemy, the forces leading to the formation of an
alliance may ultimately make the cohesion of the resulting alliance low. Al-

TABLE 3.4
Threat to Member States of the Three Emperors' League, 1881–87

Member state	Source of threat	Degree
Austria-Hungary	Russia	High
	Italy	High
Russia	Austria-Hungary	High
	Great Britain	Very high
	Germany	Moderate
Germany	France	Very high
	Russia	Moderate

though it is logical to assume that the factors contributing to alliance formation will also enhance cohesion, this is not necessarily true for a defensive alliance.

The domestic struggles each member state faced affected the cohesion of the League. There were grave consequences if the conflicting interests between Russia and Austria-Hungary in the Balkans were not contained. Austria-Hungary's control over its multiethnic population would be strained even further than it already was. Yet the fact that political authority was predicated on shared monarchical principles did enhance cohesion, albeit in a limited fashion. Table 3.4 summarizes the threats to each member state and the degree to which they were felt by the respective signatories.

COHESION

The League of the Three Emperors was reconstituted in 1881 for many of the same reasons it was initially conceived. Germany was still concerned about the possibility of a Franco-Russian alliance. Russia was concerned about the German-Austrian understanding, despite the fact that it did not yet know the substance of that agreement. Furthermore, Russia recognized the potential for conflict with Austria-Hungary and Germany. Consequently, the best strategy for Russia was to join them both. In negotiating with Austria-Hungary, Russia recognized that a defensive alliance delineating spheres of influence would benefit Russian interests.

In January and February 1880, Russia and Germany conferred on the possibilities available to them. Many of the concerns raised had been heard before: Russia desired above all to be protected against the possibility of a coalition against it and to maintain the status quo in the Straits. These objectives would be easier to achieve if Austria were part of the deal.[57]

Such strategic thinking was evidenced throughout the negotiations. All three powers had important objectives: for Russia, the Black Sea; for Austria-

Hungary, sanction of its new holdings in the Near East as well as preservation of the status quo in Turkey; and for Germany, a security system in which it was a member of an alliance of three great powers in a world of five.[58] For Russia and Austria-Hungary, it was essential to come together and agree on spheres of influence in order to avoid military hostilities against each other in the Balkans.[59] For all, preserving the peace was of primary importance. Part of the need to keep the peace was inherent in the three states' shared commitment to conservative monarchicalism.

The underlying ideological theme that drew the states together in the first League brought the three conservative monarchies together in the reconstituted League as well. When the Liberals came to power in Britain in 1880, it meant a potential disruption in European politics. While liberal politics did serve Russian interests in the Balkans by encouraging the pan-Slavic nationalist movement, in general, support for nationalist movements, as described earlier, gravely threatened Austria-Hungary's multiethnic empire, which included Slavs.

The immediate consequence of the change in British leadership was to bring to a halt Russian-German negotiations. When the congruence of interests between Britain and Germany became clear, Austria-Hungary became fearful of a potential alliance between Russia, Britain, and possibly Italy.[60] More important, Austria feared the potential alliance, which would have grave consequences for its interests, particularly in Bosnia and Herzegovina. To Austria, it became even more essential that the League be reconstituted demarcating spheres of influence between it and Russia. The direct result of this fear was the second League.

The convention, signed on June 18, 1881, in Berlin, superseded the one signed in 1873. It was largely defensive and was to be in force for three years. The treaty called for benevolent neutrality in the event of war with another state; Russia promised to respect the interests of Austria-Hungary in regard to the Treaty of Berlin; and all three states agreed to temper discord regarding the Balkans. Further, the convention specified that any territorial changes in Turkey could be broached only by mutual consent. The agreement also supported the principle of open passage through the Straits and threatened to revoke the assurances made to the Ottoman Empire in the Treaty of Berlin if this principle were violated.[61] These were the rules embodied in the agreement; they shaped the member states' behavior and expectations. The alliance, in stipulating benevolent neutrality in the event of war, offered the lowest level of security promise.

The Treaty of Berlin had granted Bulgarian independence. Once Bulgaria was established, Russia played a great part in assisting the new state to build infrastructure and develop its military and political organizations. Consequently, Russia believed Bulgaria to be firmly within its sphere of influence and beholden to Russia. Yet in the early 1880s, it became increasingly evident that Bulgaria was not going to submit to all Russian demands. An example of Bulgaria's assertion of autonomy was its decision to favor Austrian interests to build a railroad extending from Austria, through Serbia and Bulgaria, all the way to Constantinople. The Russians, already threatened by Austrian advances in the region—the signing of treaties with Serbia and later Romania—were adamantly opposed to Bulgarian compliance with the railroad construction. When Bulgaria did not concede to Russian desires, the probability of conflict between Russia and Austria-Hungary became even more likely, despite their agreement embodied in the Dreikaiserbund.[62]

Meanwhile, Austria, despite signing the Dual Alliance with Germany in 1879, felt growing distance between itself and Germany. Signing the Dreikaiserbund was tantamount, once more, to losing its status as Germany's primary ally. Further, although it allied with Russia, it was still terribly suspicious of Russian designs, particularly in Romania.[63] As tensions and suspicions grew, it became increasingly evident that the Dreikaiserbund was functioning more as a truce between Austria-Hungary and Russia than as a secure or cohesive alliance. And though it was renewed in 1884 for three years, it was not long before the same factors that tore the original League apart led to the demise of the reconstituted alliance as well.

As expected in a tethering alliance, the forces disrupting the Dreikaiserbund were also the ones most influential in its renewal. In 1883, disagreement between Russia and Bulgaria reached new heights. Austria was becoming increasingly concerned about revolutionary sentiment in Serbia and was deciding to take action. Though suspicious of each other, both Austria and Russia were facing domestic disturbances, making the possibility of hostility between them all the more untenable.[64] Further, as revolutionary sentiment continued to sweep Europe, the monarchies were ever vulnerable to erosion of their political control.

> Under present circumstances, a refusal to renew the previous arrangements, or a proposal to restrict their continuance to too short a term, would have aroused distrust, or perhaps even have led to political combinations which it was important to avoid in order to maintain pacific understanding between the three imperial courts. The understanding was more indispensable than ever, in order to strengthen the principle of monarchical order in face of increasing peril of social revolution. This common feeling was the bond which should unite sovereigns and governments in a strict solidarity.[65]

Thus, by the end of 1883 through early 1884, renewal of the alliance was negotiated and signed.[66]

Shortly after the League was renewed in 1884 it became clear that its days were numbered. With Serbia within Austria's sphere of influence, Bulgaria in Russia's (however problematic), and territorial disputes between Serbia and Bulgaria, the conflict of interests between Russia and Austria just kept growing. The fact that Russia was losing its control over Bulgaria further complicated the matter. Russia was afraid that Austria would usurp its role as defender of Bulgarian interests.[67]

In 1885, Bulgaria responded to Eastern Rumelian rebellions and desires for union with Bulgaria. Despite the fact that this is what Russia had originally wanted in the Treaty of San Stefano, at this point it threatened Russia because Bulgaria was now a free-acting agent. Further, Austrian intervention to stop Bulgaria's march south was tantamount to violation of the delineated spheres of influence; all vestiges of respect for the agreement incorporated in the Dreikaiserbund were gone.[68] The unsuccessful attempts on the part of Russia to control the Bulgarians, while Austria was making gains in Serbia, Romania, Greece, and Bulgaria, exacerbated Russian antagonism, and renewal of the League in 1887 was virtually impossible.

Germany realized it was no longer possible to reconcile the unbreachable differences between Austria-Hungary and Russia. Henceforth, Germany continued to maintain the Dual Alliance with Austria and in 1887 signed the Reinsurance Treaty with Russia. It had to be satisfied with two dyadic relationships in place of the conflict-ridden alliance of the three emperors.

The second League seemed slightly more effective than its predecessor, yet the level of cohesion was still quite low. There had been a truce of some sort between Russia and Austria-Hungary immediately following the conclusion of the alliance, one goal of the League. Yet differences over Bulgaria and the Balkans soon took precedence. The states could no longer agree over goals, let alone coordinate means for attaining them; again, as in the first League, each state's goals were different and many times in direct conflict with the others'. There was a zero-sum element to the conflict between Russia and Austria-Hungary. Consequently, Germany could only take one side or the other, indicative of a low level of cohesion.

SUMMARY

The reconstituted League demonstrates that alliances may be formed to manage interstate relations; when this is so, the level of threat internal to the alliance will be high. Cohesion of the alliance will be low, not simply because there is no uniform external threat but because of the high threat level within the alliance. This suggests that the dynamics within an alliance are as important as the external purposes they sometimes serve.

The Three Emperors' League of 1881–87 served as an attempt to medi-

TABLE 3.5
Chapter Summary: Alliances, Threat, and Cohesion

Alliance	Principal source of threat	Cohesion
Dreikaiserbund, 1873–1878	Internal to alliance	Low
Dreikaiserbund, 1881–1887	Internal to alliance	Low

ate Austro-Russian relations: it endeavored to temper those states' hostility toward one another. It failed to provide any lasting change in their attitudes to one another, even if it prevented the situation from growing any more dire in the years they managed to sustain the alliance. The alliance served no real external purpose; its principal function was to manage relations among the member states. The cohesion of the alliance was low as a result of the high level of threat internal to it. Table 3.5 summarizes the alliances, the principal source of threat, and the resulting cohesion.

Conclusion

The principal lesson from examining the two Leagues of the Three Emperors is that alliances indeed may be formed without a driving external purpose and instead are sometimes formed because of the purposes they are to serve within the alliance. The Leagues were vehicles for Russia and Austria to contain their hostility toward one another and for Germany to hedge its bets. If we pay exclusive attention to the external goals of this or any alliance, we may overlook the most important aspects of the alliance's operation.

The emperors, their chancellors, their ministers, and their ambassadors were keenly interested in keeping close watch over their rivals. Russia desired the alliances because of fear of Austria and distrust of the Austro-German combination. Austria was similarly motivated to join the Three Emperors' Leagues—by the Russian threat and the desire to keep close watch on Germany and Russia. Germany was driven by the threat from France as well as the need to hedge between Austria and Russia.

All three states had important developments that had domestic ramifications with which they needed to come to terms. Germany's unification, Austro-Hungarian loss of territory and vulnerability to pan-Slavism, and the diplomatic blow to Russia following the Congress of Berlin all dictated the need for domestic retrenchment. The League also shows how domestic politics offer a prism through which threats are perceived. Pan-Slavism and monarchical control are both examples of the nexus between domestic and international level threats. They influence how intentions of others are viewed. The Three Emperors' Leagues served as an institutional context; they were management devices to the member states as they encountered these threats. The cohesion of the alliances was very low—the member states entered into the alliances with varied goals. The very nature of these goals, managing threats among the signatories, prohibited the states from moving beyond the internal issues to confront external issues in a united way.

The Three Emperors' Leagues support the propositions from the previous chapter. They both offer evidence of the curvilinear relationship between threat and the propensity for states to ally. As the level of threat grew between Russia and Austria, the two came together in an alliance. As the level of threat continued to grow, the alliance foundered. Once threat began to recede, the states formed an alliance once more—an alliance that failed again as the level of threat between the two increased anew. As we will see in the next two chapters, it is not surprising from the vantage point of the theoretical framework that each state sought balancing alliances as the threat to each from the other grew. The hedging and balancing motivations for Germany support the theoretical framework as well. These motivations toward Russia, Austria-Hungary, and France were compatible with the tethering motivations of Germany's allies. Moreover, as anticipated, the level of cohesion varied with the level of internal threat—a high level of internal threat produced a low level of alliance cohesion, particularly in the absence of any common, external threat. Also, as expected from the predictions in the previous chapter, both alliances were of a low commitment level.

The Three Emperors' Leagues cannot be explained by a realist understanding of alliances alone. These cases highlight the importance of taking a broader view of alliance politics; they reveal the utility in moving beyond the idea that military alliances are formed to aggregate power capabilities. The Leagues also show the importance of the dynamics within alliances— an exclusive focus on external aims and objectives would miss entirely the central characteristics of the alliances in regard to both their formation and cohesion.

CHAPTER 4

The Dual and Triple Alliances

THE DUAL AND Triple Alliances were both peacetime alliances concluded by the member states in order to preserve a measure of security in a Europe fraught with uncertainty.[1] The Dual Alliance between Austria-Hungary and Germany was concluded in 1879, just after the demise of the first League of the Three Emperors and prior to its reconstitution in 1881. The Triple Alliance was signed by the member states of the Dual Alliance with Italy in 1882. These pacts represented the growing web of European alliances during the latter part of the nineteenth century. They were two of the most important alliances of the era; they were also the most long-lived of the pre–World War I period.

Despite the fact that Germany and Austria-Hungary were members of both, the two alliances were very different from one another—they were formed for different purposes, they served different functions, and they presented varying challenges to the member states. The alliances grew out of common interests, common enemies, and reciprocal antipathies. Both alliances played an important role in solidifying the division of Europe. The gulf between perceived and actual function of the alliances became increasingly noticeable in this period. This is most pronounced during the third renewal of the Triple Alliance in 1891, when it appeared that Great Britain was acceding to the alliance. The threat of another of their adversaries joining Austria, Germany, and Italy brought France and Russia together at last. For nearly forty years, the Central Powers stood at the heart of Europe, driving relations and behavior among the signatories and nonmembers alike.

The Dual Alliance

The Dual Alliance was one of the most important alliances in the post-unification pre–World War I period. And yet the dramatic events in 1877–78—the Russo-Turkish War and Russian victory over the Ottoman Empire, the Treaty of San Stefano, the Congress of Berlin and resulting treaty curtailing Russian gains, the growing animosity between Russia and other European powers—nearly overshadowed its formation. While other alliances concluded in the decades preceding the First World War resulted from sometimes agonizing negotiations, fundamental strategic aims, and coherent long-term goals, the Dual Alliance came to life rather abruptly. Nonetheless, it became the cornerstone of Austro-Hungarian and German policy; it endured to fight in the First World War and only collapsed some forty years after its formation. It foundered only in defeat of its member states in World War I. It is striking, when examining the historical record, how such a durable combination could have emerged when it was concluded at a unique moment in time.

None of the diplomats—not even Bismarck—could have anticipated or imagined the consequences of their alliance negotiations in the period 1873–1907. This is especially clear in the case of the Dual Alliance—an alliance that endured far longer than anyone could possibly have imagined in 1879. Russia and Germany were traditional friends. In fact, in the years that followed the conclusion of the Dual Alliance, Germany would continue its attempts to maintain good relations with Russia. It initiated the reconstitution of the Three Emperors' League in 1881 and signed the Reinsurance Treaty with Russia after the second League foundered in 1887.[2] Yet in 1879, tethering Russia was impossible for Austria-Hungary: the threat from Russia was too great. The Dual Alliance became both member states' insurance policy against the threats they faced and repeated tethering failures.[3] As I argue later, this alliance did not render the Franco-Russian alliance inevitable; rather, the catalyst for that alliance was the *flirt anglo-triplicien* just over a decade later. Yet the Dual Alliance does mark the onset of an era in which Germany and Austria both profoundly altered the direction of their foreign policy. Traditional friendship between Germany and Russia became subordinate to a relationship that had, until recently, been characterized by animosity. The antagonism that had marked Austro-German relations for some time began to abate with the signing of the alliance. The Dual Alliance served very effectively to heal Austro-German relations, which, as discussed in the previous chapter, had only begun to improve in the aftermath of the war in 1866.

The moment that gave rise to the alliance was one in which the threat from Russia precluded tethering with Austria. The first League of the Three Emperors unraveled; the second could not yet be forged. Austria believed war with Russia to be imminent. Germany considered Russia ungrateful for German support at the Congress of Berlin and believed Russia to be no longer reliable.[4] Germany was frustrated with Russia's failure to cooperate with the great powers of Europe, as shown by its intervening in the Ottoman Empire, fighting on to Constantinople in the Russo-Turkish War, and imposing the harsh terms of the Treaty of San Stefano.

The urgency of the moment for Germany was exacerbated by the impending retirement of Count Julius Andrássy. Bismarck thought that the departure of the Austro-Hungarian foreign minister might culminate in a change in the direction of Austrian foreign policy and pressed for an alliance before Andrássy stepped down.[5]

Austria-Hungary and Germany had a strong ideological and cultural affinity. Despite the fresh memories of the war of 1866, there were no strong differences between the two. They both maintained a commitment to monarchical conservatism. They shared language and culture. Their interests diverged generally only on issues of central importance to one and of marginal importance to the other. This facilitated the coordination of their aims, although it inhibited their joint military planning. After 1908, when Austria annexed Bosnia and war with Serbia seemed imminent, the two states began to more intimately plan their strategy in the event that such a war would come.[6]

The Dual Alliance became the cornerstone of Austro-Hungarian and German policy in the decades that followed its signing. At the moment it was negotiated, threats to both member states made this course a natural one, albeit one that definitively altered the landscape of European politics.

FORMATION

Germany

Germany was terribly frustrated with Russia in regard to Russia's war with the Ottoman Empire. Yet as a long-standing friend, it attempted to mend Russian relations with the great powers of Europe at the Congress of Berlin. Germany tried to soothe the great powers' outrage at Russia for its intervention into an area in which several had key interests. German attempts to defuse the situation culminated in Russian feelings of betrayal. This gave rise in Germany to concerns that relations with Russia would be hazardous in the future. As Bismarck's son, Herbert, wrote in the aftermath:

There has never been such an example at a Congress of a Great Power so unreservedly placing itself at the disposal of another. The result has been, not even a friendly acknowledgment, but an attitude adopted by Russia towards us, which forces us to think of the future and of how to avoid rousing the enmity of other nations on questions in which Germany is not interested. . . . But the present attitude of Russia forces me to reckon thus anxiously with the future.[7]

The newly unified Germany was preoccupied with its position on the Continent. The last thing that Germany wanted was to inspire hostility from other European states with an interest in Ottoman holdings. Germany wanted to consolidate its position in the region; it was not interested in expanding into the areas of the Ottoman Empire. It certainly did not want to risk the wrath of others over issues in which it had no interest.

Germany sought an alliance with Austria for several reasons. Above all, Germany wanted to safeguard against the possibility that a coalition including Austria and some other combination of great powers—particularly France and Great Britain—might emerge, an alliance that excluded Germany and, even worse, one that could ultimately be directed against it.[8] The Germans hoped to secure a formal relationship while Andrássy was still foreign minister. The rumors that Russia was courting France made Germany all the more interested in securing Austria as an ally.

In a report of his account of conversations with Bismarck in the summer of 1879 at Kissingen, Saburov describes Russian relations with Germany as going from one serious crisis to the next, such that one could not bear thinking about it. Germany appeared convinced that Russia was searching for new allies and that given the vehemence that Bismarck displayed, Germany would not delay its own search for new allies.[9] The tension between Germany and Russia was also expressed by the tsar in a conversation with Hans Lothal von Schweinitz, the German ambassador in St. Petersburg, in which he expressed his irritation and dissatisfaction with Germany; he further wrote a letter to the German emperor reiterating his grievances.[10]

From the German standpoint, the alliance with Austria had become absolute necessity, not only for her own protection against Russia, but also for the purpose of preventing Austria from drifting into the arms of France. The Austro-German combination would, in the last count, serve even as a barrier to an eventual Franco-Russian alliance, because, in the first place, Russia would hesitate before taking action against a united central Europe, and because, secondly, the combination of Germany and Austria would be so strong that England would join it, thus making it almost impossible for France to take the side of Russia in a future conflict.[11]

There were a couple of important factors that exacerbated German-Russian tension. One was the outbreak of a plague in Russia in late 1878.

The news reached Berlin and Vienna in January 1879 (the very moment at which fatalities were ending). Germany and Austria took coordinated and inflammatory measures—embargoing certain Russian goods, inspecting Russian ships, disinfecting certain articles before crossing the borders, certifying that Russian travelers had not been in contaminated areas for at least twenty days, and planning for the dispatch of medical personnel into the areas in question. According to the German ambassador in St. Petersburg, these measures, above all, inspired Russian fury and turned public opinion in Russia against Germany especially.[12]

A second complicating factor was the heightened Russian threat to Germany. This was manifest in the expansion and changing composition of the Russian army and the extensive railway construction that would ultimately serve to expedite Russian mobilization in the event of war with Germany. On March 21, 1879, a report by the German ambassador in St. Petersburg regarding the augmenting of the Russian army reached Bismarck. Schweinitz reported that the wartime capability of the Russian army had increased by some 400,000 men; 58,000 in peacetime. This concern was coupled by the extensive railway construction not far from the German frontier.[13] If these developments did not serve to inspire suspicion in Berlin, the Russian troop movements in Russian Poland certainly did.[14] Bismarck himself was not unduly alarmed by the military developments, but this sentiment was not shared by his military colleagues. Saburov reported that, in a conversation about the disposition of troops in early 1880, Bismarck said:

> It is true that you have much cavalry on the frontier, and that our Staff are passing sleepless nights because of this. The first time that Moltke spoke to me about it was, I think, in 1875. I told him that in the history of our previous wars, our Staff often complained that the Russian army was too far from our frontiers and did not come up quickly enough. During the war in the East, the cavalry was withdrawn. We hoped that it would not come back again. But it has come back, and the Staff has again become uneasy. Moltke spoke about it to the King, and said to him that if a similar disposition had taken place on the Austrian or French frontier, it would have been necessary to mobilise a part of the army immediately. For the moment the matter was left at that.[15]

A few months later, the matter was revisited by Saburov and Bismarck. Saburov asked Bismarck if he thought the issue was an important one between the two countries. Bismarck replied:

> As a military matter, I attach no importance to it. The danger to us is not great. The advantage which you would derive from it at the opening of a campaign is small. . . . For me the question does not lie there. I consider it important rather as a symptom of the psychological attitude of which this particular regrouping of troops as been the result. Whatever one may say, cavalry regiments on the fron-

tier have the appearance of a threat. The very men who conceived this disposition sounded our adversaries last summer at Paris on the subject of an alliance. . . . Your cavalry, I grant you, is no real danger to us; but those who put it there assuredly did not mean to give us a token of confidence. You come to say to us, "Let us be friends and allies", and behind you stands your War Minister with a pistol levelled at us. I believe your words, which represent your Sovereign's mind; but the unpleasant sight of the pistol makes me hesitate.[16]

In contrast to Bismarck, the response in military circles was to seek alternative paths to security. General Field Marshal Count Helmuth von Moltke ("The Elder") pressed for alliance with Austria-Hungary. After Bismarck sent Moltke the estimates of Russian troop increases, Moltke advocated increases in Germany's peacetime army, given the differential between the French and Russian army sizes in both peacetime and wartime.[17] Austria-Hungary was viewed as the most reliable choice of alliance partner and appropriate for strategic reasons as well. Moltke believed the Dual Monarchy to be the most advantageous ally in the event of a two-front war. A mobilization by Austria-Hungary at the same time as one by Germany would lure enemy troops away from the northeastern German frontier. Russia would likely engage in a first offensive against Austria-Hungary, allowing for a quick defeat in the east as Russia would be slow to mobilize. Germany would then be able to move its troops quickly to the western front to counter the French before the Russians could rally.[18]

The strategic advantages inherent in the choice of Austria as alliance partner were political as well as military. Bismarck believed that alliance with Austria would serve as leverage to bring Russia in line, prevent a Russo-French combination, and ensure Austria did not seek a coalition that excluded Germany. Such an alliance would also have the tremendous advantage of allowing Germany to maintain a solid understanding with Great Britain, given the strength of the Anglo-Austrian relationship and the common interests of the two states.[19] As Bismarck wrote to the German ambassador in Vienna, Prince Henry Reuss VII, on January 29, 1880, "An opposite policy is rendered impossible for us owing to the need of nursing our relations with England, a need increased by the fact that Austrian and British interests lie near together."[20]

For Bismarck, the most important factor was to ensure that German influence was not diluted by Russia. Because of the towering strength of the Russian army, Bismarck was perpetually concerned with how to ensure German independence from Russia. While German-Russian relations were generally good, Bismarck prized policy independence above all. He wanted to be at the center of all decisions; he did not want to be pressured by anyone else. After repeated attempts to smooth the path of Russia at the Congress, and repeated failures, Bismarck sought more policy independence. Alliance with Austria would grant that freedom. Austria-Hungary would be a more malleable and controllable ally.[21]

Getting the emperor to agree to a defensive alliance with Austria-Hungary, ostensibly to counter the Russians, was no mean feat on Bismarck's part. Bismarck emphasized the danger of a Franco-Russian coalition. He even sought to enlist the emperor's son, Lewis, the king of Bavaria. Hoping to get Lewis to intercede on Bismarck's behalf, Bismarck wrote him a letter exaggerating the Russian menace. He complained of the augmentations of the Russian military, the demands the Russians had placed on the Germans, the threatening nature of their policies. "I cannot resist the conviction," Bismarck wrote, "that in the future, perhaps in the near future, peace is threatened by Russia, and perhaps only by Russia."[22]

Bismarck, however, was less interested in balancing Russia than he was in balancing France. He was also concerned with maintaining good relations with Britain, managing Austria, and leveraging Russia. That Bismarck was simultaneously negotiating with Russia via Saburov on the topic of reconstituting the League of the Three Emperors supports this view. Since he is the architect of the alliance, it is fundamental to examine Bismarck's perceptions of the threat Russia posed. Quite revealing is his explanation in his memoirs that he was certainly aware of the complexities involved with the Dual Alliance.

> I regarded it as no less enjoined upon us to cultivate neighbourly relations with Russia after, than before, our defensive alliance with Austria; for perfect security against the disruption of the chosen combination is not to be had by Germany, while it is possible for her to hold in check the anti-German fits and starts of Austro-Hungarian feeling as long as German policy maintains the bridge which leads to St. Petersburg, and allows no chasm to intervene between us and Russia which cannot be spanned. Given no such irremediable breach Vienna will be able to bridle the forces hostile or alien to the German alliance. . . . In the interest of the European political equilibrium the maintenance of the Austro-Hungarian monarchy as a strong independent Great Power is for Germany an object for which she might in case of need stake her own peace with a good conscience.[23]

Bismarck continued on to say that the rivalry between Russia and Austria-Hungary actually worked to Germany's advantage, making it easier to cultivate good relations with them both.[24]

Bismarck wanted to be able to use the alliance with Austria-Hungary as leverage with Russia. The numerous hints Bismarck dropped to Saburov during their negotiations during this period suggest he viewed this as an important reason for the alliance.[25] This was even more vividly demonstrated later, in 1887, during the negotiations with Count Paul Shuvalov, the Russian ambassador to Germany, that resulted in the Reinsurance Treaty. As described in the next chapter, Bismarck used the text of the Dual Alliance to shock the Russians into compliance with his terms in their agreement.[26]

German motivations for an alliance with Austria, then, were principally balancing and hedging ones. Important tactical side benefits stood to be gained as well: to control Austria-Hungary and make sure that it would remain faithfully within Berlin's sphere of influence; to ensure British cooperation; to balance against France; and to leverage Russia back into the fold once tensions abated. The urgency of the moment was a consequence of the fact that Andrássy would be retiring, and there was no guarantee that his successor would be favorably disposed to such an agreement. One could make the argument that the level of threat between Russia and Germany precluded tethering—that Russian unreliability, the fears in Germany of a Franco-Russian alliance, and the consequent need to contemplate the possibility of a two-front war dictated such a course. Bismarck, in fact, invoked such a threat in seeking agreement from the emperor for the alliance. It appears, however, that Bismarck exaggerated the Russian threat to elicit Wilhelm's support for alliance with Austria-Hungary. After all, Bismarck never did cease his efforts at this time to reconstitute the League of the Three Emperors with Russia and Austria-Hungary.[27] The Dual Alliance did ultimately serve to provide Germany with the necessary leverage to bring Russia back into line. This highlights how Bismarck was really seeking to hedge his bets as well as balance by forming the Dual Alliance with Austria-Hungary.

Austria-Hungary

Austria-Hungary, as described in the previous chapter, had a fairly volatile relationship with Germany for many years, during their war and its aftermath. Following the Russo-Turkish War, however, the Russian threat eclipsed the German threat in a significant way. The threat level emanating from Russia to Austria reached great intensity in the aftermath of Russia's defeat of the Ottoman Empire and the failure of the tethering attempt embodied in the Three Emperors' League. Russian gains in the war and the terms of the Treaty of San Stefano generated acute Austrian animosity. Austro-Russian relations were already strained over competing aims in the Balkans. Russian victory and plans for a "big Bulgaria" outraged Austria-Hungary. Alliance with Germany would ultimately serve as a "dam against the progress of Pan Slavism" as well.[28] Since Austria-Hungary had a large Slavic population, fomenting nationalist sentiment made the Dual Monarchy's control over its population all the more tenuous.[29]

Enduring Italian animosity also contributed to Austrian insecurity. If the

Russian threat were not confronted, a Russo-Italian combination could over-whelm Austria-Hungary. As Bismarck reported to Reuss, "For me there is no doubt, that for Austria a break with Russia would mean a break with Italy, who would seize that opportunity for an attempt to annex Austrian terri-tory."[30] In short, Austria needed to secure a balancing alliance. Germany of-fered the best opportunity for partnership.

Andrássy's reaction to the threats confronting the Dual Monarchy was to favor alliance with Germany. The combination of enemies to the south and east compelled Austria-Hungary to find a solution—certainly any lingering animosity with Germany had to be put to rest. He was most preoccupied with Russia and considered it Austria-Hungary's principal enemy.[31] As his son recounts in his memoirs, "Andrássy's first thought always was to guard against the Russian danger."[32] Once the threat level was ratcheted up by the events of 1877–78, the increases in the size of the Russian army, and troop movements in the area of the Austrian frontier, Austria had to secure itself somehow. As early as the beginning of 1878 Andrássy approached Bismarck with a proposal to conclude a defensive alliance.[33]

The Dual Alliance was thus highly desirable to Austria. The one stipula-tion Andrássy insisted on was that Austria not be obligated to fight a Franco-German war. He wanted the language of the treaty to counter Russia. His difference with Bismarck stemmed from the fact that Bismarck wanted a general alliance, not one that would specifically call for joint action in the event of war with Russia. In addition to believing it would be better to have a general alliance for strategic reasons, Bismarck knew that it would be hard to sell a defensive alliance directed against Russia to his emperor. Yet he ul-timately had to capitulate to his counterpart's desires; Andrássy prevailed in the negotiations over the language of the treaty.

> Bismarck made one last attempt to coerce the Austrians into a general alliance. At one point in their negotiations, Bismarck suddenly sprang up from his couch and loomed menacingly over Andrássy. "Consider carefully what you are doing. For the last time I advise you to give way." He continued now with a raised voice and a threatening guise: "Accept my proposal, I advise you well, for otherwise"—and seeing that his threat had no visible effect in shaking Andrássy's resolution, he suddenly changed his demeanor—"otherwise I'll have to accept yours." "But," he added with a laugh, "it will cause me a hell of a lot of trouble."[34]

In sum, Austria-Hungary sought alliance with Germany for balancing purposes. Austria needed to secure itself in the face of heightened threat from Russia. Germany was by far the most attractive ally—France and Brit-ain were both more remote geographically and did not share the same com-mitment to monarchical conservatism that Germany and Austria did. Before

TABLE 4.1
Member States' Motivations for Joining the Dual Alliance, 1879

Country	Motivation for allying
Austria-Hungary	Balance Russia
Germany	Leverage Russia; prevent Austria-Hungary from allying with France or Britain against Russia; maintain good relations with Britain; preserve German autonomy; control Austria-Hungary. The Dual Alliance was a hedging and balancing alliance for Germany.

Andrássy's retirement, the Dual Alliance was signed; 1879 offered an opportunity for a lasting security arrangement for Austria. The moment did not pass unexploited. German and Austrian motivations for forming the Dual Alliance are summarized in Table 4.1.

EXTERNAL VERSUS INTERNAL THREAT

The external threat facing the Dual Alliance was different for each member state. For Germany, the principal preoccupation was that France would ultimately launch a war of revenge to regain Alsace and Lorraine. While war did not seem imminent, the need for Germany to prevent France from finding allies was a guiding strategic principle for Bismarck in this period. Russia, as described in the previous section, posed less of a threat. Bismarck did not seem very troubled by the Russian threat, although others in military circles were a bit more concerned.[35]

Austria-Hungary, by contrast, was competing fiercely with Russia in the Balkans. The Russians posed a threat to Austria-Hungary in regard to pan-Slavism and conflicting goals in the Balkans and the Straits. Tethering Russia in the Three Emperors' League had failed; Austria-Hungary had been gravely threatened by Russia's war with the Ottoman Empire. The desire for an alliance with Germany stemmed from these concerns.

The external threat to the Central Powers did not, therefore, emanate from the same source. Nor was the threat to the member states equal. The treaty of alliance addressed the event of a Russian attack on either party. Yet Germany at this time had not laid to rest its wishes for an alliance that would include Austria and Russia (the League was successfully reconstituted in 1881), whereas for Austria-Hungary, countering the Russian threat in the Balkans was the primary issue at hand. Russia was a far graver threat to Austria and Austrian interests than it was to Germany.

Pan-Slavism was an immediate and significant threat to Austria-Hungary, an unbreachable gap between Russia and Austria-Hungary. France's isolation and the French threat were far more salient to Berlin. Austria-Hungary had no real quarrel with France; this was a threat felt primarily by its ally. Yet the high level of cohesion characterizing the Dual Alliance was able to exist and persist because the threat facing each state did not emanate from the other. In the later years of the alliance, as the threat from the Franco-Russian Alliance and the Triple Entente grew, the cohesion of the Dual Alliance grew as well.

The threat internal to the alliance was low. Austro-Hungarian animosity toward Germany dimmed considerably in the mid 1870s. Instead, a nexus of common interests had emerged. The alliance was able to serve a dual purpose for Germany and Austria-Hungary. In addition to providing a dam against pan-Slavism, the alliance was heralded as a natural alliance, bringing all Germans together into an intimate relationship, an enduring partnership. The alliance functioned as an institution for the two states—it incorporated both formal and informal rules that constrained each other's activity and behavior as well as shaped their expectations. Cooperation between them did grow over time. The alliance proved to be a very popular policy choice.[36]

The signing of the alliance was greeted warmly in both Germany and Austria because of the common historical ties the countries shared. Austria-Hungary and Germany maintained close cultural ties and a commitment to monarchical conservatism. The Germans in Germany and those of Austria had "for a thousand years . . . been in the same empire, and their present political severance from one another dated back scarcely a decade."[37] In Germany, there was the sentimental belief that the fates of Germany and Austria were inextricably bound.[38] Bismarck, in talking about the alliance, spoke of "the ties of blood, the possession of a common language, and of historical memories—the same general considerations which had earlier been the strength of the great German movement and which were still largely responsible for the pro-German tendencies of German opinion."[39]

In Austria, similar feelings existed. "Austro-Germans, especially those with Pan-German leanings, and the Magyar ruling caste looked upon the diplomatic bond with Germany as something natural and altogether desirable."[40] Germany was the perfect ally for Austria's desire to maintain German hegemony in Austria.[41] Such commonality in background provided a basis for strong relations between the states. To this end, too, continuing conflict between the two states would be problematic.[42] The popularity of the alliance and the nexus of common historical and cultural ties also reveal that by 1879 Austro-German relations were quite positive and the level of

TABLE 4.2
Threats to Member States of the Dual Alliance, 1879

Member state	Source of threat	Degree
Austria–Hungary	Russia	Very high
	Italy	High
Germany	France	Very high

threat within the alliance was low. Table 4.2 provides a summary of threats facing the Dual Alliance member states.

COHESION

The Dual Alliance was an agreement to uphold the "imperative duty as Monarchs to provide for the security of Their Empires and the peace of Their subjects, under all circumstances."[43] It stated that if either country were attacked by Russia, the other was obligated to assist "with the whole war strength of their Empires, and accordingly only to conclude peace together and upon mutual agreement."[44] In the event of an attack by another power, the allies were obliged to observe benevolent neutrality, unless that other power was assisted by Russia. In that case, the states would be required to assist with their whole fighting force until a mutual peace agreement was signed.[45] The alliance was concluded for a period of five years. It was renewed in 1883 and 1902, when it was agreed that the treaty would automatically be prolonged, providing no negotiation to the contrary took place.[46] The alliance had a moderate commitment level, as it specified the conditions for intervention. As it turned out, the Dual Alliance remained in effect until the two powers were defeated at the end of World War I in 1918.

The text of the treaty presents the primary goals of the alliance as countering the Russians. As seen in the previous section, however, that is a little misleading. German goals were to prevent Austria from allying with France. For Austria-Hungary, the principal goal was security vis à vis Russia. Mutual goals were harder to distill at least initially, although subsequently there was significant convergence in the Central Powers' aims.

Over time, the two states' goals and interests became increasingly intertwined; they continually adopted the other's interests as their own. At the time of the initial conclusion of the alliance, Austria-Hungary had no significant quarrel with France, Germany's primary foe. In fact, they shared the common interest of supporting the papacy and Catholic interests throughout Europe. Germany, despite intermittent periods of significant tension, had relatively warm relations with Russia—Austria-Hungary's primary rival. Emperor Wilhelm of Germany and the Tsar Alexander were in fact closely related (Wilhelm was Alexander's uncle) and quite fond of each other. Yet during the course of the alliance between Germany and Austria, incrementally each power took on the other's enemies and interests. German policy choices ensured tension with Russia, and Austria's relations with France deteriorated as well.[47] The institutional aspects of the alliance in this case served to deepen the member states' cooperation over time.[48]

This convergence happened slowly. During the first years of the alliance, Germany was unwilling to commit to becoming embroiled in a war over Austria's aspirations in the Balkans. It was not until the end of the 1880s that Wilhelm II assured Franz Joseph that Austrian mobilization, for whatever reason, would be immediately followed by German mobilization.[49] This promise did not wholly resolve the conflict between the two states over Austria's Balkan policy, although it facilitated allegiance to the alliance and coordination of policy regarding threats to each other's security interests.[50]

In addition, Bismarck did not believe that the tension that characterized Russo-German relations at the time that the alliance was signed would be long term. Yet over the lifetime of the alliance, Germany could not sustain good relations with Russia and simultaneously maintain its alliance with Austria. Consequently, Austria's conflict with Russia became Germany's, just as Germany's quarrel with France became Austria's. In the early years of the alliance, it was clear that Germany had no intention of supporting Austria-Hungary militarily as a consequence of Austria's Balkan policy, and Austria-Hungary did not intend to get embroiled in a war between Germany and France. Yet over time, as the tension between the two blocs increased, this changed as well.

As discussed in the preceding chapter, the League of the Three Emperors was reconstituted from 1881 to 1887. In 1887, when relations between Austria and Russia disintegrated to the point where the League could no longer operate, Germany maintained its commitment to the Dual Alliance. Although Germany signed the Reinsurance Treaty with Russia following the end of the League, the Treaty did not abrogate the Dual Alliance. As one scholar notes, "much has been made of Bismarck's dishonesty in making the Reinsurance treaty. There was certainly no dishonesty towards the Austrians. He had always insisted that he could not support them in Bulgaria nor at the Straits."[51] In spite of the Reinsurance Treaty, it is clear that the cohesion of the Dual Alliance increased from 1890 on. The subsequent German decision not to renew the Reinsurance Treaty facilitated closer Austro-German relations. By 1890, Germany believed that "a Russian solution of the Straits question was 'absolutely impossible' and that no changes could be allowed in the Near East without a previous agreement between Germany and Austria-Hungary."[52]

The level of cohesion of the Dual Alliance during its peacetime years was therefore quite high. The two powers, during the course of their alliance, managed to coordinate their aims and effectively implement policy intended to attain them. This was particularly true during the crises that peppered the pre–World War I period. The member states successfully coordinated their mutual goals as expressed in the treaty of alliance as well as strategy to attain those goals. The cohesion of the alliance actually precluded a resolution of the growing conflict between the members of the Dual Alliance and Russia and France. The heightened antagonism, in part a consequence of the cohesion of the Dual Alliance, became more acute in the latter half of the 1890s.

The two states' close coordination of strategy during crises had some effect on the military planning of the two as well. From 1879 to 1908 there was little discussion between the two states about their military strategy, nor did the states' war planning change. There was virtually no revision at this time in the German plans for a two-front war. Moltke hoped that alliance with Austria would make the probability of victory in the east more likely, but the allocation of troops to the east and west did not change.[53]

The annexation of Bosnia and Herzegovina by Austria-Hungary in 1908 and the ensuing crisis led to a tightening of ties between Austria and Germany. Ultimately, Germany gave Austria its support, and in early 1909 the Germans and Austrians entered into a correspondence concerning their military cooperation in the event of war between Austria and Serbia.[54] Germany assured Austria that if Russia intervened in a war between Austria and Serbia, it would constitute *casus foederis*.[55] From this time on, the cohesion of the Dual Alliance increased as a function of the growing threat of the Triple Entente.

SUMMARY

The alliance between Austria-Hungary and Germany was a fairly cohesive one. In its early years, the goals of the alliance were defensive and limited. Not much effort was required to fulfill them. The interests of the states, while not wholly consistent, were not in direct conflict with each other. The absence of a uniform external threat did not inhibit cohesion; nor did the fact that Austria-Hungary was more threatened than its alliance partner. Stresses and strains did appear, particularly over Austrian policy in the Balkans, but nevertheless the Central Powers managed to coordinate their goals and strategies to attain them. Convergence over time in the two states' aims was a manifestation of their alliance's cohesion.

The alliance also became increasingly institutionalized over time. Ultimately, despite the fact that the Dual Alliance was intended by Germany to leverage Russia back into the fold, it had the opposite effect of driving Russia into the arms of France.[56] The low level of threat within the alliance provided permissive conditions for a durable combination to emerge. This longest-lived alliance of the period altered the course of European history in a very profound way.

The Triple Alliance

The Triple Alliance between Austria-Hungary, Germany, and Italy was formed in 1882. It is puzzling at first glance to understand why or how in 1915 Italy could abandon this alliance of thirty-three years and less than a month later join a major war against its former allies. Yet an examination of the relations among the states of the Triple Alliance turns the puzzle into a question of why Italy joined the alliance in the first place and remained a member of it for so long. In other words, the puzzle is not Italy's defection but rather its cooperation. The Triple Alliance is yet another case of allied adversaries: Italy and Austria-Hungary were historic enemies. The Triple Alliance was a tethering alliance, designed to keep the hostilities between Austria-Hungary and Italy in check. It successfully served this purpose—until 1915. The alliance was never terribly cohesive, and the threat level within the alliance was always high. But the member states managed to renew it five times over the course of four decades and thereby keep the peace among them.

FORMATION

Italy

Following the Congress of Vienna in 1814, Austria gained Trento and Trieste. From that time, Austria dominated nearly the whole of the Italian peninsula, and all revolts against its authority were brutally suppressed.[57] In the quest for the unification of Italy in the late 1850s and 1860s, much of the territory controlled by Austria came under Italian authority. The Dual Monarchy, however, had yet to relinquish Trento and Trieste. In addition to Italian bitterness toward Austria for its brutality during the years of Italian subordination, the popular irredentist movement clamored for the cession of Trento and Trieste.

The Triple Alliance was formed at a time when Italy was seeking to enhance its prestige. The Congress of Berlin was a political and diplomatic disaster for Italy. It had hoped to press for territorial compensation for Austrian gains in the Balkans. Italy, unrealistically, especially hoped that Austria would cede Trento and Trieste. The failure of Count Corti, minister of Foreign Affairs, to secure any significant gain, coupled with the rumors that Tunisia, an important Italian interest, had been promised by the attending powers to France, was a terrible blow to Italian aspirations.[58]

Further, irredentist pressures culminated in a series of crises between 1878 and 1880. On May 29, 1881, in the wake of the bey of Tunis acknowledging the supremacy of France, Sidney Sonnino, a member of Parliament at the time and later prime minister and minister of Foreign Affairs, wrote a very influential article in the *Rassegna settimanale*.[59] In the article, Sonnino argued that Italy should resolve the question of irredentism and seek closer relations with Austria.[60] "This friendship represents for us the free disposition of all of our land and sea forces; it represents, it is useless to delude ourselves, the authority of our words in the concert of Europe. . . . *Friendship with Austria is for us an indispensable condition for a conclusive and industrious policy*."[61] Italy, threatened by France and by Austria, needed to contain the level of external threat it faced. As Sonnino continued, "*Isolation is equivalent to annihilation*, it would be more dangerous than the search for foreign alliances, provided this search for alliances was conducted with clear, constant and shrewd purpose."[62]

Why Italy chose to ally with its "hereditary" enemy can only be explained by viewing alliances as mechanisms for conflict management. As Edoardo de Launay, the Italian ambassador in Berlin, wrote to Italian prime minister Antonio di Rudini, "With Austria-Hungary we have contracted a 'mariage de raison,' which rests on a certain foundation of suspicion."[63] The "mariage de raison" was concluded in order to keep the peace between them.

Italy sought an alliance with the Central Powers to prevent isolation and contain the level of threat it was experiencing from France and Austria simultaneously. Those threats echoed from within the country; the Italian government urgently needed to consolidate its control over the population. Irredentism and the threats to monarchical interests from France were very grave. The tactical side benefits of the alliance for Italy were significant. Alliance with Austria, with a diminution of irredentist fervor, would allow the Italian monarchy to solidify its grip. Further, alliance with the Central Powers would guarantee for Italy enhanced prestige in Europe. The alliance was in fact a diplomatic coup. Italy was allied with one of the most powerful countries on the Continent and at the same time confronted a diminished fear of being attacked by the stronger Austria-Hungary.[64]

Other side benefits of the alliance would be gained in the Balkans where Austria-Hungary's and Italy's competing aspirations were manifest. In the words of Luigi Salvatorelli, "Italy wanted to transform the Austro-Russian duet in the Balkans into an Austrian-Russian-Italian trio."[65] The alliance offered an opportunity for Italy to anticipate gains in the Balkans, to be acquired as a consequence of Italy's guarantee to maintain neutrality in the event of an Austrian war with Russia.

The tethering motivations that underpinned the alliance became even clearer over time. This is most vividly portrayed in the successive renewals. By the 1891 negotiations regarding the third renewal, relations were fraught with tension and suspicion. In a letter from Launay to Rudini, Launay described the mutual threat between Italy and Austria and suggested that Germany inspired more confidence and exercised influence over Austria.[66] As animosity between the two rivals grew, tethering became more essential; Germany became instrumental to Italy as a means of influencing Austria. Indeed, Italy required German pressure on Austria-Hungary in order to obtain the modifications to the separate treaty with Austria-Hungary that Italy desired. The separate treaty manifested the tethering motivations on the part of Italy and Austria-Hungary.[67]

By the time of the fourth renewal, in 1902, the alliance itself was fundamental to maintaining the peace between Italy and Austria-Hungary. Rumors were rife among diplomatic circles that the hostility of the Italian public and irredentist sentiments would create a rupture in the Triple Alliance.[68] Renewing the treaty of alliance became essential to ensuring that the distrust and suspicion between Italy and Austria did not escalate.[69] The renewal of the alliance in July 1902 stemmed the immediate threat; it did not do so for long, however. By 1904, the threat between Italy and Austria reached new heights.[70] The Italians were gravely concerned by an augmentation of Austrian troops along the Italian frontier. The Triple Alliance was seen as the last best hope to manage the hostility between the two states.[71]

The alliance did not serve to decrease the level of threat Italy faced. It was that very threat from Austria that impelled Italy to maintain its commitment to the alliance,[72] despite the fact that the "extraordinary Austrian armaments" along the border did not exactly give rise to feelings of being "completely and securely tranquil."[73] A report in March 1905 gave an overview of the Austrian forces on or near the Italian frontier and addressed the increases of these forces between 1887 and 1905.[74] In passing along the findings of the report, Duc d' Avarna, the Italian ambassador in Vienna, wrote to Minister of Foreign Affairs Tomaso Tittoni that there were "voices circulating in every center of Vienna speaking of war with Italy as if it is inevitable."[75]

The tenuous peace, due in no small part to the Triple Alliance itself, continued, though the threat did not diminish. The very motivation on the part of Italy for maintaining the alliance was to stave off the possibility of armed conflict between it and Austria.[76] The alliance served to constrain states' behavior and activity as well as to shape their expectations. The desire to keep the peace carried Italy through the fifth renewal of the treaty in 1912. As Avarna wrote to Antonio, Marquis di Sangiuliano, the Italian minister of Foreign Affairs from 1905 to 1906 and 1910 to 1914,

> If we are very persistent in the wish for us to detach from the Triple Alliance without taking into careful consideration our convenience, we will find ourselves alone on the Austro-Hungarian front and in that case any incident that were to excite our public opinion radically hostile to Austria-Hungary would sour the reciprocal relations in a way as to render inevitable in time an armed conflict between the two states.[77]

The continued and heightened threat between Austria and Italy perpetually gave rise to the fear that Italy would not renew the alliance. It simultaneously gave added vigor to the tethering motivations that underpinned the alliance from the beginning.[78]

The alliance, as suggested by the German newspapers, also offered "the opportunity to dissipate the clouds over Italy."[79] In fact, the press in all countries was filled with speculation regarding the alliance's fate. On December 9, 1912, for example, the German paper *Vossiche Zeitung* ran an article stating: "The oscillations of Italian politics derives [*sic*] from its antagonism with Austria in the Adriatic and of the preponderant strength of England in the Mediterranean. This has aggravated the attitude of Austria against its Italian subjects and of the irredentist agitation in Italy."[80]

The Italians were neither unaware nor unmoved by Austrian animosity toward them. As Avarna reflected in a letter to Sangiuliano on December 28, 1911, "there is always a certain mistrust and a certain latent antipathy that will never be fully eliminated, but it does not and will not impede the maintenance of an alliance in the supreme interests of the two states."[81] This only served to highlight to the Italians the need for and the purpose of the Triple Alliance.[82]

While member states of the Triple Alliance benefited from the alliance precisely because of their conflicts of interest, the alliance itself never mitigated the existing distrust between the adversaries. In fact, each renewal of the agreement brought the tethering motivations to the fore once again. As Avarna wrote to Tittoni: "The continuing and reciprocal mistrust that exists in Italy against Austria-Hungary, and in Austria-Hungary against Italy, sleeps for some time and then returns periodically in certain seasons of the year."[83] Italy and Austria were never able to eliminate the threat that emanated from one to the other and vice versa. The threat became all the more pronounced with successive renewals. As seen in the case of the two Leagues of the Three Emperors, the Triple Alliance is an example of a peacetime alliance concluded for conflict resolution, an alliance to ensure the peace between two adversaries. So profound were the differences between Austria and Italy, so ingrained the sources of their hostility, that the only way the two could keep the peace was to become allies.[84]

Austria-Hungary

The motivations behind Austrian adhesion to the Triple Alliance were quite straightforward. Italy was regarded by Austria as a threat—not so great that it could not be managed in the context of an alliance, but great enough so as to render the alliance with Italy an important way of reducing Austrian insecurity.

The principal reason Austria was interested in alliance with Italy was to ensure "that her ally would not attack her in the rear in case she should become involved in a war with Russia."[85] It was the very threat of Italy's involvement in a war against Austria that made it an attractive ally for the Austro-Hungarian Empire. Given that Austria had two threatening adversaries on its borders—Russia and Italy—tethering those threats was an important motivation underpinning Austrian alliance policy. Should tethering Russia fail, Austria needed to be able to secure Italian neutrality in the event of war with Russia.[86]

There were key tactical side benefits involved. Above all, it was crucial for Austria to prevent Italy from seeking to secure itself elsewhere, especially if that elsewhere were France, Russia, or both. The challenge for Austria, then, was to make concessions with Italy for the sole purpose of preventing Italy from attacking its southern frontier in the event of war with Russia, to guarantee Italian neutrality, and to ensure Italy would not seek alliance with Russia. "By restraining our ally we should alienate her, and might drive her into the opposite camp, there to seek opportunities for expansion."[87] Haymerlé acknowledged that containing Italy was important to Austrian interests.[88]

Although Austria was hopeful that alliance with Italy would mean that troops that would otherwise have to defend an attack from the south could be deployed to the east to fight the Russians, the Austro-Hungarian Empire continued its preparations in the event of war with Italy.[89] Subsequent renewals illuminate even more starkly that Austria viewed Italy as an enemy and sought to tether it.

By the second renewal in 1887, the situation in the Balkans and Austro-Russian hostility were even more dangerous. The heightened possibility of war with Russia meant that Austria needed to continue to contain Italy. Italy had grown stronger militarily and financially in the years since the initial treaty. This, coupled with the graver threat from Russia, meant that it was all the more essential for Austria to tether Italy. By as early as 1884, Austrian plans for war had changed. The new plan called for more troops to be deployed to the east, with fewer divisions solely for defensive purposes on the southern frontier. The need to maintain such a deployment required containing Italian hostility through a tethering alliance.[90]

The third renewal in 1891 was motivated by tethering objectives as well. Early in the year, the Triple Alliance experienced a threatening development. The Italian government of Francesco Crispi, ardent supporter of the alliance, fell. Crispi was replaced by Rudini, a francophile. Germany and Austria both viewed this development with trepidation. Rumors from trustworthy sources to the effect that Italy was being seriously courted by France were picked up by the Austro-Hungarian ambassador at Rome, Baron Bruck.

> These disquieting tidings were in contradiction to the official declarations of Rudini, who repeatedly gave assurances of his loyalty to the Triple Alliance; but Kálnoky and Caprivi both lacked faith in the trustworthiness of his protestations. The latter particularly considered it most important under the circumstances to bind the unreliable ally to the Central Powers by still another tie. The drive grew month by month more urgent.[91]

The urgency derived from heightened threat that Italy would join France and Russia as they proceeded to negotiate their alliance, discussed in the next chapter.

The final renewal of the treaty in 1912 was also motivated by Austria out of a desire to tether. War planning in Austria during 1910–11 included scenarios in the event of war with Russia (War Case R), in the event of war with Italy (War Case I), and in the event of war with Serbia and Montenegro (War Case B). The Austrians' worst nightmare was War Case R + I + B; they did not believe they had sufficient strength to fight a three-front war.[92] "[T]hus the chief Austro-Hungarian diplomatic goal became the avoidance of such a constellation."[93] They did so by maintaining their commitment to their alliance with Italy, to neutralize the Italian threat. In other words, the Austrians continued their tethering relationship to Italy; the Triple Alliance, and particularly the Austro-Italian relationship within it, was generated and maintained as a consequence of conflicting, not common, interests.

Germany

Germany derived most benefit from alliance with Italy by averting an escalation in hostility, by preventing Italy from seeking to secure itself elsewhere, and by balancing France. Germany's motivations in concluding the Triple Alliance were to tether and to balance. The threat that Italy alone posed was not great, but nevertheless Germany needed to forestall growing antipathy between the two countries. Further, were Italy to ally with France, the resulting alliance would present a serious threat indeed. Germany was completely uninterested in capability aggregation; rather, German diplomats sought to tether Italy so as to contain and manage the level of threat it faced. The very possibility of adversarial relations made Germany receptive to alliance with Italy. Certainly the Germans were not enamored of the Italians, nor was there the sense that Italy and Germany shared common interests.

Germany's fundamental mistrust of Italy was articulated by Bismarck himself. In conversation with Haymerlé regarding policy toward Rome, Bismarck called Italian foreign policy "jackal policy." "Insatiable Italy," said Bismarck, "with furtive glance, roves restlessly hither and thither, instinctively drawn on by the odor of corruption and calamity—always ready to attack anybody from the rear and make off with a bit of plunder."[94] Controlling, restraining, and tethering Italy were infinitely preferable to allowing its "jackal policy" to come at Germany's expense.

The Italian threat to Germany derived not from its military capabilities but from the possibility that the Central Powers would have an additional front in the event of war with France, Russia, or both. As Busch wrote to Reuss on February 28, 1882:

> I admit that Italy's military weakness and her limited ability to act outside her frontiers make the comparative strength and the hoped for mutual services very unequal. But it would be an advantage not to be despised, if, supposing France in alliance with Russia undertook a war, Italy were on our side, even though it were but nominally and without her doing much. We should thus be free to employ elsewhere the troops, which we should otherwise have to place in or near the Alps.[95]

While Germany sought alliances in this period to secure itself against France, this does not cover all of its motivations for concluding the Triple Alliance. Germany wanted to ensure that in the event of war, Italy would not be an opponent. Germany wanted to tether Italy, to guarantee at the least its neutrality in the case of war. Although Italian military capabilities were not overwhelming to Germany or to Austria, Italy did have the third most powerful fleet at the time the initial treaty of alliance was concluded.[96]

Germany wanted to come to terms with Italy, too, as consequence of Italy's conflict with Austria. If Italy became embroiled in war with Austria, a German ally, it would involve Germany by default. German leaders certainly thought in these terms. When Count Launay approached Bismarck about the possibility of an alliance, he was told that "the key to the situation is in Vienna." [97] This is corroborated by a memo by Bismarck to the emperor, January 31, 1882, in which he states that he told Launay "that the key of the door leading to us was to be found in Vienna." [98] Germany wanted to ensure that Austrian-Italian animosity was contained; if Austria and Italy could come to agreement, war between the two would be averted. This was consistent with the thinking of Austrian diplomats. As the German ambassador at Vienna, Reuss, wrote to Bismarck on March 18, 1882: "The Minister [Count Gustav Kálnoky] told me that the longer he thought about it, the more necessary it seemed to him to bind Italy by a formal Agreement, and he thinks that he shares this view with Your Highness." [99] In fact, the first article of the treaty of alliance stipulates that none of the member states will enter an alliance or go to war against each other. [100]

Subsequent renewals of the treaty of alliance highlighted German tethering motivations even more. The second renewal came not long after Italy's occupation of the port of Massowah (discussed below in the section on cohesion). This heightened Bismarck's sense that Italy needed to be watched more carefully than ever and was best tethered via alliance. Keeping Italy in line was even more urgent at the time of the third renewal, when France was courting Italy, attempting to detach it from the Triple Alliance. [101] "The menacing spectre of a coalition of France, Russia and Italy, directed against the Central Powers, rose once more before Bismarck's eyes and spurred him on to make every attempt to avert the peril." [102] German-Italian relations were fraught with tension, distrust, and suspicion; therefore an alliance between them was prized in Berlin. Forming an alliance with a state so as to avoid war with it is a clear manifestation of tethering.

The latter renewals of the alliance were also motivated by a German desire to tether Italy. The prolongation of the alliance in 1902 and 1912 were important so as to ensure that Italy would not join the enemy camp. As the son of Austrian foreign minister Andrássy recounted: "From this period the German General Staff were convinced that no positive assistance from Italy could be relied on. The only value of the alliance in their eyes was the fact— an important fact, however,—that it at least would prevent Italy from turning against us, so that the entire Austro-Hungarian military strength could be devoted to common cause." [103]

The Triple Alliance was concluded and prolonged for the purpose of managing and containing the conflicts of interest among the signatories. The alliance was not concluded in order to bolster any one state's capabilities per se but rather to ensure that in the event of hostilities, adversarial relations among the member states would not culminate in war. In May 1915, however, the inability of the alliance to fulfill that mission was quite vivid. Thirty-three years after the signing of the alliance, Italy broke with the Triple Alli-

TABLE 4.3
Member States' Motivations for Joining the Triple Alliance, 1882

Country	Motivation
Italy	Tether Austria-Hungary Balance France
Austria-Hungary	Tether Italy
Germany	Keep peace between Austria-Hungary and Italy; tether Italy; balance France

ance and joined the Entente Powers in a war against its former allies. The Triple Alliance managed to keep the peace among the member states for a very long time. It did not succeed, however, in reducing the level of threat internal to the alliance. The member states' motivations for forging the Triple Alliance are summarized in Table 4.3.

EXTERNAL VERSUS INTERNAL THREAT

The story of the Triple Alliance is quite similar to the one described in Chapter 3 on the Leagues of the Three Emperors. The threat to each member state was different, and for two members, threat emanated from the other. Nevertheless, a significant difference is that the impetus for the alliance did contain an element of external threat. I will first address the external threats facing the member states and then turn to a discussion of the internal threats.

One external threat confronting the alliance at inception was from France. As discussed earlier, France was Germany's principal adversary, particularly in the aftermath of their war in 1870.[104] At the moment the alliance was formed, Italy, too, was experiencing difficulties in its traditional friendship with France. Despite the fact that France had been instrumental in advancing Italian interests in its fight for unification, by the late 1870s relations were straining over colonial aspirations in North Africa. Tunis, just across the Mediterranean from Italy, represented the ripest acquisition on Italy's agenda. The Italian population there was, in 1878, the largest foreign contingent in the city—some 20,000 compared to the 200 or so French nationals.[105] Yet France, quite firmly in possession of Algeria, believed a preponderance of influence in a neighboring state to Algeria by any European great power, even a friendly one, would be threatening. Further, if Italy were in possession of Tunis, it would then have both sides of the Mediterranean at its narrowest point. Consequently, the French were determined to keep Italy out of Tunis and to claim it as France's own. In 1881, the French military occupied Tunis, and it was turned into one more of France's colonial protectorates in North Africa.[106] Italy was outraged by France's appropriation of coveted territory to which it felt it had both a legal and moral right. This anti-French sentiment provided an impetus for Italy to align itself with Germany against France. The French threat to Italy also included conflict over the papacy. The struggle between the papacy and the Italian House of Savoy for political authority over Rome heightened tension between Italy and France, as France championed the authority of the Catholic Church.[107]

German-French hostility had, of course, been severe since the Franco-Prussian War, and relations deteriorated further in the early 1880s. It thus became increasingly important to Germany that Italian-French hostilities remain unabated, ensuring the prevention of an alliance between them in the event of war. Although relations between Italy and France were hostile, the two did have a history of cooperation, particularly in the unification of Italy, and the rapprochement between the two at the turn of the century raised fears in Germany that Italy might defect from the Triple Alliance.[108] Hence a mutual adversary drew Italy and Germany together.[109] Austria-Hungary was the exception in the Triple Alliance in that it did not confront a threat from France. The primary Austrian threat came from Russia.

The internal threats to the alliance were not unrelated to those the member states faced from outside. For Italy, the need to secure Austria-Hungary as an ally was heightened because of its conflicts with France. The biggest advantage to Italy from the alliance was that it was guaranteed against an attack by Austria in the event of conflict with France, and in the latter case, it had the military support of Germany.[110] For Austria-Hungary, the strong irredentist movement in Italy that clamored for the return by Austria of Italian territory was a problem. Because Italy still sought claim to Trento and Trieste, Austria-Hungary needed to ensure that in the event of a war with Russia, its southern flank would not be vulnerable to an attack by Italy.[111] The alliance was thus used as a threat-reducing strategy, to eliminate the number of fronts the member states would have to fight in the event of war. The consequence, however, was that the threat internal to the alliance was quite high.

The level of threat within the alliance created conflict and divisions. The reciprocal threat between Austria and Italy was so high that war between the allies was a possibility. The Macedonian problem heightened Italy's disenchantment with Austria-Hungary. In 1903, a Macedonian revolt was reignited and spread to Turkey. Austria and Russia both sent troops; Austria and Italy sent warships. Two months later, to resolve the problem, Austria and Russia coordinated a program of reform to submit to Turkey. Italy was excluded from these proceedings. Austro-Hungarian policy was to prevent

Italy from maintaining any influence in the area. As the German documents revealed:

> Austria-Hungary does not intend to establish herself in Albania; but she cannot allow Italy to do so either. The propaganda carried on by Italy in Albania was either useless or designed to prepare a future Italian annexation. The freedom of the Adriatic, which would be ended if Italy established herself on the Albanian coast, was one of the questions for which the Hapsburg Monarchy would, in case of need, be obliged to fight.[112]

Following the first Moroccan crisis and during the Algeciras conference, tensions among the Triplice members grew. Germany blamed Italy for its inability to achieve German aims; Italy, having signed the Mediterranean agreements with France in 1902, was incapable of supporting its German ally's position without violating the spirit of its agreements with France. The lack of Italian support of Germany escalated the suspicion and distrust between the allies. Ironically, this increased distrust made it even more important that Italy be kept in the alliance—as the threat within the alliance increased, it was more important to maintain the alliance to keep the peace. The dangers revealed by the Algeciras conference heightened Austria's and Germany's desire to renew the Triple Alliance when it came time to do so in 1907.[113] Ladislas Szögyény-Marich, the Austro-Hungarian ambassador to Germany (1892–1914), reported Emperor Wilhelm of Germany saying to him at the time that "it was really monstrous for any one to give thought to the possibility of war against an ally . . . however in case Italy should show hostility to Austria-Hungary, he would seize with real enthusiasm the opportunity to join Austria-Hungary and to turn loose upon her his whole military strength."[114]

The antipathy between Austria and Italy continued unabated. When Italy annexed Tripoli in 1911, the Austrian chief of the General Staff, Franz Conrad von Hötzendorf, advocated preventive war against Italy and Serbia. He detailed his thoughts in a letter to Austrian foreign minister Alois Aehrenthal, contending that Austria should take action to counter Italy, "thus frustrating for a long time to come her designs on Italian territory of the Dual Monarchy, her plans for mastery of the Adriatic, and her activities in the Balkans." Conrad continued, arguing

> that the Dual Monarchy should take a position decidedly unfavorable to Italy's move in Tripoli, assure for herself a complete freedom of action, and, in case Italy opens hostilities in Tripoli, either attack Italy or secure at least equivalent indemnification in some other region.[115]

Conrad was dismissed for advocating war against his country's ally—the Austrian political elite realized that the occupation of Tripoli would inevitably anger Britain and France.[116] Although war did not come, that Austria's chief military strategist would advocate it reveals the depth of Austro-Italian antagonism.

In all, the threat level among the Triple Alliance member states was quite high; the primary motivation for maintaining the alliance was to prevent war among the signatories. Germany and Austria-Hungary persisted in tethering Italy because they saw it as the only alternative to Italy's repudiation of their alliance and realignment with the opposite camp. The Italian threat teetered on the brink of the tethering/balancing threshold; it could still be managed via alliance, but just barely. The Central Powers wanted to avoid Italy's balancing against them for as long as they possibly could. As a consequence, they worked hard on threat management. Italy, by the 1890s, believed itself to be allied with the only state that posed a grievous threat to its security. It, too, worked at threat management in the hope that the alliance would continue to keep the peace for as long as possible.[117]

When it ultimately became clear that Italy would need to make a choice, and it would not remain on the sidelines once the First World War erupted, it decided not to fight on the side of its allied adversaries. The war pushed Italy over the edge; it went from seeking to tether to seeking to balance. As early as September 1914, Italy drafted a war plan against Austria.[118] Italy's primary interest was to regain territory still within Austrian control, and to do so, it was imperative to fight Austria-Hungary. Doing so alongside the Entente was inevitable. As Antonio Salandra, prime minister of Italy at the time of the Great War, wrote,

> Italy had never been able to reconcile herself to the results of the inglorious war of '66. The acquisition of territory in Venetia had been considerable, but the young Kingdom had not gained proportionately in moral position or military reputation. . . . All possibility of defence on the Eastern frontier was negatived by the wedge-like Trentino, which facilitated the descent of an enemy safely established in command of the passes and heights. . . . Even after '66 — even after '70 — Italy found herself incomplete. The flame of patriotic aspiration, even if diminished and dimmed, had been handed on to us by the heros of the Risorgimento, and each of us carried in his heart a spark of the irredentist spirit.[119]

Hence, once again, the theme of internal threat to member states of an alliance, and resultant conflict and absence of cohesion, played itself out in the Triple Alliance. Fear of one another brought the member states together in an alliance, and differences were inevitable. No unifying force of a common external threat existed, as the threats each state faced were different. Both Italy and Germany were threatened by France, but Italy was also threatened by Austria. Austria was Italy's "hereditary enemy"; an alliance between the two states could not encompass mutual aims and goals and a

TABLE 4.4
Threats to Member States of the Triple Alliance, 1882

Member state	Source of threat	Degree
Italy	Austria-Hungary	High
Austria-Hungary	Italy	High
	Russia	Very high
Germany	France	Very high

unified strategy for attaining them. Table 4.4 summarizes the threats confronting the members of the Triple Alliance.

COHESION

The treaty of the Triple Alliance is interesting because it was a formal alliance with a significant commitment level and yet, with successive renewals, the treaty itself became the very tool for a truce between Italy and its allies. The first treaty was fairly straightforward. It stated that the signatories should come to the others' aid if attacked by any other great power. It more specifically identified an attack by France on Italy or Germany as grounds for assistance by the member states. If one of the allies initiated war with another great power, the others were, at a minimum, to observe benevolent neutrality. The treaty obligated the three states to consult in the event of war and to ensure mutual cooperation in concluding peace. The treaty was to remain a secret and to be subject to renewal after five years. Upon ratification, an additional declaration by Italy was attached stating that the provisions of the alliance excluded action directed against England.[120]

The alliance had a moderate commitment level, as it specified the circumstances under which the allies would come to each other's aid. Over time, the contents of the alliance became more and more specific; the issues of contention between Italy and Austria-Hungary were broached, and resolution was attempted. Over time, the institutional function of the alliance also became clearer. Rules were set out, particularly those designed to constrain member states' activity and behavior as well as shape their expectations. The second treaty of the Triple Alliance, concluded in 1887, was an extension of the first yet had two separate treaties attached. One between Austria-Hungary and Italy addressed the territorial interests of the two states in the Balkans and the Adriatic—the first attempt to resolve problems between the two in these areas. The second treaty between Germany and Italy addressed the conflicts between Italy and France in the Mediterranean and North Africa. It described what would constitute *casus foederis* for Italy.[121]

The third treaty of alliance between Germany, Italy, and Austria-Hungary, concluded in 1891, incorporated the separate agreements signed by Italy and Germany and by Italy and Austria-Hungary. It was more detailed and added an article addressing Germany's and Italy's efforts to maintain the territorial status quo in Cyrenaica, Tripolitania, and Tunisia. This treaty formally added Article VII, which came to symbolize the difficulties between Austria and Italy. This article stated that

> Austria-Hungary and Italy, having in mind only the maintenance, so far as possible, of the territorial status quo in the Orient, engage to use their influence to forestall any territorial modification which might be injurious to one or the other of the Powers signatory to the present Treaty. To this end, they shall communicate to one another all information of a nature to enlighten each other mutually concerning their own dispositions, as well as those of the other Powers.
>
> However, if, in the course of events, the maintenance of the status quo in the regions of the Balkans or of the Ottoman coasts and islands in the Adriatic and in the Aegean Sea should become impossible, and if, whether in consequence of the action of a third Power or otherwise, Austria-Hungary or Italy should find themselves under the necessity of modifying it by a temporary or permanent occupation on their part, this occupation shall take place only after a previous agreement between the two Powers, based upon the principle of a reciprocal compensation for every advantage, territorial or other, which each of them might obtain beyond the present status quo, and giving satisfaction to the interests and well founded claims of the two Parties.[122]

Here we see the institutional function of the alliance quite clearly, although this article was subject to numerous disputes over interpretation; much of the conflict between Austria-Hungary and Italy manifested itself in debate over Article VII. The fourth treaty of alliance, signed in 1902, contained an only slightly modified version of this article, as did the fifth treaty, signed in 1912.[123]

Distrust among the members, particularly Austria-Hungary and Italy, constantly came to the fore. In 1885, the Italians, without informing their allies of their intentions, occupied the Egyptian port of Massowah. This act dismayed Germany and Austria-Hungary, who believed that such action was in direct violation of the terms of the alliance.[124] When Italy annexed Tripoli in 1911 with no notice to its allies, the cohesion of the alliance similarly suffered a blow. This event also heightened fears within diplomatic circles as to Italy's future intentions. "The mode then of the attack of Italy on Turkey has strengthened in some Austrian circles the fear that Italy will one day do the same against Austria."[125]

It was often unclear to the member states what purpose, other than ensuring the peace between Austria-Hungary and Italy, the alliance served. As Count Gustav Kálnoky, the minister of Foreign Affairs of Austria-Hungary

(1881–95), said when the subject of renewing the Triple Alliance arose in 1886–87:

> The more evident it becomes to friend and foe that Austria-Hungary will have to defend single-handed her lawful interests on her southeastern frontiers, the more our enemies are heartened, and our friends discouraged by this fact, the greater care we must take to assume no obligations which would involve us in complications outside our own sphere of interests. At a moment when our people are speculating, with pardonable solicitude, as to the perils which may be-set the monarchy to the southeast, and as to the sufficiency of our forces to with-stand the various hostile elements which threaten us in that quarter, it would be indeed a heavy responsibility unnecessarily to assume obligations which might draw us into a conflict with France over incidents in the far west, or in Tripoli or Morocco, where we have no interests whatever, and bind us . . . for the purpose of protecting Italy and her shores against French attacks by land and on sea.[126]

For a state to declare it has no stake in its ally's crucial area of interest indicates quite clearly that their goals are not shared, to say nothing of their capacity to implement those goals.

Yet for Italy, it was not the absence of central interests between it and its ally that was a problem, it was the conflict over those interests that was most salient. For example, Austria's Balkan policy was a source of unending Italian displeasure. As Francesco Crispi, premier (1887–91, 1893–96) and acting minister of Foreign Affairs in Italy (1887–91), said in 1880 to the Italian Chamber:

> By the Treaty of Berlin, Austria acquired with Bosnia and Herzegovina an in-vulnerable frontier in the Near East and ought to rest content. We without en-vying her ill-gotten gains must be willing that she shall stay there, but that she shall not ask for more than the treaty gives her. We, gentlemen, in our own in-terests and in accordance with the principles of our great revolution must be the protector and friend of the little states in the Near East. The time-honoured idea, which Mazzini was the first to formulate, of a confederation in the Balkan pen-insula is the only one which can avert major disasters and prevent Russia from reaching the Adriatic or Austria the Aegean.[127]

"In other words," one scholar notes,

> Austro-Italian differences were due not only to the unresolved problem of the unredeemed provinces, but also, even if not fully realized by Italy in 1878, to Bal-kan questions in which Austria would not brook Italian interference. These dif-ferences were to remain latent until 1914; once the European conflagration had burst out, they made Italians conscious that their place could not be elsewhere than in the opposite camp to Austria.[128]

Once Italy had given voice to issues of dispute in the Balkans, friction be-tween Austria-Hungary and Italy grew. Article VII of the third treaty of alliance was not specific enough to resolve disputes. Rather, it, too, was continually subject to dispute over interpretation.[129] The protocol between Italy and Austria-Hungary attached to the second treaty of alliance, and later converted into Article VII of the third, fourth, and fifth treaties, was an attempt to resolve the differences between them. Yet it was not effective. Austria-Hungary's Balkan policy, competition between Italy and Austria-Hungary over Albania, and continuing resentment on the part of Italy for Trento and Trieste made relations between the allies largely divisive and ridden with conflict. The level of cohesion, although it varied over time, was low.[130]

From 1900 to 1915, the level of cohesion of the Triple Alliance did vary. Despite the fact that relations, particularly between Austria and Italy were divisive,[131] the alliance members managed to coordinate their policy during the Balkan Wars,[132] and in fact in 1913 the three members signed a naval agreement specifying a plan of operation in the event of hostilities between the Triple Alliance and the Triple Entente. It outlined a command structure, communications, and a division of responsibility for the plan.[133] This reflects a moderate level of cohesion, yet it did not last. Even at the height of its cohesion, when the member states concluded the naval agreement, the army staffs of the allies did not exchange information, and the question of command coordination was not raised. As a consequence of this, the member states were unable to coordinate their policy or implement it effectively.[134] Furthermore, that same year Austria-Hungary passed the "Hohenlohe decrees," which dismissed all Italian citizens from public employment in Trieste.[135] Such an act was inflammatory and could only bring the issues of conflict between Italy and Austria to the fore again.

As seen in the previous case studies, certain domestic issues had ramifications at the international level that affected the threat level the allies experienced. The heightened threat level in turn influenced the dynamics and cohesion of the alliance. The Italian irredentist movement, based on the notion of "the reclamation of Italy's *terra irredenta* ('Unredeemed land')" had a very powerful effect on both the populace and decision makers.[136] This movement, though often employed with respect to issues of imperialist claims to places like Tunis, at its heart was centered on Italian-speaking populated territories. While this movement's power waxed and waned over the period of time during which the Triple Alliance endured, as we have seen, it was nevertheless an important wedge between the two states. As described above, in 1913, at the height of the alliance's cohesion, when the alliance was renewed for the fifth time and a naval agreement was concluded by the member states, the Hohenlohe decrees were passed. This set fire to irredentism, and despite the fact that in November the Austro-Hungarian emperor Franz Joseph did not approve of the laws and it became clear that the decrees would not be implemented, the cohesion enjoyed by the alliance earlier that year could not be regained. Irredentism was brought to the forefront of Italian politics once more.[137] At every point it was raised, it came with a threat to Austria-Hungary.

Irredentism reflected Italy's desire for great power status and was also a manifestation of the antagonism Italy felt toward Austria for its subjugation of its Italian population. As Francesco Crispi wrote in recollecting a conversation with Herbert Bismarck (the son of Prince Otto von Bismarck), "If the Italians in Austria were well treated and their autonomy respected, our own people would have no reason to complain, and all excuse for the Irredentist movement would be removed."[130] Crispi went on to recount that "Austria is not beloved in Italy. She has not known how to make us forget her domination on Italian soil, but rather keeps the memory of it green by her present rule at Trieste."[139] As is clear from Crispi's words, irredentism's force was grounded in nationalist pride, and as much as it was a cry for "unredeemed land," it also served as a vehicle to voice hostility toward Austria for its treatment of Italians within Austrian political control.

Irredentism represented a central conflict with and posed a direct threat to Austria-Hungary. The idea incorporated an expansionist element as well. The ultimate desire for Italy was to win territory from the Habsburg Empire. The irredentist movement fueled the threat level from Italy to Austria-Hungary by revealing hostile intent. As a consequence, when irredentist sentiment was strong, the cohesion of the alliance decreased. When the issue was shifted to the back burner, and thus the threat within the alliance diminished, cohesion was enhanced.

Austria, predominantly Catholic, largely considered itself guardian of Catholic interests. It is difficult to determine how much Italian-Austrian relations were affected by their conflicting religious goals. Yet the conflict over the Catholic Church represents another way in which the goals of the Triple Alliance differed and how cohesion of the alliance was low.[140] This issue is somewhat confused further by the fact that Germany also battled the influence of the church (see the discussion of Kulturkampf in the preceding chapter), and so on this issue Italy and Germany agreed.[141]

As a final note regarding the ideological goals of the alliance, it is worth pointing out that scholars disagree on whether liberalism or monarchical conservatism played a role in the dynamics of the alliance. It has been argued that Italy defected to the Allied Powers' camp once war came because it could not remain allied with the conservative monarchies of Germany and Austria-Hungary, given Italy's liberal tendencies.[142] Yet it has also been argued that one should not underestimate the significance attributed to the Treaty [of alliance] by the allied sovereigns and their chief statesmen as a safeguard of the monarchical principles and a protection against "destructive" social movements. If the desire for strengthening the monarchical power had been one of the reasons for the rapprochement between Italy and the two Empires then the conclusion of the Triple Alliance must be regarded as the triumph of this idea—a triumph, primarily, of the House of Savoy which had not yet been firmly established in Italy.[143]

Aside from a minor role that the Triple Alliance played in legitimizing Italy's monarchical authority, however, these issues were really not central to the operation of the alliance. Agreement on the goal of monarchical conservatism was not enough to make the alliance cohesive. The theme that underscored the history of the Triple Alliance was one of conflict rather than cohesion. It was a case of allied adversaries, and despite its endurance, the members were unable to overcome the conflicts of interest that characterized their individual agendas.

SUMMARY

The Triple Alliance was not cohesive. The reasons the states chose to ally were the very factors that inhibited them from coordinating goals or implementing joint policy. Italy and Austria-Hungary were historic adversaries, and nothing short of Austria relinquishing the Italian provinces still in Habsburg possession would have resolved the conflicts besetting the Triple Alliance. Austria agreed to the alliance with Italy in order to ensure that it would not have to fight a two-front war in the event of an Austro-Russian conflict. By 1907, hostility among the members was so high that Germany and Austria were compelled to renew their alliance with Italy to prevent Italy's open defection to the Entente.

The alliance, despite its explicit defensive purpose, actually was a tool for keeping the peace among the member states. The absence of an overarching common threat to all three states inhibited the ability of the allies to coordinate their policy goals and pursue them jointly. As such, the Triple Alliance demonstrates the curvilinear relationship between the level of threat between states and the propensity for those states to ally in times of peace. The conflict between Italy and Austria-Hungary was a deeply entrenched one; the level of threat that emanated from one to the other was quite high. Yet war between them, though considered as an option at times, proved avoidable from 1881 to 1913. War only ensued when Italy was presented with the opportunity to redeem the provinces it had never relinquished hope of attaining. Italy may not have initiated a war to regain the Italian

TABLE 4.5
Chapter Summary: Alliances, Threat, and Cohesion

Alliance	Principal source of threat	Cohesion
Dual Alliance, 1879–1914	External	High
Triple Alliance, 1882–1914	Internal	Low

provinces in Habsburg control on its own; yet once the Great War began, it seized the opportunity. At this point, maintaining the alliance was impossible; Italy switched camps and less than a month later was fighting against its former allies.

Given the history of relations between Italy and Austria, this shift is not surprising. The puzzle is, why did they ally in the first place? A traditional understanding of alliances as vehicles for capability aggregation cannot explain their partnership. The answer to the puzzle lies in the gains presented to the members in managing their conflict through an alliance. This also helps us understand why allies are not only unreliable but frequently fight one another. Italy was guaranteed against any attack by Austria-Hungary; Austria-Hungary was guaranteed that Italy would not combine with Russia and initiate a two-front war. These gains could only be reaped during times of peace; allies with conflicting interests and divergent enemies could only exist in the absence of system-wide war. Once the war began, the importance of common enemies predominated. Austria-Hungary and Italy were enemies—allied enemies for some time, yet enemies nevertheless. The outbreak of the First World War could only mean the end of the Triple Alliance. Table 4.5 summarizes the threats and cohesion to both the Dual and Triple Alliances.

Conclusion

The Dual and Triple Alliances were formed within three years of each other, with two of the same signatories in each. The alliances, however, were very different from each other. The Dual Alliance actually was able to have external goals and purposes, while the Triple Alliance, despite Italy's and Germany's balancing motives against France, was principally to serve as a managing device among the member states. The Triple Alliance was primarily formed and maintained to keep the peace between Italy and Austria-Hungary. It did so for thirty-three years.

The Dual and Triple Alliances provide evidence for the argument that the relationship between alliance formation and threat is curvilinear, as well as the idea that both internal and external threats drive cohesion. The Dual Alliance was, in essence, a balancing alliance, with hedging motives, too, on the part of Germany. The level of threat within the alliance was low, and the level of external threat was moderate; the cohesion of the alliance was fairly high as a consequence. While the alliance may be understood or explained by the realist perspective, its successor, the Triple Alliance cannot. To provide a realist explanation of the Triple Alliance would miss the most important features of that agreement. In that case, the level of threat between and among the signatories was significant. The level of threat within the alliance eclipsed any common external threat. At numerous points throughout the thirty-three-year existence of the alliance, it appeared that the level of threat would lead to a defection on the part of Italy from the alliance. Italy teetered on the brink for many years, and defection finally came in 1915.

The alliances thus reveal that when the level of threat outside the alliance is greater than inside, cohesion will be relatively easy to attain, as was the case in the Dual Alliance. If threat is greater inside the alliance, it will be hard for states to coordinate goals and means to attain them, as was true in the Triple Alliance. The Triple Alliance did not lack cohesion because of the absence of an external threat; it did so because the level of threat internal to the alliance was high.

Despite the lack of cohesion of the Triple Alliance, it was perceived by Russia and France to be threatening—a menace to their respective interests. The danger of using an alliance to manage signatories' relations is that nonmembers may perceive it very differently from its intended purpose. Thus, the Triple Alliance, in particular, with the near adhesion of Great Britain in 1891, was precisely what brought into being the first exclusively balancing alliance of the period—the Franco-Russian Alliance. France and Russia both sought to balance, to secure themselves against the Triple Alliance when they perceived that Great Britain would be joining it.

CHAPTER 5

The Franco-Russian Alliance
and the Triple Entente

THREE TREATIES formed the Triple Entente: the Franco-Russian Alliance of 1891/94, the Entente Cordiale between Britain and France of 1904, and the 1907 Anglo-Russian Convention. The Triple Entente marked a key turning point in European history, one that culminated in a war more costly in lives and treasure than anyone could have imagined. The coalescence of great power alliances—Germany, Austria-Hungary, and Italy on the one side and Great Britain, France, and Russia on the other—heightened the threat perceived by each state. Yet these alliances were largely forged to manage relations among the signatories. This was certainly the case with the Triple Entente.

The bilateral agreements that formed the Triple Entente, with the exception of the first, were undertaken to manage the threat from each state to the other. The Entente Cordiale, which was fundamental to British foreign policy from its inception, was concluded primarily as a consequence of British fears of Russia and France and French fears of Britain. An understanding with France opened the door to reducing the threat Britain faced in the Far East and its antagonisms with Russia. Indeed, the Anglo-Russian rapprochement, ultimately provocative to the Triple Alliance member states, was embarked upon to manage and contain the signatories' distrust. Despite the fact that the Triple Entente sealed the fate of the great powers of Europe, the purpose of the agreements at the time they were signed had almost nothing to do with the external goals that the alliance ultimately fulfilled. The great powers of Europe were victims of the alliance paradox.

This chapter explores the motivations that led to the formation of the Triple Entente and assesses the cohesion of the alliance over time. Each dual agreement constituting the Entente is examined. Both Russia and France perceived Great Britain as an adversary and were drawn together by the mutual threat it posed. The danger of British adhesion to the Triple Alliance made the alliance of France and Russia a natural one. The Franco-Russian combination was a balancing alliance.

The Entente Cordiale was characterized by tethering incentives. The reciprocal level of threat between France and Britain brought about this agreement. The two states feared becoming embroiled in a war against each other. The Fashoda crisis in 1898 illuminated the tensions between them and signaled the dangers of having competing colonial interests. Further, as hostility between their respective allies grew in the first two years of the new century and culminated in war in 1904, Britain and France became all the more fearful that they would each be drawn into the war on opposing sides. The clash of allied and colonial interests brought tethering motives to the fore. The Entente Cordiale paved the way to improved relations between the signatories. It also became an important turning point in the orientation of British policy. Until 1904, British war planning had been exclusively directed against France and Russia.

The Anglo-Russian Convention was also forged by tethering motivations on the part of both states. The Entente Cordiale had successfully kept the peace between France and Britain during the Russo-Japanese War. Britain and Russia wanted to ensure that peace between them would continue. British efforts to tether via agreement with Russia should not be construed as contra Germany. Russia was painstakingly careful to keep Germany apprised of the negotiations. In fact, rather than allying against Germany, both Russia and Britain sought to maintain good relations with Germany at that time.

The Triple Entente, then, at its inception in 1907 was an alliance that incorporated balancing and tethering motives. At the outset, it lacked cohesion, as expected in an alliance with a high level of internal threat and only a moderate level of external threat. Over time, however, the alliance gradually became more cohesive; there was more planning and coordination of goals and strategy to attain those goals among the member states. This occurred as the perceived external threat to the signatories increased and came to eclipse the internal threat originally experienced by the states. Interestingly, the threat the Triple Entente came to counter was the very one it was ultimately instrumental in creating.

Just as the Triple Alliance served to heighten the threat experienced by France and Russia, despite the fact that the alliance was formed principally to keep the peace among the signatories, the Entente had the same effect on Germany and the Triple Alliance. Although none of the member states of the Triple Entente meant to encircle Germany in the early twentieth century, that was how their behavior was ultimately viewed. The Entente heightened insecurity in the international system. The formation of the Triple Entente was undertaken with a view to improving the relations of Great Britain, France, and Russia in order to reduce the possibility that Britain would find itself at war with France or Russia. Yet the unintended consequence of those states coming together was to signal to the Triple Alliance that a counter-point alliance had been formed. The Triple Entente served well to keep the peace among the member states of the alliance; it also served, however, to fuel the alliance paradox. The Triple Entente took the great powers of Europe one step closer to the possibility of war.

The Franco-Russian Alliance

The Franco-Russian Alliance marks a crucial turning point in the diplomacy of the pre–World War I period. It was both a manifestation and a cause of the heightened level of threat experienced by states in the waning years of the nineteenth century. The Franco-Russian Alliance was the first exclusively balancing alliance concluded; the effects of it on the constellations of powers in the system were manifold.

To understand the advent of the Franco-Russian combination, it is important to consider the consequences of the alliances that came before it, described in the previous chapters. Although the Triple Alliance was formed and maintained principally as a tethering alliance—to manage and constrain hostility between Austria and Italy and for Germany to control Austria—a damaging effect of the alliance was to isolate and threaten nonmember states.

The Triple Alliance was initially concluded just after the Three Emperors' League was reconstituted in 1882. Hence, Russia and Austria had an effective vehicle for constraining their hostility toward one another, and Russia was not wholly isolated. The League failed in the same year that the Triple Alliance was renewed the second time, in 1887. Yet because Russia concluded the Reinsurance Treaty with Germany at that time, it was still not left completely excluded from the security arrangements in Europe.[1] All of this changed, however, in 1890 when the Reinsurance Treaty expired and it was clear that Germany would not be prolonging it. Russian isolation and the threats it faced from Austria and Great Britain came more sharply into focus. This was especially true since at the same moment the Triple Alliance was renewed for the third time, and it appeared that Britain might be joining it.

France was experiencing heightened threat and isolation at this point as well. The consequences of the network of agreements and alliances among these great powers in the 1870s through the 1880s had been profound for France. One of the principal objectives of Bismarckian diplomacy had been to isolate France and draw a wedge between it and any possible ally. French isolation, coupled with its antagonistic relationships with Germany, Britain, and Italy, meant that the threat level it experienced was quite significant. As with Russia, the third renewal of the Triple Alliance and the perceived adhesion of Great Britain raised the level of threat to France to new heights.

Thus, in 1891 both Russia and France were isolated. Both were threatened by the third renewal of the Triple Alliance and the rampant rumors of British adhesion to it. As will be described below, a balancing alliance between them was the natural result. The Franco-Russian Alliance was the first exclusively balancing alliance to arise in this period. It ushered in an era of seeking military solutions to diplomatic problems.

FORMATION

Russia

Until 1890, Russia sought to secure itself through tethering one of its gravest enemies, Austria-Hungary. The repeated attempts to constrain and manage the threat that emanated from its principal rival in the Balkans, however, failed in the face of a growing fear that war would be inevitable with Austria and that Germany would not maintain benevolent neutrality. Until 1890, Russia had been at least modestly successful in retaining understandings with Germany to neutralize the possibility that Germany would support Austria-Hungary in a war against Russia. These fears, however, were present from the late 1880s and only continued to grow.

In 1887, negotiations were under way between Count Paul Shuvalov, the Russian ambassador to Germany, and Bismarck, which resulted in the Reinsurance Treaty. One of Russia's principal goals was to protect against the danger of a European coalition at a time when all the powers were proving hostile to Russia and to guard against this possibility by securing an alliance with Russia's most powerful neighboring state.[2] During the drafting of the treaty's first article, the issue of Germany's behavior in the event of a war between Austria-Hungary and Russia arose. To this, Bismarck told Shuvalov that in the event of such a war, Germany could not guarantee neutrality, and, to Shuvalov's astonishment, Bismarck revealed the existence of the agreement that had been signed between Austria and Germany in 1879 — the Dual Alliance — and renewed in 1884 for five additional years.[3] This was the first Russia learned of the existence of the Austro-German agreement. As a consequence, Bismarck informed Shuvalov, Austria would have to be exempted from the powers with which Germany would retain benevolent neutrality in the event of war with Russia, if Russia were the initiator of hostilities. During the fourth meeting with Bismarck, Shuvalov extracted a similar exemption for France, in the event of war between France and Germany. Bismarck was unhappy with this demand, stating,

> You demand of us our neutrality in case of war between You and England, Turkey or Italy and You accord us only a half neutrality only in case of war between us and France! We admit that this half neutrality is the equivalent of that which we promise You in case of war between You and Austria, but You still have three whole promises. Is that fair?[4]

Shuvalov prevailed, knowing that the tsar's and Russian foreign minister Giers's views were that Russian neutrality in a Franco-German war was the equivalent of Germany maintaining neutrality in a war between Austria and Russia.[5]

The negotiations culminating in the Reinsurance Treaty were important for a number of reasons. First, Shuvalov's reports reflect the level of threat Russia was facing. The concerns he raised about confronting a world of hostile powers, the desire to secure German amity, and the need to leave the door open to France were all results of his threat perception. Shuvalov's reports to the tsar also illuminate how essential the treaty was to providing a modicum of safety in an otherwise hostile world. Russia's sense of isolation and perception of threat were elevated by the revelation of the Austro-German alliance that had been drafted in such a way as to be directed against Russia. Bismarck's ploy of pulling the text of the agreement out of his briefcase to show Shuvalov during the negotiations had the desired effect of compelling Russia to accept his terms by amplifying Russia's need to successfully conclude the agreement. Seeing that the alliance singled out Russia as an important target of Austro-German collusion exacerbated the threat Russia faced and, in equal measure, intensified the importance of the Reinsurance Treaty in securing German neutrality in the event of war with any of its enemies, save Austria-Hungary.

Given this backdrop, the events of 1890 and 1891 and the emergence of the Franco-Russian combination are hardly surprising. Russia was already threatened by Austria. When Russia discovered the existence of the Dual Alliance, its perception of that threat was elevated. Russia's link to Germany was held only by the tenuous thread of the Reinsurance Treaty. The fall of Bismarck, the nonrenewal of the Reinsurance Treaty, and the apparent adhesion of another enemy, Great Britain, to the Triple Alliance only worsened Russia's strategic situation.

The deaths of Emperors Wilhelm I and Frederick III in March and June of 1888, respectively, and the accession of Wilhelm II in June 1888 marked important changes as well. In German military circles, sentiments had become increasingly tied to Austria and suspicious of Russia. It seemed that Wilhelm II was of a similar mindset.[6] The distance between Bismarck's and Wilhelm II's ideas regarding the direction of German foreign policy became clear in the year following Wilhelm's assumption of the throne. By May 1889, the kaiser was growing irritated with Bismarck's pro-Russian stance. He viewed the chancellor's strategy of binding Germany to Russia to avoid a Franco-Russian combination as problematic and was even more averse to supporting Russian policy in the east. The kaiser was threatened by the pro-Russian parties' successes in Romania and Serbia in the early months of 1889, and this, coupled by an antagonizing speech made by the tsar in May, heightened Wilhelm's concern that Russia was preparing for action that would offend Austria and Britain. Bismarck's response to these developments was to draw closer to Russia; the kaiser's reaction was very much to the contrary.[7] The kaiser viewed Russia as more threatening than did Bismarck; Wilhelm wanted to balance against Russia, while Bismarck wanted to tether it. We see here again that threat perception of the key decision makers is the most important indicator for predicting alliance choices.

The divergence in foreign policy objectives between Wilhelm and Bismarck led the kaiser to declare that "if Bismarck is unwilling to act against the Russians, our ways must part. I have already told him through Herbert that my patience with Russia is at an end."[8] The conflict between Wilhelm II and Bismarck on foreign policy became insurmountable when they disagreed on domestic policy as well. They clashed over how to deal with liberal forces at work within Germany. The combined effect of these differences of opinion culminated in Bismarck's fall from power in March 1890, just three months before the Reinsurance Treaty was due to expire.[9]

Bismarck's fall greatly agitated Russian diplomats.[10] At first the Russians believed that the Reinsurance Treaty would be renewed nonetheless.[11] The reality, however, soon emerged that no such action would be forthcoming by Germany. In May 1890, Russian foreign minister Giers suggested that the Reinsurance Treaty be renewed without the second article, which stated that Germany supported a preponderance of Russian influence in Bulgaria. Germany declined even this offer.[12] The lapse of the Reinsurance Treaty, coming with Bismarck's downfall, served to heighten Russian fears regarding German intentions.

Suspicions of Germany were compounded by a bill introduced in the Reichstag that increased the army troop level in peacetime by 18,574 men. Declarations were made by Minister of War Verdy du Vernois and Field Marshal von Moltke suggesting that German military strength should be increased to a point at which it could not be exceeded by any other state. The military budget went up accordingly.[13]

A final, crucial catalyst that compelled Russia to balance was the renewal of the Triple Alliance and rumored adhesion of Great Britain to it. The strain in Russo–German relations and continued hostility between Austria and Russia had already heightened Russian fears; the rumors that its enemy, England, was joining the Triple Alliance raised those fears to intolerable levels. Just as the Reinsurance Treaty expired in June 1890, Britain and Germany concluded their negotiations of the Heligoland Treaty, effectively removing the principal source of rivalry between the two great powers. As Antoine Laboulaye, the French ambassador to Russia, reported to French foreign minister Alexandre Ribot on June 22, 1890, the Heligoland agreement was viewed as "the symptom of European rapprochement between the two Cabinets of London and Berlin."[14] In this agreement, Germany ceded claims to territory in east Africa in return for the British cession of the Heligoland island to Germany.[15] The Russian decision to balance is, in a sense, overdetermined —it experienced heightened threat from Austria, from Germany, and from Great Britain, all of which would lead us to expect balancing behavior.

As will be discussed in further detail below, relations between Britain and the Triple Alliance were never as close as they were in 1890 and 1891. Many European diplomats believed that Britain's adhesion to the Triple Alliance was imminent. As Ribot reported to the prime minister and Minister of War Charles Freycinet on August 6, 1891, "Russia is evidently preoccupied with its assurances of our eventual assistance against Britain which is in effect considered from now on bound to the Triple Alliance."[16]

Russo–British rivalry centered, above all, on the colonial holdings and frontiers in Central Asia.[17] Britain feared the Russian southern advance in the region and the implications for the security of India; British holdings in India blocked Russia's continued expansion of influence and served as a "perpetual challenge" to Russia.[18] As early as January 1890, Laboulaye reported to Foreign Affairs minister Eugene Spuller that Russia wanted assurances from France to resist British preponderance of influence in Persia.[19] Animosity between Great Britain and Russia continued unabated in the subsequent period. An article published in the *Standard* on July 27, 1891, for example, characterized the Russians as "people proved to be barbarous and contemptuous of Western Civilization."[20] The magnified threat based on the belief that Britain was joining the Triple Alliance drove Russia to France.

As Russian foreign minister Giers wrote to Mohrenheim, the Russian ambassador in Paris,

> [T]he situation created in Europe by the manifest renewal of the Triple Alliance, and the more or less probable adhesion of Great Britain to the political aims that this alliance pursues, motivated, during a recent stay here of M. Laboulaye, an exchange of ideas to define the attitude . . . of our respective governments, which

being outside of all leagues, are nonetheless sincerely desirous of surrounding the maintenance of peace with the most efficacious guarantees.[21]

The negotiations were thus under way. Russia and France sought to combine their fates, ending each country's isolation. The negotiations culminated in an agreement that endured until the Russian Revolution in 1917.

France

Franco-German antagonism in the period following German unification through the First World War is well known and well documented. That Bismarck did all he could in his long stay in power to maintain French isolation and to prevent France from launching a war of revenge is similarly well known.[22] During the years leading up to the Franco-Russian Alliance, however, what preoccupied the French decision-making elite was France's rivalry with Britain, its strained relations with Italy, and the overwhelming fear that Britain had permanently and irrevocably aligned itself with Germany. While Franco-German hostility provides a crucial backdrop to the threat level faced by France, France, as did Russia, faced exacerbated threat by the renewal of the Triple Alliance and the belief that Britain was joining this alliance.[23]

It is important not to underestimate the impact that British alignment decisions had on France and Russia. In the post–World War II period, the popular narrative regarding the rise of hostility in the pre–World War I period has largely been attributed to the growth of German power. According to this narrative, German ambitions and increased military power drove the Entente member states to balance against it. The rise in systemic threat culminated in the First World War. Yet the Franco-Russian Alliance marks the turning point in the diplomatic history of the pre–World War I period, driving the great powers to seek military rather than diplomatic solutions to the problems they faced, and this alliance emerged largely in response to the British threat.[24]

The sources of threat confronting France in 1890 emanated from Germany, from Italy, and from Great Britain. The defeat in 1870 and terms of peace that France accepted in 1871 scarred France and influenced its foreign policy for decades to come. Since losing Alsace and Lorraine, France had never given up hope of regaining them. Since 1871, Germany had done all it could to ensure that France remain isolated and incapable of launching the war of revenge that both seemed to view as ultimately inevitable.[25] Further, Anglo-French relations were divided at nearly every turn. Relations were strained on policies covering many points of the globe—the Newfoundland fisheries, Egypt, Siam, and the Mediterranean.[26]

France viewed German policy and alignment decisions in the aftermath of the 1870 war as designed to counter, isolate, and threaten it. As Jules Herbette, French ambassador in Berlin, wrote to Ribot, the Triple Alliance was a Bismarckian plan to counter France at every turn.[27] Against the backdrop of a hostile and powerful Germany, three important and interrelated developments provided the impetus that drove France to agreement with Russia: the ongoing problems with Italy in the Mediterranean; the explicit guarantees made by Britain to support Italy regarding maintenance of the status quo in the Mediterranean; and the renewal of the Triple Alliance and perceived certainty that Britain had formally or informally acceded to it, via its promises to Italy and intimacy with Germany.[28]

While still unaware of the Mediterranean agreements forged by Britain with Italy and Austria, the French were only too aware that certain promises had been made by England to Italy. Not only were rumors rife in the press, but explicit statements were made by Italian prime minister Rudini and King Humbert of Italy that left little doubt in the minds of the French decision makers that Anglo-Italian collusion over policy in the Mediterranean had taken place. This was very threatening to France, particularly as the nature of the agreements was still ambiguous.

The ambiguity was experienced not only by France; in a series of discussions in the House of Commons, English radical leader Henry Labouchère repeatedly raised the question of the accord existing between Great Britain and Italy. Sir James Fergusson, undersecretary of state for Foreign Affairs, in response to these queries, admitted that there had indeed been communication between the two governments in 1887, but he was vague as to the nature of the agreement that had been reached. At each point the question was raised, Fergusson argued that the British government could not bind Britain to any course of action in the absence of parliamentary approval, though, again, he made it clear that informal guarantees had been made.

In a June 5, 1891, dispatch from William Henry Waddington, French ambassador to Britain, to Ribot, an "annexe" including an article published in the *Times* quoted Fergusson's reply to Labouchère: "Italian statesmen are well aware that Her Majesty's Government are at one with them in desiring that there shall be no disturbance of the existing order in the Mediterranean and adjacent seas, and that the sympathies of this country would be on the side of those who would maintain a policy so important for the British interests involved." The article continued, "France may feel annoyed by the thought that England and Italy have common interests, but if so it must follow that she cherishes designs hostile to one or both."[29] Further, Waddington's report to Ribot on June 23, 1891, stated that public opinion was "alive with the idea" that Britain and Italy had bound themselves by their communal interests in the status quo in the Mediterranean. The *Standard* reported that there was a similar accord between Britain and Austria-Hungary concerning the status quo in the Balkans.[30] Needless to say, the French followed these parliamentary proceedings and press reports very closely.[31]

In the middle of the attacks by Labouchère on Fergusson in the House of Commons, Waddington sought assurances and clarification from Lord Salisbury. Salisbury, to the frustration of Waddington, was decidedly ambiguous, leaving the French to infer for themselves as to what Britain had committed. Waddington interpreted his conversation with Salisbury to mean that if France were to attack Italy, the Parliament would immediately discuss and decide whether to send the British fleet to join Italy. But if Italy attacked France, Britain might maintain neutrality. This would depend on public opinion, the composition of Parliament, and the series of events that led up to the attack.[32] French decision makers were very preoccupied by the uncertainty regarding British intentions and alignment strategy.

The press was also rife with allusions to British cooperation with the Triple Alliance. Waddington attached these reports to his dispatches and monitored the reports very closely. In an "annexe" to his June 4, 1891, dispatch to Ribot, he included an article from the *Standard* of the same date, underlining the part of the article that stated: "We all know what would be, and what must be, the attitude and conduct of England if Russia were to make war on Austria or Turkey. We all equally know what would be, and what must be, the attitude of England were France to assail Italy, at any rate at sea."[33]

By the end of June and beginning of July 1891, the renewal of the Triple Alliance and Britain's status regarding this alliance were the key preoccupations of the French government. Nearly all dispatches from Herbette in Germany, from Waddington in London, and from Laboulaye in Russia at this time reported what they learned about the situation. The press reports, particularly from London, left little doubt in the minds of those monitoring the situation that Britain had become at least an informal member of the alliance.

In a dispatch from Waddington to Ribot on June 30, 1891, an "annexe" containing coverage of the renewal of the alliance in the *Standard* was attached. The article claimed that Germany was a most peaceful and contented power, and although all it and its allies desired was to be left alone, to live peacefully with its neighbors, belligerent France refused to comply with this wish. Ever since France recovered from its defeat, it had clamored for a return of the territories it had lost to Germany; Germany thus had no choice —it could either attack France for its open threats or secure powerful friends who would help Germany defy French designs. Of the Russians, the article stated: "Russia professes not to meditate any direct assault on the Austro-

Hungarian Empire. But it openly proclaims and ostentatiously pursued a policy, the execution of which would deal a mortal blow at that Power." [34]

The *Morning Post* of July 1, 1891, reported that

> so strong were the feelings [in France] aroused by the conviction that England, by a naval understanding with Italy had joined the Triple, or rather the Quadruple Alliance, and had thus become an enemy of France. . . . France now knew that England had been false to her; for when it would have been so easy to have remained neutral, she had chosen to point her guns openly at her neighbour across the Channel, with the inevitable consequence that all chance of an honest good feeling between the two countries had disappeared. . . . France would never forgive England for having secretly acceded to the Triple Alliance. [35]

The British press was unabashedly anti-French and jubilant regarding the renewal of the Triple Alliance. The announcement of the alliance's third renewal and British collusion with the member states frightened France badly. Were that not enough, the very moment that the renewal was announced, the German emperor visited England. The dispatches from London were filled with news of this visit, its meaning, and the press coverage of the visit. The *Standard* of July 11, 1891, captured the essence of the sentiment in England at this time:

> Germany, Austria-Hungary, and Italy have proclaimed aloud their determination to respect and, as far as in them lies, to protect public tranquility. How is it possible that English Statesmen would not hear such a declaration with satisfaction and sympathy? How is it possible that England should not virtually, though not formally, be the ally of Powers that dedicate their wealth, their strength, their arms, their whole policy to the furtherance of so noble and sacred an end? . . . We have welcomed the German Emperor as one of our race and blood. We have greeted him also as a truly great, conscientious, and extraordinary able Ruler. But the chief force and fervour of his reception have arisen from the feeling that he is our friend and ally—the friend and ally of all who deprecate war and detest the carnage of the battlefield. [36]

The *Standard* of July 4, 1891, reported Germany and England as being

> friends and allies of ancient standing. . . . It can have been neither by accident, nor the mere inspiration of an arbitrary statesmanship, that the two peoples should have found themselves in the same camp, animated by the same purposes, and struggling for the same ends, whenever a great political and military issue was being fought out. . . . [If a conspiracy against the stability of the European system emerges again] it would once more be met by the union of England's naval strength with the military strength of Germany. [37]

Meanwhile, in Germany, the conviction was even greater than in Britain that England was linked to the Triple Alliance, as Herbette reported to Ribot on June 6, 1891. According to the French ambassador in Berlin, the idea reported in the German press was not solely the existence of the Triple Alliance but a "system of alliances" of which Britain was formally a part.[38] Later the same month, on June 28, 1891, Herbette wrote to Ribot that "the accession more or less intimate of England to the Triple Alliance will have the consequence of tightening the bonds that bind Russia to France."[39] This is precisely what happened.

Heightened French and Russian insecurity as a consequence of British informal adhesion to the Triple Alliance brought the two states to the negotiating table. Laboulaye reported in a dispatch to Ribot on July 18, 1891, after meeting with Giers, that in the course of their conversation, the renewal of the Triple Alliance came up and the indirect accession of England. The question was then raised as to whether this event would make "one step more down the path of the entente" desirable.[40] Ribot's response to Laboulaye was to say that the renewal of the Triple Alliance "operating in the conditions that you know means that France must fortify the guarantees of its entente with Russia to ensure a certain equilibrium of forces in Europe."[41] On the same day, Ribot sent an additional dispatch to Laboulaye with an "annexe" entitled "Premier Project D'Arrangement." In it, Ribot wrote that the anticipated extension of the Triple Alliance, coinciding with an exchange of views between Britain and one of the Allied Powers, which had the effect of assuring the Triple Alliance of the more or less direct assistance of Britain, has caused the rapprochement of France and Russia.[42]

The negotiations between Russia and France, sparked by the British intimacy with the Triple Alliance, culminated in an understanding between the two states. The agreement specifically cited the renewal of the Triple Alliance and British adhesion to it as the reason the two desired to enhance their understanding and take measures in concert if threatened by aggression.[43]

The "Definition of Understanding" between the two states was signed in August 1891. The agreement stated that "the situation created in Europe by the open renewal of the Triple Alliance and the more or less probable adhesion of Great Britain to the political aims which that alliance pursues" prompted the two governments to come to an agreement.[44] The understanding was embodied in two points: to consult in response to any situation that might culminate in war and to reach an agreement regarding action in the event that war seemed imminent.[45]

The alliance formally came into existence in 1894, with the approval of a military convention. This distinction from the preceding cases is noteworthy. The Franco-Russian Alliance was one that centered on the security and military interests of the two states; it was not a conflict management or resolution mechanism. It also embodied a higher commitment level than the preceding alliances. In this sense, the Franco-Russian Alliance foreshadowed

TABLE 5.1
Member States' Motivations for Joining the Franco-Russian Alliance, 1891/94

Country	Motivation for allying
Russia	Balance Austria-Hungary, Great Britain, Germany
France	Balance Germany, Great Britain

the First World War. The signing of the alliance began a period of seeking military solutions to problems that divided the states of Europe. Table 5.1 provides an overview of French and Russian motivations for forming their alliance.

EXTERNAL VERSUS INTERNAL THREAT

The level of external threat was the most important factor in the formation and cohesion of the Franco-Russian Alliance. France and Russia allied as a direct result of the level of threat emanating from the Triple Alliance. For Russia, the primary foe in the Balkans was Austria-Hungary; in Asia, it was Britain. With rumors that Britain—one of the most powerful countries of Europe—was joining the Triple Alliance and the German decision not to renew the Reinsurance Treaty, there was no check on either of Russia's most threatening adversaries.[46] In the past, Germany had mediated the hostility between Austria and Russia. The German decision to allow the Reinsurance Treaty to lapse left the conflict open to escalating hostility. Russian military leaders were convinced that war with Austria-Hungary was imminent. To deal with Austria, they needed to deal with Germany. Russo-German hostilities were considered in military circles to be possible. As each state's military preparations began to take the position that war was conceivable, the dynamics of the conflict process were set in motion. The competition born of large militaries, mutual anxieties, and public and private perception of reciprocal threat all made it even more probable. The mutual preparations for war, in other words, made war more likely.[47]

The Triple Alliance itself became a foe. French leaders saw Germany as the most threatening member, but Britain's flirtation with and Italy's adherence to the alliance contributed to their increasing level of anxiety. The German threat was compounded in 1893 when a German army bill that increased the peace strength of German forces was passed. This threat was exacerbated by heightened antagonism with Britain, manifest in France's stand against Britain in Siam and British appeals to Germany for help.

Russia's quarrel with Germany grew largely out of hostility toward Austria and Britain. Germany increasingly became the target of Russian enmity as a consequence of Germany's place at the core of the Triple Alliance. The German decision to augment its military, coupled with the brewing conflict in Central Asia between Russia and Britain, led the tsar to believe that only an alliance with France would offer protection against the Triple Alliance and England.[48]

In the early 1900s, the level of external threat the alliance faced continued to grow; the alliance, as a consequence, became more cohesive. Tension between the Triple Alliance and the Franco-Russian Alliance rose in conjunction with several international developments. The two Moroccan crises and the Balkan Wars demonstrated the increasingly intractable conflicts of interests between the two adversarial coalitions. The tsar was instrumental in creating the Balkan League. Russia's defeat of Turkey and growth of the Russian satellite, Serbia, worried the Triple Alliance. The alliance was swiftly renewed, and Germany increased its army to unprecedented numbers.[49]

The German military buildup threatened both France and Russia. In response, France restored three years of compulsory military service. Tension between Russia and Germany was very high as well.[50] Russian reliance on France financially and the 1905 revolution in Russia made the tsar ever more concerned with maintaining the alliance with France to ensure Russian security and the wherewithal to confront the diverse array of threats facing him.[51]

Over time, the increase in the level of external threat had an important effect on the Franco-Russian Alliance. In particular, French and Russian military plans became more fully integrated. In 1912, the two states signed the Naval Convention to supplement the Military Convention of 1894, which had stipulated the combined action of the land armies. The Naval Convention called for complete and full cooperation and coordination of the two navies. The chiefs of General Staff of both France and Russia were called upon to communicate directly with one another, and a convention for the exchange of information between the Russian navy and the French navy was appended to the Naval Convention.[52] The exchange of information on a monthly basis represented an increasing level of alliance cohesion.

The Franco-Russian Alliance is the first alliance of the period under investigation that was solely the direct result of external threat. This is illuminated by the fact that the Franco-Russian Alliance commenced in the form of a military convention signed in 1894. In the previous four cases examined, political, not military, understandings gave the alliances life. The political and military goals in both Leagues of the Three Emperors, the Dual Alliance, and the Triple Alliance were intertwined. In August 1891, the agreement signed between France and Russia was not considered to be constitutive of a formal alliance. The Military Convention was a document instructing the two states as to what would constitute *casus foederis* and called for joint mobilization directed against the Triple Alliance. The physical form of this alliance was therefore distinct from the alliances investigated in Chapters 3 and 4, and this follows from the fact that the previously examined alliances were primarily political and diplomatic tools. All but the Dual Alliance were cases of allied adversaries, and their primary functions were as conflict management and resolution tools, not military arrangements with the goal of addressing a common, external threat.

The internal threat that existed within the Franco-Russian Alliance was negligible. Perhaps the only element of internal threat that existed emanated from the differences in structure and ideology of the governments. The two states of this alliance had vastly different ideological orientations. The success of the French Revolution symbolized a triumph for republicanism. Russia epitomized conservative monarchical autocratism that eschewed republicanism in any and every form. "The Russian autocrat was filled with disgust and hatred for Republican radicalism of France and his dislike was enhanced by the aversion of a deeply religious nature to the so called 'atheism' which appeared to be inseparable from political 'revolution.'"[53] The same aversion could be found in France; many despised the corrupt conservativism that the tsar represented.

The unimportance of the basic ideological contradiction between France and Russia is even more clearly illuminated when examining French loans to Russia. The damage incurred by Russia in the Russo-Japanese War and the need for finances to suppress the 1905 revolution made the influx of funds from France acutely necessary. The fact that France loaned money to the tsar to allow him to maintain power illustrates the degree to which security concerns overrode domestic sentiment in France about the corruptness of the Russian monarchy.[54] The desire of France to maintain the tsar's authority in Russia, despite the fundamental ideological differences between the two, was a product of the threat posed by Germany and continuing differences between France and Germany in Morocco. The cohesion of the Franco-Russian Alliance rose and fell as a function of the threat that emanated from the Triple Alliance, not according to the ideological underpinnings of the two allies.

Russia subordinated ideological considerations as well. At this time, the tsar and the kaiser met at Björkö and discussed the possibility of signing a treaty of alliance. Yet "the Paris Bourse made a stronger appeal than monarchical solidarity; and Nicholas II had to undo his own work."[55] It is, however, worth noting that changes in the French government made the Russians wary and suspicious of France. In 1892, while negotiations for the alliance were under way, a crisis in the French Parliament over relations between church and state arose unexpectedly. Its consequences were so far-reaching

TABLE 5.2
Threats to Member States of the Franco-Russian Alliance, 1891/94

Member state	Source of threat	Degree
Russia	Austria-Hungary	Very high
	Great Britain	Very high
	Germany	Very high
France	Germany	Very high
	Great Britain	Very high

that it culminated in the fall of the cabinet. The dismay this created in Russia was substantial. Russian leaders viewed this incident as yet another example of the instability of the French governing system.[56]

Despite the fact that Russia was concerned about this instability, negotiations for the Military Convention did ultimately continue, and the alliance nevertheless was formed. Again, the level of threat emanating from the Triple Alliance mitigated the concern over the French republican state, which was subject to rapid changes in its key leadership positions. Table 5.2 summarizes the threats faced by France and Russia.

COHESION

The cohesion of the Franco-Russian Alliance varied with the level of external threat emanating from the Triple Alliance. Its cohesion waned in periods when the threat levels were unequal or when the source of the threat to each member state was different. The fact that the Franco-Russian Alliance was a balancing alliance and that the external threat level was greater than the internal made cohesion effectively easier to attain than in the previous alliances examined. Interestingly, despite the fact that Russo-German relations improved dramatically and were quite cordial throughout the duration of this alliance—a point that will be returned to in the discussion of the Triple Entente—and despite the antipathy both felt toward the other's system of governance, in many ways this alliance became the cornerstone of each country's foreign policy in the two decades that preceded the First World War.

The Franco-Russian Alliance, then, was relatively cohesive, more so from the turn of the century on than before; the two states were largely able to agree on goals and coordinate policy to attain them effectively. One of the reasons for a high level of cohesion was that the goals of the alliance were limited and more precisely defined than in the previous alliances analyzed. The alliance came to life with a military convention that specified the conditions under which each would mobilize its forces, identified the number of troops each would mobilize, and called for joint planning and implementation of all military operations. This gave the alliance specific goals with guidelines for attaining them. "In short, the Alliance implied a rigid reorganization of material and moral resources which could be summed in the single word: Order."[57]

The cohesion of the alliance suffered a little bit at first, partly because of the confusion over terms of the convention. The first two articles contained an implicit contradiction. The first stated that Russia would mobilize on France's behalf in the event of an attack on France by Germany "or by Italy supported by Germany." France was to mobilize on Russia's behalf in the event that Russia was attacked by Germany "or by Austria supported by Germany."[58] Yet the second article stated that "in case the forces of the Triple Alliance, *or of one of the Powers composing it*, should mobilize, France and Russia . . . shall mobilize immediately and simultaneously the whole of their forces."[59] The first article implied that an attack by Italy alone on France would not obligate Russia to mobilize, as an attack on Russia by Austria alone would not constitute an obligation for France to mobilize on behalf of France's ally. Yet the second article stated that any member of the Triple Alliance attacking either member of the Franco-Russian Alliance would constitute *casus foederis* for the other.[60]

In addition to contradictions within the treaty, Russia and France had divergent goals in their colonial interests. For Russia, interests in Asia and the Balkans were central; for France, the Middle East and North Africa were key. Neither state wanted to become embroiled in a war over the other's imperialist interests.

There were limits to the extent the allies could agree on goals and strategy, particularly in the early years of the alliance. At its inception, Russia was concerned that France would entangle it in a war of revenge against Germany. Germany, while threatening to Russia, was not the focal point of its enmity. This was evidenced in the negotiations that preceded the signing of the agreement. The Russians were adamant that their relationship with Germany be preserved. The situation was already worse than they wanted, and they certainly did not want their relations to deteriorate any further. Similarly, France was reluctant to openly confront Austria or Britain, the states that most threatened Russia.[61]

Ultimately, France and Russia compromised. France made a tentative commitment to mobilize in the event of hostilities between Russia and Austria, and Russia made a tentative commitment to mobilize in the event of hostilities between France and Germany.[62] The advent of the Gladstone ministry in England lessened the tensions between Britain and Russia, making a French commitment to mobilize in the event of hostilities between Britain and Russia less urgent. However, the Anglo-Russian conflict in Asia made an agreement between France and Russia all the more necessary for Russian security, even if the French refused to come out openly against the British.[63]

Following the signing of the Military Convention, the cohesion of the Franco-Russian Alliance grew over time. Overall, cohesion remained relatively high.

> The bonds of friendship uniting the two Governments grew closer and closer. Successive French ministries . . . could not do enough to curry favor with tsarism. By 1895 the Alliance had reached the point of forcing France to support Russia against Japan in connection with the treaty of Shimonoseki, to send three warships . . . to attend the opening of the Kiel canal . . . and to refrain from intervening to put a stop to the Armenian massacres because Russia's interest required that the reform of the Ottoman Empire should be deferred; and the infatuation went on growing with the years.[64]

During the early years of the alliance, there were crises that the states did not face as a united front. Russian anger when, in the scramble for Chinese ports, Britain took Weihaiwei did not meet with French support. Nor did the Russians feel compelled to support the French in Fashoda when, in 1898, France and Britain confronted each other in the Sudan over their competing interests in Egypt. This crisis nearly brought France and Britain to war. Russian support to France was not forthcoming, and ultimately France capitulated to Britain.[65]

Yet by the turn of the century, the Franco-Russian Alliance was becoming more cohesive. France and Russia did consult and coordinate their plans when the Boer War broke out in 1899; the French withdrew their support for collaboration with the British on a Baghdad railway because of Russian objections, and the allies coordinated their policy on the Macedonian issue. Further, the French did lend moral, though not military, support to Russia during its war with Japan. This was true despite the fact that France had concluded the Entente Cordiale with Japan's ally, Great Britain, in 1904. By the time of the Algeciras conference in early 1906, Russia was thoroughly committed to taking the part of its ally: "For Russia, in order to relieve the fears of the French, prepared to give her ally unflinching support at the forthcoming conference on Morocco, and began to consider sympathetically the possibility of an understanding with Great Britain."[66]

The allies agreed on goals that were limited, and policy was coordinated to attain them, despite the independent policies they pursued at various times. The goals of the alliance in its early years were primarily to end each state's isolation and to give some measure of security to each against the

Triple Alliance that had a close association with Britain. By and large, the Franco-Russian Alliance performed these functions.

As time went on, the two states also increasingly adopted the other's adversaries as their own. This was especially true of France and Austria. France had no quarrel with Austria at the time the Franco-Russian Alliance was concluded. Yet as time passed, the French began to view Austria as a potential adversary.[67] Likewise, the conflict and hostility between Russia and Germany grew over the course of the years that Russia was allied with France. Both of these developments were a result of the two states becoming a unit and adopting a common agenda, as well as their adversaries being united in an alliance and doing the same. Germany adopted Austria's interests more and more, and its conflict with Russia grew as a consequence. This occurred in tandem with Russia increasingly adopting France's concerns and growing more hostile toward Germany by default. The same was true for Austria and France. As each state became more closely identified with its ally, its ally's adversaries perceived that state as hostile: my enemy's friend is my enemy.[68]

The interests of France and Russia became more intertwined over time. The cohesion of their alliance was enhanced. As their interests became more connected, the level of threat emanating from the adversarial coalition was increased because each was adopting its ally's enemies, increasing in turn the level of cohesion of their alliance.

SUMMARY

The story of the Franco-Russian Alliance offers a departure from the theme of the preceding alliances explored in Chapters 3 and 4 (excluding the Dual Alliance). Instead of a peacetime alliance of adversaries seeking to manage their conflicts of interest, the Franco-Russian Alliance was a balancing alliance that came to life with a military convention; as such, it was a turning point in the prelude to the Great War. The alliance was formed as a response to the increasing level of threat emanating from Germany, Austria-Hungary, and Great Britain. The alliance marked the end of French isolation and offered security to an isolated Russia following the lapse of the Reinsurance Treaty. The end of Germany's role as a moderator of the conflict between Russia and Austria allowed that hostility to increase and placed Germany firmly in Austria's camp. This served to heighten the level of hostility between Russia and Germany. Further, the concern that Britain would join the Triple Alliance provided another reason for France and Russia to come together. At that time, relations between Britain and France and between Britain and Russia were antagonistic, another unifying common threat to France and Russia that illuminated the benefits of an alliance between them.

The Franco-Russian Alliance came into being with the signing of a military convention in 1894. Its purpose was thus underscored: it was an alliance intended to coordinate military planning between France and Russia in the event of war with the Triple Alliance. The Franco-Russian Alliance was not a vehicle for managing adversarial relations; it was a vehicle to balance the ever-growing threat emanating from a hostile coalition. The alliance solidified the conflicts between the two coalitions and ushered in an era of military, not diplomatic, solutions to conflicts that had remained unresolved since the beginning of the nineteenth century.

The Triple Entente

The Triple Entente between Britain, France, and Russia came into existence with the signing of two dual agreements in addition to the Franco-Russian Alliance: the Anglo-French Entente Cordiale of 1904 and the Anglo-Russian Agreement of 1907. It is a difficult alliance to examine because, as Serge Sazonov (Russian minister for Foreign Affairs 1910–16) noted as late as February 1914, the Triple Entente's "real existence is not better authenticated than the existence of the sea serpent."[69] The elusive nature of the Entente was the result of divergent interests of the signatories as well as the reluctance of Great Britain to tie itself too closely with the other powers. The Anglo-Japanese Alliance of 1902 marked Britain's first significant departure from the policy of "splendid isolation." This alliance was palatable because the "area of entanglement" was rather limited.[70] With Russia, and particularly France, the areas of coordination of respective policies grew from 1904 to 1914, yet a formal treaty of alliance would have aroused public opinion in Britain already opposed to the Entente.[71]

The Triple Entente represents yet another case of an alliance being born in peacetime to resolve conflict between and among its signatories. The convention of April 8, 1904, between Britain and France, termed the Entente Cordiale, was a resolution of colonial disputes between the states. The convention between Russia and Britain of 1907 was also an agreement to resolve colonial conflicts between the signatories. While the growing German threat to Britain did play a role in the transformation of these understandings into an alliance in everything but name, the impetus for the agreements arose out of a desire to avoid military hostilities between the member states. At the time that Britain signed the Entente Cordiale with France, its relations with Germany were still warm. In fact, up through 1901 Britain was negotiating with Germany regarding a possible alliance. The two remained on good terms for years beyond.[72] The German threat was not the central factor affecting the formation of the Entente; rather, for Britain, there was a need to contain the threat of France and especially Russia. "As in 1903, Britain was driven towards France not directly by fear of Germany but by fear of Russia."[73] British war plans through late 1904 were primarily against the Franco-Russian Alliance; the *flirt anglo-triplicien* had been going on for years.[74]

In 1903, the biggest threat to Britain's security was Russia, and the best way for Britain to contain that threat was to seek an agreement with Russia's closest ally, France. When the war between Russia and Japan began in 1904, the need for an understanding between Britain and France was even more important to avoid each being drawn into the war on opposite sides.[75]

THE ENTENTE CORDIALE

The second bilateral agreement of the three states forming the Triple Entente was the Entente Cordiale forged in 1904 between France and England. This agreement, negotiated to manage conflicts of interest that threatened to culminate in war, proved to be of crucial historical importance. It was the agreement that the British prime minister invoked in 1914 in his declaration of war on the Central Powers. Despite the low commitment level of the agreement, it marked the reorientation of policy on the part of both great powers for the decade after its conclusion.[76] The operation of the Entente Cordiale was believed to "change the balance of powers in Europe. [In France], the effect was tremendous."[77]

Anglo-French relations, as described earlier, were characterized by hostility, suspicion, and antagonism for the bulk of the pre–World War I period. In 1891, British flirtation with the Triple Alliance culminated in the Franco-Russian Alliance; the end of that decade brought the two states nearly to war in Fashoda. Speculation concerning a Franco-British war centered on the damage that would be wrought by both sides. Lt. Col. Douglas Dawson, military attaché at the British embassy in Paris, noted to Edmund Monson that

> M. Beaulieu thinks England will content herself with Fashoda, but if, as people suppose, she really wants war what will be the result?
> France must resign herself to the fact that England's navy is incomparably superior to her own. France cannot pretend to face, at the same time, the German army and the English navy without ruining herself. War with England must result in the destruction of the French fleet.
> How would the war affect Great Britain? First she would use up her fleets, for nothing is so destructive as the maintenance of permanent blockades. Meanwhile, the French fleets would be well nursed in the ports. England's commerce, from her extended position, would suffer much worse than that of France, and

if the latter resorted to corsair or cruiser warfare, England would run a real danger. . . . [The English] know the French to be an obstinate race, and as nine-tenths of Frenchmen will not suffer by the war, it will last an eternity, an eventuality which England fears most of all.[78]

War between the two states would have been costly and an endeavor neither party could contemplate.

From 1898 through 1901, the British attempted to come to an understanding with Germany. Their efforts toward this end intensified after the onset of the Boer War in October 1899.[79] On November 30, 1899, Joseph Chamberlain declared:

I cannot conceive any point which can arise in the immediate future which would buy ourselves and the Germans into antagonism of interests. On the contrary, I can see many things which must be a cause of anxiety to the statesmen of Europe, but in which our interests are clearly the same as the interests of Germany and in which that understanding . . . if extended to Germany, do more, perhaps than any combination of arms in order to preserve the peace of the world. . . . [A] new Triple Alliance between the Teutonic race and the two branches of the Anglo-Saxon race will be a still more potent influence in the future of the world.[80]

British attempts to conclude an alliance with Germany, however, were not well received by the latter power. The Germans were keen to maintain their friendship with Russia and to continue their commitment to the nearly twenty-year-old Triple Alliance. British diplomats nonetheless continued their attempts. In 1901, the permanent secretary at the Foreign Office even drafted a treaty by which Britain would become a member of the Triple Alliance. Lord William Lansdowne was very much in favor of strengthening British relations with Germany and formalizing them if possible. He willingly considered adhesion to the Triple Alliance and the draft Anglo-German convention, though Salisbury was critical of it.[81] These attempts on the part of Great Britain came "for the first time after the first German naval bill, and for the second time soon after the ratification of the second naval programme in 1900 which provided for the construction of a power battle fleet."[82]

This is of special note because, once again, it reveals the misleading nature of the popular narrative of Britain being driven to France and to Russia as a consequence of the growing German threat. These developments similarly remind us of a point that will be elaborated on in more detail later in this chapter—that Anglo-Russian relations were quite hostile throughout this period. It echoes the sentiment expressed by Keith Neilson, who writes that studies of pre–World War I British foreign and defense policies are flawed as they are based on the incorrect "assumption that Britain was destined to go to war with Germany in 1914." As he notes, this comes from reading history "backwards" and neglects the key fact that "in 1894, Russia was Britain's most persistent and formidable opponent."[83] This was a principal reason why Britain had an incentive to tether with France, Russia's ally.[84]

Great Britain

Britain at the turn of the century realized that the spread of its imperial empire, coupled with increasingly complex and ambitious imperial aspirations and holdings of the other great powers, compounded the likelihood of becoming embroiled in a war. The Boer War was particularly illuminating in that regard. That Britain struggled to quell this uprising revealed how difficult it would be for it to defend itself in the event of war with Russia or France, or both, while defending its other colonial holdings around the world.[85]

The concerns culminated in an attempt to tighten the bonds between Britain and Germany. From 1898 through 1901, the British made overtures to Germany in the hopes of formalizing an agreement. While these efforts ultimately came to naught, Britain, as mentioned previously, went so far as to draft an agreement providing for British adhesion to the Triple Alliance. Kaiser Wilhelm, in his correspondence with Tsar Nicholas, told him of the British offer of an alliance. The kaiser then proceeded to ask what the tsar would be willing to offer if he were to decline.[86]

An alliance with Germany, however, was not a welcome thought to all in Britain. As Francis Bertie said in November 1901, "If we bind ourselves by a formal defensive alliance and practically join the Triplice we shall never be on decent terms with France our neighbour in Europe and in many parts of the world, or with Russia whose frontiers are coterminous with ours or nearly so over a large portion of Asia."[87] Tethering was paramount; rapprochement with France would lessen colonial tensions and facilitate improvement in British relations with Russia.[88] "In 1903 it was above all fear of Russia, a fear caused principally by India's apparent vulnerability to overland attack, which led Balfour to favour a settlement with France."[89] At this time, Great Britain had no intention of antagonizing Germany.[90]

There were important tactical side benefits to alliance with France. One was a principal force driving Britain to France—de-escalating tensions with Russia. As Lord Cromer wrote to British prime minister Arthur James Balfour on October 15, 1903:

> I had wished to press on your attention the very great importance of the present negotiations with France. . . . The question is not merely one of settling our Egyptian difficulties . . . it extends to a far wider sphere. . . . I cannot help regarding an understanding with France as possibly a stepping-stone to a general

understanding with Russia, and that this possibly again may prepare the ground for some reduction in our enormous military and naval expenditure.[91]

Threat reduction via entente was the most important factor driving British policy at this time. The level of threat with Russia was too great to manage with a direct agreement; tethering France was the most promising avenue open to Britain to avoid war with France and Russia. As Balfour himself declared: "If Japan goes to war, who is going to lay odds that we are not at loggerheads with Russia within six months?"[92]

As hostilities heated up between the British ally, Japan, and France's ally, Russia, an agreement with France became ever more important. As Lansdowne wrote to Monson on December 26, 1904: "The New Year will be full of anxiety for us all. I incline myself to the belief that the closeness of our relations with France, and of her relations with Russia, may prove useful to all concerned when the time comes for bringing the war to a close."[93]

Britain greatly hoped that the "negotiations between France and England would finally succeed in putting an end to the antagonism undoubtedly existing at this present moment and for long years past, between England and Russia."[94] The side benefits accruing to Britain from its alliance with France were immediately realized. At the height of tension between Britain and Russia, French intervention defused the crisis. In October 1904, the Russian fleet was on its way to the Far East. En route, it fired on British fishing boats that were mistaken for Japanese torpedo boats, killing seven British fishermen. France was able to de-escalate the explosive situation, and a peaceful arrangement was reached.[95]

France

Relations between France and Britain reached their low point in the Fashoda crisis and its aftermath. By the fall of 1899, French minister of Foreign Affairs Théophile Delcassé sincerely believed that Britain "might be plotting the destruction of the French fleet."[96] Although the Franco-Russian Alliance was fundamental to the orientation of French foreign policy, the allies had divergent colonial holdings; as a consequence, they were averse to becoming embroiled in each other's imperial conflicts. During the Fashoda crisis, Russia was less supportive than France had hoped. Because France did not have the aid of its ally in Egypt against Britain, it had to back down.[97]

The British threat toward France was exacerbated by the rumors in diplomatic circles regarding an Anglo-German agreement. The French, incorrectly, supposed that this was an agreement that Germany was advocating. As Paul Cambon, French ambassador in London 1898–1920, wrote to his mother on October 24, 1900, "It appears more profitable to Germany than to England and I think that it was proposed by Germany."[98] Tension between Britain and France in Morocco and fears of Anglo-German cooperation both increased the threat level experienced by France at the turn of the century.

By the early 1900s, the situation was improving. The level of threat from Britain had receded somewhat. At that moment, however, there was growing hostility between Russia and Japan. Neither Britain nor France wanted to be drawn into a war against each other on behalf of their allies. The uncertainty that this situation generated preoccupied French decision makers.[99] The result was the desire to tether Great Britain in order to contain hostility between Russia and France, as well as to reap the side benefit of reducing tension between Russia and Britain.[100]

The British understood these fears well. Even before the Russo-Japanese War, Cecil Spring Rice wrote to Francis Bertie, on November 23, 1902:

> With regard to the alliance between France and Russia although French relations with a third power must be dependent to a great extent on the relations of that power with Russia—there was nothing in the Treaty of Alliance which could oblige France to join Russia in a single handed war with England—though public opinion would probably force the government's hand.[101]

Certainly the agreement came at a fortuitous moment—the Malacca and Dogger Bank incidents dictated French intervention to ensure that Britain and Russia did not come to blows. Lansdowne was effusive in his appreciation of French diffusion of the North Sea incident.[102]

In this crisis, Britain and Russia had been on the brink of war. War had been so near that the British Channel Fleet at Gibraltar was told to inform the Admiralty the instant any Russian ships at Vigo left port. Their orders were to "detain cruisers on passage home until further orders."[103] A telegram from the vice admiral of the Channel Fleet at Gibraltar to the Admiralty stated that the Russian fleet had left Vigo, and he had "steam for full speed ready and am prepared to proceed immediately" with eleven battleships, three cruisers, seven torpedo boats, and three torpedo boat destroyers.[104] The telegram continued, "when ordered to act I shall order all Russian Fleet at Tangiers into Gibraltar and if disobey they will be sunk and I shall then proceed to meet Vigo Fleet my Cruisers already having orders never to leave them." The French were able to intervene once more and defuse the situation.

We see, then, that the Entente Cordiale succeeded in tethering Britain and France. This was essential as their respective allies became embroiled in war. The benefit of their agreement was realized immediately, as France brought Britain and Russia back from teetering on the edge of war. The

TABLE 5.3
Member States' Motivations for Joining the Entente Cordiale, 1904

Country	Motivation
Great Britain	Tether France
	Gain small measure of control over Russian threat
France	Tether Great Britain
	Inhibit military conflict between Great Britain and France as well as Great Britain and Russia.

Entente Cordiale also served to pave the way for the third bilateral agreement comprising the Triple Entente, the Anglo-Russian Agreement of 1907. Table 5.3 contains a summary of the member states' motivations for joining the Entente Cordiale.

SUMMARY

The Entente Cordiale was a manifestation of tethering motives on the part of the French and the British. The states sought to reduce tension and hostility because of the threat of war between them. The resolution of the two states' conflicting colonial holdings and aspirations set the stage for enhanced cooperation. It also set the stage for a similar reduction in threat between Britain and Russia, something that would become a priority once the Russo-Japanese War was over.

THE ANGLO-RUSSIAN CONVENTION OF 1907

Contrary to the popular narrative, the Anglo-Russian Convention of 1907 was not inspired by fear of Germany.[105] As noted in the preceding section, Britain and Russia had been on the verge of war. That crisis made it ever clearer that coming together in an entente of some kind, resolving their severe colonial disputes, was the only route to keep the peace between them. Once the threat between them receded to a level at which they could tether, the two states' desire to keep the peace culminated in the agreement of 1907.

Great Britain

Britain had been driven to France in part by its fears of Russia, in the hopes that it could reduce the chance the conflict between their two respective allies would spread. At the time, in 1904, an agreement with Russia directly was impossible. France, however, especially Delcassé, was committed to facilitating such a diminution in threat. As Bertie wrote to Lansdowne on January 17, 1905:

> Monsieur Delcassé called on me yesterday to return a private visit which I paid him on the 15th. . . . His great desire is, he says, to bring about rapprochement between England and Russia for if those two Powers and France acted together peace would have a long reign.[106]

> Indeed, as early as April 27, 1904, M. [Maurice] Bompard hoped that the same beneficial influences that had been so successful in the negotiations between France and England would finally succeed in putting an end to the antagonism undoubtedly existing at this present moment and for long years past, between England and Russia.[107]

In the same letter, Spring Rice communicated Bompard's conviction that British safety and security rested in coming to terms with Russia: "[R]emove this supposed antagonism and you remove all danger to India. But if you maintain that your possession of India gives you the right to impose a veto on Russian development throughout the continent of Asia, Russia can only reply by a menace in India itself."[108] Those fears were temporarily eclipsed by a greater threat during the period when Russia and Japan were at war. This conflict made it all the more essential for Britain to tether by securing the lines of communication and cooperation with France and with Russia, while maintaining cordial relations with Germany. Britain did not have a desire to align itself with France and Russia at the expense of Germany. It had never been the intention of Britain to signal a warning to Germany.

The Russo-Japanese War and the near clash with Russia renewed Britain's desire to ensure it would not be so vulnerable vis à vis the great powers of Europe. Its relations with France had improved noticeably after the Entente Cordiale was concluded; yet its relations with Russia were still tense. The early years of the twentieth century were ones in which Britain concentrated its energies on tethering heightened animosities with Russia—its principal remaining foe. Tethering via agreement with Russia became a possible course of action, as the threat level receded from its high point during the Russo-Japanese War.

These sentiments were expressed as early as 1900 by Chamberlain:

> It is certain that we are not strong enough by ourselves to prevent [Russia] from accomplishing such an annexation [in northern China], and both in China and elsewhere it is in our interest that Germany should turn herself across the path of Russia. An alliance between Germany and Russia, entailing as it would the cooperation of France is the one thing we have to dread, and the clash of German and Russian interests whether in China or Asia Minor would be a guarantee of our safety.

> I think then our policy clearly is to encourage good relations between our-

selves and Germany, as well as between ourselves and Japan and the United States, and we should endeavour to make use of the present opportunity to emphasize the breach between Russia and Germany and Russia and Japan.[109]

Great Britain sought to tether Russia, while simultaneously seeking the tactical side benefit of capitalizing on a rift between Russia and Germany. The agreements provided an institutional basis for cooperation among the signatories.

At the beginning of the twentieth century, Britain faced important questions regarding the orientation of its foreign policy. One possible path was to forge an agreement with Germany. As discussed earlier in the chapter, it tried to do so yet failed. It had the motivation to form an agreement; Germany did not. At the same time, Britain needed to ameliorate tensions with Russia. This was especially important as it became embroiled in the Boer War. "This could be done either by direct negotiations with Russia or by joining in some sort of coalition designed to limit Russian aims. In the period from March 1901 to the signing of the Anglo-Japanese alliance in January 1902, Lansdowne attempted both options."[110]

Unfortunately, these attempts also came to nothing, and, as one would expect, the signing of the Anglo-Japanese Alliance heightened Russian suspicions of both states' intentions. As previously mentioned, the Russo-Japanese War was a period of intense anxiety for British diplomats. Britain and Russia came to the brink of war not once but twice. The war did not come to ensnare France and Britain only as a consequence of attentive diplomacy on the part of Britain and France particularly. In the aftermath of the war, the strategic context of great power diplomacy was in flux. The fall of Delcassé, the Algeciras conference, rumors regarding the meeting between the tsar and kaiser at Björkö—all raised concerns in Great Britain regarding its position in the international system and its relations with the other great powers in Europe. At this point, in 1905, Anglo-German relations were not antagonistic, yet concerns over German intentions existed, as did anxiety regarding French loyalty and the orientation of Russian policy.[111] Britain's strategy of trying to balance against Russia had failed; as the threat receded in the aftermath of the Russo-Japanese War, its next step was to attempt to tether, just as we would anticipate.

The Liberal government in Britain desired to improve its relations with Russia. Tethering via agreement with Russia became all the more important as the path behind it lay strewn with failed attempts to balance with Germany.

An agreement with Russia would prevent a European coalition which might isolate England. A bargain in Central Asia as to the safety of India was, also, undoubtedly preferable to an expensive policy of preparation against her on the North-West Frontier, and to tying up troops, which in fact the British did not have, on the Hindu Kush at a time when the uncertain situation in Europe could make such a policy dangerous to the safety of the British Isles themselves.[112]

Tethering motivations were at the forefront of British foreign minister Edward Grey's mind as Britain embarked upon its negotiations with Russia. As he wrote to the British ambassador to Russia, Sir Arthur Nicholson, on November 16, 1906, "The benefit from an arrangement with Russia is that we should be set free from any such apprehension [of Russia attacking India's frontier] and this is precisely what we ask in the settlement."[113]

As will be discussed in greater detail later, it was essential for Britain, if it pursued rapprochement with Russia, to maintain good relations with Germany. Russia would not have entered the Anglo-Russian Convention in the absence of German approval and agreement. To illustrate, in early January 1907, Nicholson wrote a long report to the home office, to Grey, analyzing Russian relations with all of the other major powers in the international system. Of Russo-German relations, he wrote: "Relations between the Russian Court and Government and those of Germany are at the present time intimate and cordiale. I should be inclined to go further, and to state that German influence is to-day predominant both at the Court and in Government circles."[114]

Nicholson was far more uncertain regarding the Russian position vis à vis Britain. He addressed both the sources of suspicion and the sources of opportunity in coming to an understanding with Russia.[115] In no way was the forging of an agreement with Russia a strategy on the part of Britain to encircle Germany.[116]

The principal reasons for forming the agreement were the belief that the British army was insufficient to meet the Russians in a war along the northwest frontier and to prevent the Russians from coming to a formal agreement with Germany that would have the potential of being directed against Britain. In short, the British sought to tether by arriving at an agreement with Russia to resolve their colonial disputes.

Russia

The Russo-Japanese War proved to be a near fatal catastrophe for the tsarist autocracy. The crushing defeat of Russia's Baltic fleet in the straits of Tsushima in the spring of 1905 by Japan humiliated the Russian navy and the tsarist government as a whole. Military defeat was made all the more traumatic for Russia by domestic instability within the country. With the tsar and his government disgraced militarily, revolution erupted across Russia. Tsar Nicholas was determined to maintain autocratic government at home, but Russian losses against Japan undermined his legitimacy and strengthened the revolutionaries' influence.[117] Their challenge to autocratic authority, backed by widespread labor unrest and peasant revolts, nearly toppled the tsar. The Russian autocracy was profoundly vulnerable at home and abroad at this moment of history.

In the midst of the difficulties confronting the tsar domestically and of Russia's war with Japan, Nicholas and Wilhelm were vacationing in the Baltic Sea and the Gulf of Finland. They decided to meet at Björkö. The kaiser asked his Foreign Office for a copy of the draft alliance from the year past, which called for a defensive agreement for each to come to the other's aid in the event of an attack by a third party. At their meeting, the kaiser prevailed upon the tsar to sign the agreement, and he ultimately did.[118]

The Treaty of Björkö was thus a treaty of defensive alliance. More specifically, its first article stipulated that in the event that one of the two empires was attacked by a European power, its ally would aid with all land and sea forces. The second article specified that the powers would not conclude a separate peace. The third article indicated that the treaty would be in force when the peace between Russia and Japan was concluded and would remain valid unless denounced a year in advance. The fourth article stated that the tsar would initiate discussions with France to have it accede to the alliance.[119]

The treaty was short-lived. When Tsar Nicholas revealed to Russian minister of Foreign Affairs Vladimir Lamsdorff what he had done, the latter undertook all he could to get Russia out of the agreement. Lamsdorff convinced Russian prime minister Sergei Witte that it was essential to back out of the agreement, and the two combined convinced the tsar that the alliance was incompatible with their agreement with France. Ultimately, on December 2, 1905, Russia communicated to Germany that it deemed the agreement inoperative.[120] Although the Björkö treaty never really saw the light of day, it does illustrate that Russo-German relations had dramatically improved by this point. An agreement between them ultimately was impossible, however, given each state's existing alliance obligations.[121] Had Lamsdorff not been concerned that formalizing relations with Germany would undermine Russia's relationship with France, the Russo-German alliance may have endured.

By 1906, the worst of the domestic crisis in Russia had passed. Witte's October manifesto gave sufficient satisfaction to the liberal opposition, and the creation of the Duma, despite its limited powers, took the wind out of the sails of the liberal challengers to autocratic authority. Yet Russia's position internationally remained vulnerable. Its defeat by Japan revealed how thinly stretched it was regarding its colonial holdings and the vulnerabilities associated with attempting to defend its far-flung empire.

As Russia tried to determine how best to orient its foreign policy, Alexander Izvolsky took over the Foreign Affairs Ministry in May 1906. In this period, as in many moments past and to come, there were arguments favoring the reconstitution of the conservative Dreikaiserbund.[122] Yet foremost in Izvolsky's mind was to resolve Russia's problems in Asia by ensuring its eastern frontier would not be continually beset by conflict. One of the first things he did toward this end was to open negotiations with Great Britain and Japan.[123] Witte described the abrupt change in policy:

> The Anglo-Russian Convention signed on August 18, 1907, marked a sharp turn from our policy of rapprochement, or rather flirtation, with Germany to one of rapprochement, or rather flirtation, with England. Since such ladies as Germany and England are inclined to be jealous, and since they are as clever as we, we put ourselves into an ambiguous position from which we try to escape by assuring each in turn that we love only her and are only flirting with the other.[124]

Since Russia was committed to convincing both Britain and Germany of its "love" for each, the key problem for Russia as it negotiated the agreement with Britain was to keep Germany happy. Thus, throughout the course of the negotiations with the British, the Russians kept the Germans apprised of developments and sought Germany's approval before advancing.

In October 1906, Izvolsky made a trip to Paris and stopped in Berlin en route for an audience with the kaiser.[125] After Izvolsky's return to St. Petersburg, he resumed negotiations with Sir Arthur Nicholson. Nicholson reported to Grey on November 7, 1906, that Izvolsky was relieved after having been uneasy as to the attitude Germany would take regarding the negotiations with Britain. Izvolsky had feared that Germany would see it as a move to encircle it, and he now felt comfortable that Germany understood that there was no such intention embodied in the agreement. Izvolsky was tremendously pleased. Izvolsky "wished to reassure me that he had found in his conversations at Berlin no suspicions or misgivings."[126]

In a report to Grey on November 21, 1906, Nicholson stated that "M. Isvolsky is radiant over the speech of Prince Bülow so far as it relates to our discussions, and the nightmare which was haunting him of German interference at a later date has been dissolved. He seemed to have been anxiously and endurably nervous on this point."[127] The perception that Russia was so under the influence of Berlin during the course of its negotiations with Britain gave rise to continual rumors in French and British diplomatic circles that the Russians had forged an arrangement with Germany. Repeated and emphatic denials by the Russian government allowed the rapprochement to proceed.[128] The British viewed Russian tethering behavior for what it was. As Nicholson reported to Grey on March 26, 1907: "But while admitting

TABLE 5.4
Member States' Motivations for Joining
the Anglo-Russian Convention, 1907

Country	Motivation
Great Britain	Tether Russia
Russia	Tether Great Britain

that many motives impel the Emperor and his Govt. to draw nearer to Germany, and to accept as an unfortunate necessity the alliance with France, it seems to me that more powerful factors than personal sympathy will counteract to a great extent the tendency to drift too much in the orbit of Berlin." [129]

Nicholson went on to explain that Russia needed France and agreements with Britain to "husband" its resources and to keep its hands free for recovering its position as a European power.[130] Even on the eve of the final signing of the convention in August 1907, when the tsar and kaiser met, Izvolsky spoke to Bülow about the agreement and assured him that its contents in no way would undermine German interests.[131] In a second communication to Grey on August 10, 1907, Hugh James O'Beirne reported his impressions to Grey after meeting with Izvolsky. He wrote that Izvolsky "found Emperor William and the Chancellor in the most amiable disposition. Prince Bülow had shown himself quite free from suspicions as to the aims of the pending negotiations between Great Britain and Russia. His Highness had expressed himself as perfectly satisfied with the explanations given to him." [132]

The Russians sought to tether Britain, yet not at the expense of close relations with Germany. This strategy appeared successful, as Sir Francis Lascelles, the British ambassador at Berlin, reported to Grey in a letter of October 1, 1907: "I have the honour to report that the publication of the Anglo-Russian Convention has on the whole been very favourably received in the German press. . . . The present Convention goes far to allay this fear [of war between England and Russia], at any rate for some time to come, and, taken as a whole, it may be regarded as a triumph of British diplomacy." [133]

The forging of the last of the dual agreements constituting the Triple Entente, then, was not at all undertaken in response to a growing German threat. Nor was it formed to counter the Triple Alliance. The Triple Entente had three parts to it—balancing by France and Russia, tethering between France and Britain, and tethering between Russia and Britain. At its signing in August 1907, no one could have foretold that the Entente Powers would be at war against Austria and Germany a mere seven years later. Table 5.4 summarizes the motivations of Britain and Russia.

EXTERNAL THREAT VERSUS INTERNAL THREAT

At the inception of the Triple Entente, the level of threat internal to the alliance was far greater than the external threat. Threat played an important role in the formation of the Triple Entente—the threat of Austria-Hungary to Russia and Germany to France gave rise to the Franco-Russian Alliance; the reciprocal threats from France to Britain and from Russia to Britain gave rise to the Entente Cordiale and the Anglo-Russian Convention, respectively.[134] The conflicting colonial policies of France and Britain had continually brought the two as close to hostilities as they were in 1898–99 during the Fashoda crisis.[135] In 1904, the most fearful prospect to France and the United Kingdom was becoming embroiled in the Russo-Japanese War on opposite sides.

Gradually, the external threat did grow and had the important effect of enhancing the cohesion of the Entente. The Moroccan crisis of April–December 1905 raised fears in Britain and particularly in France of growing German belligerence. This perceived aggressiveness only increased as time went on. The turning point for enhanced Entente cohesion was a direct result of an increased perceived external threat. The second Moroccan crisis confirmed to the member states of the Entente that Germany was a threat that needed to be countered. The German threat was exacerbated by Germany's ambitious naval program. German efforts to vastly increase its military and naval strength began in 1898 and were accelerated in the early 1900s. In 1907–8, the annexation crisis in which Austria-Hungary sought to take over Bosnia and Herzegovina did heighten the threat, particularly between Austria and Russia. The threat was exacerbated by the "naval scare" of 1908–9, which manifested growing Anglo-German rivalry in the seas.[136] The rivalry between these two great powers precipitated a desire on the part of Germany to conclude a naval understanding with Britain. These efforts were frustrated by Admiral Alfred von Tirpitz, the secretary to the German Admiralty 1897–1916, whose forceful personality undermined each attempt.[137]

In 1912, following the Agadir crisis, the threat continued to escalate and went hand in hand with an arms race that exacerbated tension throughout Europe. In Germany, the General Staff had increased its "establishment" in 1911 and 1912. In 1913, legislation was introduced for significant increases in Germany's peacetime force.[138] These developments did not go unanswered in Germany's rival states. As German capabilities increased, the threat it posed to the members of the Triple Entente increased as well. Their response was to coordinate more closely their goals and the means to attain them.

TABLE 5.5
Threats to Member States of the Triple Entente, 1904/7–14

Member state	Source of threat	Degree
France	Germany	Very high
Great Britain	Russia	High
Russia	Great Britain	High
	Austria-Hungary	Very high

While the Triple Entente was not formed to counter a threatening Germany, as the threat grew the cohesion of the alliance was enhanced. While the Russian threat to Britain continued, it was eventually surpassed by the increasing German one. Consequently, the conflict between the allies was managed, and the Triple Entente members became increasingly unified in their policy against Germany. Following the Agadir crisis of 1911, military and naval conversations and agreements were concluded between the member states. The threats to the member states of the Triple Entente are summarized in Table 5.5

COHESION

To assess the cohesion of an alliance, it is useful to examine the text of the treaty of alliance to determine if the parties were then able to coordinate their goals and strategy to attain their stated goals. In this case, no such tool is available, since the documents creating the Entente were dual agreements addressing the resolution of colonial disputes. Yet the ability of the member states to successfully resolve the issues in dispute indicates that the level of cohesion was significant. By contrast, in the two Leagues of the Three Emperors, Austria-Hungary and Russia were unable to successfully uphold the terms of the treaties. Austria-Hungary and Italy failed to do so as well with regard to the Triple Alliance.

Further, despite the loose design of the Entente—the commitment level is the lowest of all of the alliances under review—and the absence of central joint goals, the states were able to lend support to one another during the crises and conflicts that continually cropped up in the decade following 1904. In reviewing this history, each state's different agenda becomes clear, as each pursued its plans relatively independently of the others. Yet as time passed and the German threat to each grew, the Entente members increasingly intertwined their policies; they consulted each other more frequently, and they slowly began to integrate their war planning. Early British reluctance to turn the Entente into a defensive alliance never completely dissipated; yet British planning with France especially became increasingly intimate. The cohesion of the Entente was relatively low in 1907–10. Following the second Moroccan crisis in 1911, cohesion increased.

In 1908, Austria-Hungary annexed Bosnia and Herzegovina. This act, in direct violation of the Treaty of Berlin, could only bring to the fore once again the conflict between Russia and Austria-Hungary in the Balkans. Serbia demanded territorial compensation, and Russia was compelled to support Serbia in this demand. Russia insisted that the issue of Austro-Hungarian annexation be referred to an international conference. Russia refused to recognize the annexation, and Austria-Hungary refused to agree to a conference. As tension escalated and it appeared that Austria-Hungary was taking steps toward preparing to invade Serbia, it became apparent that Russia would not be getting the unconditional support of France or Britain to aid Serbia in attaining its demands. Russia, consequently, abandoned Serbia.[139] As explained in a telegram from Izvolsky to the Russian minister at Belgrade,

> We have been able to convince ourselves through various sources that the Powers are not disposed to support the idea of a territorial aggrandizement of Serbia. The Royal Government must deduce from this that all efforts to move the Powers to support such demands would remain futile and that Serbia can be assured of the sympathies of the Powers only if she refrains from insisting upon demands which must lead to an armed conflict with Austria. We deem it necessary to warn the Royal Government against adopting any attitude which might expose it to danger. . . . At the same time, we believe that the Serbian Government must, under the prevailing circumstances, clearly declare to these Powers, that it does not insist on its territorial demands and that it will rely upon the decision of the Powers in all pending questions.[140]

On the one hand, Russian capitulation to its allies' pressure indicates an ability of the Entente members to coordinate goals and strategy. On the other, the fact that Russia's allies were unwilling to view Russian response to an Austrian attack on Serbia with possible German intervention as *casus foederis* indicates that, at this time, the members of the Entente had divergent goals. By 1911–12, France accepted the potential scenario described above as *casus foederis*; the cohesion of the alliance did increase.[141]

In 1910, however, the Entente's cohesion ebbed. The Potsdam conversation between Russia and Germany concerning the Near East made both Britain and France uneasy. Compounding French anxiety were the secret naval talks between Germany and Britain.[142] The Entente recovered quickly, however; in 1911 the second Moroccan crisis erupted, and the cohesion of the Triple Entente increased in response to the escalating German threat.

Competing French and German interests in Morocco had come to a head in 1905, and the Algeciras conference in 1906 had been an attempt to settle those differences. Yet in 1911 the sultan of Morocco appealed to France for help in defending him against insurgent tribes threatening Fez. Complying with this appeal, France occupied Fez. In response, Germany sent the gunboat *Panther* to Agadir. The British stood up quite firmly for France, and ultimately Germany capitulated. Both France and Britain had an interest in containing the Germans. The Russians had wanted to remain aloof from the tension between its allies and Germany. Russia had not wanted to be dragged into a war over French interests in Morocco, just as France was unwilling to be dragged into a war over the Balkans. This very reluctance became an incentive for the two to tighten their relations, which was accomplished through talks the next year.[143] "From the Agadir crisis and the Anglo-German negotiations of the early part of 1912 the Triple Entente emerged stronger than ever."[144]

Following the Agadir crisis, the Entente's cohesion continued to increase. By early 1913, the French and the British had thorough military and naval plans in the event of war.

> The Entente Cordiale, conceived in part because of Britain's strategic interests in Moroccan ports, had progressively evolved into a friendly partnership with military and naval features directed against Germany. As a result, by early 1913 there existed not only detailed military and naval preparations but also the guarantee of consultation in times of danger.[145]

On the Russian side of the alliance, planning was not as comprehensive, yet it was still significant.

> St. Petersburg . . . had given a precise pledge to attack on a certain day with a specified number of troops; wartime communication between the allies were arranged; rail facilities for the attack were carefully considered. The Anglo-French talks were even more detailed because of the very nature of the operation—the movement of the B.E.F. [British Expeditionary Force] across the Channel and to the zone of concentration required more staff coordination.[146]

The level of coordination and cooperation between the allies was very high, although there was residual suspicion in Britain toward Russia, and naval conversations between them had little significant substance.[147]

The cohesion of the Triple Entente was relatively high by the time the Great War began. The powers were coordinating their goals, consulting each other, and pursuing joint policy in order to attain those goals. Above all, it was the desire to contain the growing threat of Germany that transformed the Entente from agreements to settle colonial disputes into a defensive alliance in everything but name.

TABLE 5.6
Chapter Summary: Alliances, Threat, and Cohesion

Alliance	Principal source of threat	Cohesion
Franco-Russian Alliance	External to alliance	High
Triple Entente	Initially internal to the alliance; ultimately external to the alliance	Initially low; ultimately higher

SUMMARY

The Triple Entente was a case of a peacetime conflict management alliance that was transformed into a defensive alliance to counter a common external threat. This case demonstrates clearly that when the level of external threat eclipses the level of internal threat, internal disputes may be successfully resolved, and cohesion in the face of the external adversary is enhanced. Despite the loose design of the Triple Entente, its member states increasingly coordinated their policy and consulted one another more and more frequently. By 1914, the states' decisions were more influenced by the threats they faced together than they were by their divergent interests. A summary of the Franco-Russian Alliance's and Triple Entente's threat and cohesion can be found in Table 5.6.

Conclusion

The coming together of France and Russia against the Triple Alliance signaled the end of a period when alliances were primarily used to manage conflicts among great powers. The failure of the two Leagues of the Three Emperors to effectively manage conflict between Austria-Hungary and Russia, the lapsing of the Reinsurance Treaty, the ongoing conflict between France and Germany, and increasing animosity between Britain and Germany all marked the onset of escalating conflict, which ultimately culminated in the First World War. The Triple Entente, though formed to manage internal conflicts of interest, adapted to these changing realities. Conflicts of interest between the two coalitions became more entrenched, and effective management of them within an alliance became impossible. As a consequence, the alliances begin to function as a tool for security aggrandizement vis à vis an external threat. The cohesion of the alliances, as a result of increasing threat, was enhanced.

The Triple Entente was formed in part to secure France and Russia against Britain and the Triple Alliance and later to improve Anglo-French and

Anglo-Russian relations. The Triple Entente was not at its inception designed to be directed against the Triple Alliance or to serve as a counterbalancing alliance. Just as British flirtation with the Triple Alliance catalyzed the Franco-Russian Alliance, the tethering arrangements were ultimately threatening to Germany and the Triple Alliance. As alliances serve very important internal functions in regard to member states, they have external consequences that may not be intended.

The cohesion of the Triple Entente, ironically, was served by the heightened external threat that the alliance itself helped to create. It successfully managed the conflicts of interest among the member states to the detriment of the strategic context, exacerbating the level of threat in the system, heightening suspicion and mistrust in such a way that all the great powers of Europe began to regard the system as one of competing alignments. The states of Europe were trapped in the alliance paradox.

Military alliances are manifestations of relationships of enmity and amity; they drive those relationships as well. When formed, regardless of the intention of coming together in the first place, they shape the constellations of states in the system as well. This is never clearer as it is in the case of the Triple Entente, whose purpose came to be something altogether different than the intention embodied by the states at the time of the alliance's creation.

The Franco-Russian Alliance and the Triple Entente illustrate again the utility in understanding alliance formation as a curvilinear function of threat. France and Russia experienced heightened threat from Germany and Great Britain especially at the beginning of the 1890s, and both sought to balance against those threats. As the threat between France and Britain receded, a tethering agreement was possible between them. As the level of threat between Russia and Britain diminished, in no small part due to the Entente Cordiale, a tethering arrangement became possible for them as well.

The Triple Entente also reveals how the cohesion of alliances is a result of the balance between internal and external threat. In its early years, the cohesion was low as a consequence of high internal threat. This was transformed over time as the level of external threat ultimately eclipsed the level of threat emanating from within the alliance itself. The forging of the Entente, to keep the peace among the member states, had the negative effect of making war between it and the Triple Alliance all the more conceivable.

CHAPTER 6

Alliances and the Great War:
The Central Powers and the Triple Entente

THE CALM THAT pervaded Europe in the summer of 1914 was shattered in July. The assassination of the heir apparent to the Dual Monarchy's throne triggered a fierce desire in Austria to deal with Serbia once and for all. The assassination set off a chain of events that culminated in the bloodiest war the world had seen to date.

The Austro-Hungarian chief of General Staff, Franz Conrad von Höt-zendorf, had pushed for war for some time. We saw in Chapter 4 that he advocated war against Italy repeatedly. In 1913, he expanded his military planning to the most ambitious program of all—war against Albania, Montenegro, Russia, Serbia, and Russian Poland. In the months leading up to the July crisis, his attention was focused on war plans against Montenegro, Romania, Russia, and Serbia.[1] With the assassination of Archduke Franz Ferdinand, Conrad's call to arms fell on more receptive ears. Both the emperor and Foreign Minister Leopold Berchtold believed decisive action against the Serbs was necessary. The two approached the German kaiser via letter to determine the German response in the event of Austrian intervention in Serbia. Wilhelm II assured his Austro-Hungarian counterpart that Germany would support its ally of thirty-five years completely. Austria-Hungary thus issued an ultimatum to Serbia, seeking entry to search for the murderers of Franz Joseph. Serbia rebuffed the ultimatum, and Austria mobilized for war. The fear of a long war compelled Germany to mobilize as well; the Schlieffen Plan depended on a swift preemptive offensive attack in the west to defeat France, in order to shift German forces to the east to meet the slower-mobilizing Russian forces. The Entente powers, learning of the Central Powers' mobilizations, began the process of mobilizing as well. By August, Europe was at war.[2]

When war finally came, how did the alliances fare? By this time Austria-Hungary and Germany had been allies for thirty-five years; Italy had been a part of their alliance for thirty-two of those years. France and Russia had been allies for twenty years; Britain had been allies with France and Russia for eleven and seven years, respectively. Since the two alliances that fought the war had managed to maintain the cohesion of their alliances during peacetime, the question of whether they were able to sustain their unity throughout the war is a natural one. The alliance that struggled the most with cohesion during peacetime disintegrated immediately with war. Italy declared neutrality in 1914; in May 1915 it joined the war on the opposite side of its former allies. The tethering combination of the Triple Alliance was the first allied casualty of World War I.

The Dual Alliance fared better. Its durability was proven throughout the war, though the alliance suffered from division and a lack of cohesion. The Entente experienced a mixed fate. The alliance endured fairly cohesively until 1917. The Russian Revolution and separate peace at Brest Litovsk marred the cohesion of the alliance, although it did not prevent victory in 1918.

In this chapter, I examine each alliance in turn, exploring the wartime challenges to unity and analyzing the factors that affected cohesion. If threat alone influences cohesion during wartime, alliances should be more cohesive when they are losing than when they are winning. The empirical evidence for this proposition is considered case by case. As a whole, I argue that there are sharp differences between peacetime and wartime determinants of alliance cohesion. As discussed in the second chapter, I focus here on three central aspects of coordinated alliance behavior. I assess the level of cohesion according to the capacity of the member states of the alliances to coordinate their war-fighting strategy; the ability of member states to agree on war aims; and the ability of a wartime alliance to prevent the conclusion of a separate peace.

The function of intra-alliance bargaining and negotiation is even more essential during wartime than peacetime. Further, the consequences of alliance cohesion matter as well. During peacetime, enhanced cohesion is both a product and producer of increased threat. During wartime, it has direct implications on the prosecution of a war. War will continue without separate peace and without negotiated peace as long as the coalitions fighting them stand together. The stakes during wartime are far greater than during peacetime. Alliance cohesion, in other words, will be of enormous importance to who wins a war and how easy or hard war termination will be.[3]

The Central Powers

Of any of the alliances in the pre–World War I period, the Central Powers had the biggest advantage in regard to cohesion. After all, this was an alliance that had already proved durable and cohesive in its thirty-five-year existence prior to the war. In addition, unlike the Entente, it was not conceived as a tethering alliance; the member states did not have the deep conflicts of interest and tradition of suspicion that plagued its rival coalition. And yet the Central Powers had not exploited this advantage to the utmost, since its joint war planning prior to war was minimal.

Still worse, the alliance was from the start riddled with problems, beginning with the German preoccupation with the western front from the onset of war, neglecting its original commitment to Austria-Hungary to launch an offensive against Russia. Tensions between the allies culminated in the Sixtus Affair of 1916–17, in which the new emperor of Austria-Hungary dispatched his brother-in-law to try to negotiate a separate peace for Austria-Hungary with the Entente Powers. From the beginning to the end of the war, the alliance was plagued with challenges to its cohesion. The alliance was virtually unrecognizable as the stable and cohesive Dual Alliance; the alliance during wartime was dramatically different than it was during the peacetime years.

THREAT

This section briefly sketches the progression of victories and defeats for the Central Powers and the threat that rose and fell accordingly. It also details the threats that faced Germany and Austria-Hungary individually. Because the two confronted very different situations and because the threat level each faced was so different, the effect on cohesion was devastating for the Central Powers. Having different enemies during peacetime was not a problem and could even lead to compatible alliance strategies. During wartime, however, it was disastrous. The wartime situation dramatically transformed the member states' relationship from one of amity to one of enmity. In fact, by 1917, Austria-Hungary feared Germany more than the states with which it was at war. It was Germany, after all, that had tried to induce Italy to stay out of the war by offering bits of Habsburg lands; it was Germany, after all, that was developing its ambitious Mitteleuropa plan that would ultimately serve to preserve Austrian subordination to the German empire for all time.

In 1914, when the war first began, the Central Powers had high hopes. It was not long before they were dashed. Almost immediately it became apparent that the Schlieffen Plan was going to fail; the French were not easily defeated, the Russians were mobilizing faster than Germany had anticipated, and the British entered the war right away. As early as the Battle of the Marne in early September, it appeared that quick victory would be elusive. The German defeat at Marne was made all the worse by the failed "race to the sea" and the Battle of Ypres; the principal lessons were that defense dominated and that the Schlieffen Plan was flawed—there would be no quick, one-front war in the west, followed by another short, one-front war in the east. After the initial battles, trench warfare became the tactical strategy adopted, resulting in a stalemated, bloody, and drawn-out war.[4]

Disappointments early in the war were not the sole province of Germany. In the east, things were going very poorly for the Central Powers as well. Austria had initially mobilized against Serbia and at the last minute had to redirect to face Russia. The delay was costly. Early defeats in Galicia were painful, Austrian losses devastating.[5]

Yet despite the major setbacks for the Central Powers in the first months of the war, and the heightened threat of defeat that accompanied them, the Central Powers did not become more cohesive. On the contrary, as discussed below, the division within the alliance was even more pronounced.

In 1915, threat in the form of imminent defeat for the Central Powers receded. Victories against Russia in the spring and summer boosted the hopes of the allies. Their triple offensive culminated in a dramatic Russian retreat.[6] In September, Bulgaria joined the side of the Central Powers; with the additional support, the invasion and occupation of Serbia, Montenegro, and a portion of Albania were successfully undertaken.[7] The successes experienced by the alliance in this period, however, did not alter the conflict and division that characterized the alliance. Neither defeat nor success facilitated the cohesion of the alliance.

The deterioration of the alliance continued throughout 1916, which was a year of setbacks for the alliance. Hostility, conflict, and division were the overriding characteristics of the alliance in this period.[8] By 1916, Austria-Hungary was on the verge of collapse. Though saved in 1915 by German and Bulgarian intervention, the Habsburgs in 1915 had seen Italy joining the fray and opening up yet another front against them. Their losses were staggering. Conrad's staff reported that the Habsburg army lost 170,000 men each month in the east in the spring of 1915 and 200,000 men in September alone. The total casualties for 1915 were said to be 2,118,000.[9] Strategic errors plagued the Austrian military effort as well. Conrad's desire to defeat Italy led to his transfer of six infantry divisions from the east to the south. A Russian offensive at Lutsk culminated in disaster for Austria-Hungary as a consequence. Estimates put Austro-Hungarian losses at some 750,000 soldiers. This disaster brought about near total Austrian dependence on its German ally.[10]

Events on the western front in 1916 were not terribly encouraging for the Central Powers either. Germany had hoped to compel France to conclude a separate peace by bringing enormous pressure to bear at Verdun. The campaign failed and was very costly to both sides. The Battle on the Somme was similarly discouraging. The defeats in these two battles alone cost the Germans nearly 800,000 men.[11]

Despite the disasters of 1916 for the Central Powers and the consequent heightened threat to the alliance, the two states did not draw closer together and stand united against the Entente. If anything, as the situation deteriorated, German disdain for Austria-Hungary grew, and Austrian skepticism toward its German ally did as well.

The failures on the ground in 1916 led the German High Command to conclude that attention would have to turn to the seas. As Erich Ludendorff recounted: "Unrestricted submarine warfare was now the only means left to secure a victorious end to the war within a reasonable time."[12] This decision, in addition to the famous Zimmerman telegram proposing an alliance to Mexico and supporting the reconquering of Texas, New Mexico, and Arizona, as anticipated by the German High Command, brought the Americans into the war. The year 1917 also brought, however, the Russian Revolution and a separate peace at Brest Litovsk. Romania followed, concluding an armistice with Germany in December. For Austria-Hungary, only Italy remained.[13]

Despite the Central Powers' victory against Italy at Caporetto, the Austrian army was completely drained. In addition to the staggering number of casualties, Austria-Hungary was unable to feed or clothe its army or its population. The situation was so dire that Austria-Hungary actually seized a convoy of barges with Romanian grain making its way to Germany. Ludendorff was so angered by his ally's action, he wanted to declare war.[14]

Although the mood was mixed for the Central Powers in 1917, the alliance continued to suffer. It was dramatically clear by 1917 that victory or defeat for them rested exclusively with Germany. Austria-Hungary, as discussed in detail below, with the death of Franz Joseph and the accession of Karl, tried in vain to conclude a secret separate peace with the Entente.

By 1918, the situation confronting Austria-Hungary was even more dire. Germany, too, was beginning to crumble. Hunger was pervasive, and mutinies in the navy and strikes among German workers punctuated the winter of 1917/18.[15] Allied successes in the spring and summer of 1918 chipped away at Germany, culminating in what Ludendorff called "the black day of the German army" on August 8, 1918. A surprise attack allowed Britain to advance six to eight miles that day, eroding German morale. It was then that Ludendorff began to realize that the war must end.[16] The following month, as the British broke through the famous Hindenburg line, Paul von Benckendorf Hindenburg, chief of the German General Staff (1916–18), and Ludendorff decided armistice was necessary.[17] Even at this moment of consummate threat, the Central Powers were unable to rally as a united team, in spite of their nearly forty-year history as allies.

The Central Powers, despite the ebb and flow of threat that came with victory and defeat, were unable to sustain a cohesive alliance. This was true because the level and source of threat confronting the two states were different. The principal threat during the war to Austria-Hungary came from the east. Germany, in contrast, was preoccupied by the western front.[18] Throughout the war, Germany resisted sacrificing gains in the west for victories in the east.[19] This created enormous tension between the allies, as will be described in more detail in the subsequent section on cohesion.

Italy and Romania were primarily threatening to Austria-Hungary. Germany believed that Austria should make territorial concessions to them to prevent their defection to the Entente; Austria-Hungary, however, was not amenable to such dismemberment.[20] In essence, Austria-Hungary and Germany, despite fighting the same war as allies, had different enemies. Just as Italy and Romania principally had quarrels with Austria, Britain and France were largely the enemies of Germany, not Austria. The threat level throughout the war was higher to Austria-Hungary than Germany. From the beginning, the only victories Austria-Hungary was able to secure were with the assistance of Germany. Facing Serbia, Russia, Italy, and Romania, the war continued to spread, and the Habsburg army simply was not up to the task.[21] The difference in source and level of threat had a profound effect on cohesion, as did the fact that Austria was significantly threatened by its ally. The level of internal threat, more than the level of external threat, inhibited cohesion, to which I now turn.

COHESION

The wartime experience of the Central Powers in regard to cohesion could not have been more different from its peacetime years. The cohesion of the alliance in its first thirty-five years was significant; the wartime years left the alliance utterly bereft of unity. The alliance, in fact, is a fascinating study precisely because the contrast between the peacetime and wartime years could not be more vivid. From the first offensive of the war, when Moltke disappointed Conrad by failing to launch an offensive against Russia from Prussia as he had promised, the allies were divided. They proved largely unable to coordinate their strategies—indeed, the Germans frequently kept the Austrians in the dark regarding their impending plans. Their war aims not only diverged but frequently came at the expense of the other, and though neither state concluded a separate peace, it was not for lack of trying.

One major factor that undermined the wartime cohesion of the Central Powers was the absence of close military planning between the two states during the peacetime years. Disagreements persisted between the two Central Powers over the control of troops; over German strategy to win over allies at Austria-Hungary's territorial expense; over the primacy of the eastern or western front; over the disposition of Russian Poland; over troop support and military and economic aid; over how comprehensive their war aims should be; and over the question of whether to end the war in compromise peace. From the earliest moments in the war, the only thing the two allies could agree on was the desire to win the war. This section analyzes the cohesion of the Central Powers during its wartime years by examining how the states coordinated their strategy, the extent to which they shared war aims, and their ability to avoid the conclusion of a separate peace.

Coordination of Strategy

The joint planning for war between Germany and Austria was minimal prior to the war. In 1882, during the tenure of German general field marshal Count Helmuth von Moltke ("The Elder") and Austrian chief of staff General Frederick Beck-Rzikowsky, the allies had their initial conversations regarding strategy. Germany and Austria-Hungary agreed that in the event of a two-front war, Germany and Austria-Hungary would launch major offensives in tandem. They did not, however, address the issue of a unified command structure. This remained unresolved in the peacetime years and created significant difficulties for the allies once war came. Other problems cropped up during the German-Austrian discussions as well. Germany presumed Austria-Hungary would augment its military capabilities as well as improve its process of mobilization, which it did not.[22]

During the period in which Alfred Waldersee served as chief of the German General Staff, from 1888 to 1891, the allies experienced fairly close relations, although there were no major changes in their strategic planning. The most dramatic changes that took place in German planning came with Count Alfred von Schlieffen, who took over from Waldersee in 1891 and served as chief of the German General Staff until 1905. Schlieffen had no confidence in Austrian capabilities and, in contrast to relations under his predecessor, Austro-German military conversations came virtually to a halt by 1896.[23] In 1899, Schlieffen's disdain of Austria-Hungary was apparent as he noted on a memo, "To count on the intercession of our ally!! What an illusion."[24]

The Schlieffen Plan, for which this German chief of General Staff was most famous, evolved over the years subsequent to its development, yet its central concept remained. The bulk of German troops—over four-fifths of them—would initially confront France. Most of the German forces would cut through Belgium and try to outflank the French field army. Soon thereafter the French would be encircled and annihilated, leaving ample time for the German troops to be moved to the east to meet the Russian offensive, which would be in its initial stages.[25] In contrast to the plans that preceded it, the Schlieffen Plan was principally preoccupied with an initial, decisive assault against France. Schlieffen's concentration on the idea of a knockout blow in the west and only subsequent attention to the east caused consternation in Vienna. Ultimately, the allies suspended their conversations until 1909, during the annexation crisis, at which time Austria-Hungary took over Bosnia and Herzegovina.[26]

At this time, Austrian chief of staff Conrad and German chief of staff Helmuth von Moltke ("The Younger") began a correspondence in which they exchanged their views on planning for war. This exchange continued for several years. Conrad insisted on extracting a German promise to launch a simultaneous offensive against Russia. Moltke agreed, writing, "I will not hesitate to make the attack to support the simultaneous Austrian offensive. Your Excellency can count absolutely upon this assurance, which has been extensively considered . . . should the allies' intentions be disturbed by enemy action, immediate reciprocal information is required."[27]

This promise was not fulfilled when war finally came. The Germans were unable to effectively pull off the quick offensive in the west. This meant that attention to the east had to be deferred. Austria-Hungary, failing in its offensive in Galicia, blamed Germany for the lack of success. The plan that Moltke and Conrad had agreed upon never materialized. This was devastating for Austria, as Conrad had conceived of his initial offensive in Galicia with the assumption that the Germans would help with a powerful thrust of their own. Without the German attack to support the Austrian offensive, it failed miserably. Conrad was enraged and blamed Germany for the betrayal.[28] His bitterness persisted throughout the war, making cooperation between Austria and Germany all the more difficult. The failure of Germany to make good on its promise for swift support on the eastern front was thus costly, both in terms of Austrian casualties as well as in terms of Austrian goodwill toward its ally.[29] The rumors in late 1914 that a unified eastern command was being developed led Conrad to exclaim that he was "sick and tired" of the "egotistical ally" and to submit his resignation. It was rejected.[30]

For its part, Germany was not terribly pleased with its ally from the outset of the war either. Germany had been counting on an all-out Austrian offensive against Russia in the initial stages of the war. Conrad, however, preoccupied by Serbia, altered his plans without informing Moltke.[31] Austria-Hungary failed miserably in its first campaign and was from the early days of the war extremely dependent on Germany to assist its efforts. Conrad bombarded Moltke with telegrams as early as August 23, 28, 30 and September 1 demanding German support.[32] In April 1915, Ludendorff, the German chief of staff on the eastern front, wrote to Moltke "The Younger" disparaging the Austrians in every way imaginable, calling them arrogant, incompetent, chronic failures, and "miserable people."[33] The bitterness was so severe that by the end of the war, Hindenburg and Ludendorff thought Germany's next war would be against Austria-Hungary.[34]

The antagonism between the allies persisted throughout the war. It interfered with the ability of the states to coordinate their strategies. From the start of the war, each ally conducted campaigns with little regard or communication with each other. This was especially true of the Germans. For example, the German plans at Verdun were not only not coordinated with Vienna, the Germans actually fed Conrad's representative disinformation regarding the German buildup.[35]

Despite the antipathy, however, there was some coordination. By the spring of 1915, a large number of German forces were shifted to the eastern front. After successes in the Polish campaign, the Germans turned their attention to the Balkans and launched a campaign to subjugate Serbia and open the Danube route to Bulgaria and Turkey.[36] Concurrently, major Anglo-French offensives commenced in the west. Despite the fact that Entente forces were superior to German forces in the west at that time, the Germans continued to concentrate on the east. This show of German support of its ally indicates some cohesion of the Central Powers. In fact, Austrian failure in its Volhynia offensive meant even more German divisions had to be committed in the campaign against Serbia. Nevertheless, friction between the Central Powers continued over command of the operations as well as over coordination of the campaign.[37]

By 1916, Germany decided to once again turn its attention west. Ironically, by participating in the war in the Balkans, Germany had brought to the fore competing ambitions of its allies. Ultimately, Erich von Falkenhayn, the chief of the German General Staff (1914–16), decided that Germany's fate would be settled in the west, not the east, and focused the German fighting resources there once more.[38] The fighting on the eastern front started to wind down in 1917. The Russian Revolution resulted in the Russian treaty of surrender at Brest Litovsk in December.[39] Following the diminution of fighting on the eastern front, Austria-Hungary actually sent contingents to fight on the western front.[40] But for the most part, the western front remained principally Germany's theater. By 1918, Austria-Hungary was completely sapped.[41]

The coordination of military strategy required the specification of detailed command and control issues, such as agreement on troop deployments. Yet for Austria-Hungary and Germany, though they had agreed in principle to certain arrangements, the details remained unresolved. Further, communication between the two was problematic.[42] This produced conflict over military control of troops and priorities of front from the earliest moments of the war.[43] There was no unified command of their forces; the troops were separate armies with separate orders, and there were constant conflicts over where each state's troops should be deployed. Only in critical moments, when it was clear that Germany needed to send support to its ally or face continuing the war alone, was grudging cooperation elicited.[44] As a consequence of the differences between the two allies, division over the disposition of Poland, and a growing desire to end the war in Austria-Hungary, sentiment in Austria-Hungary was often that the war was not being fought for Austrian interests or aims.[45] It is these aims that I turn to next.

War Aims

Recounting in detail the war aims of Germany and Austria-Hungary during the First World War is beyond the scope of this section and has been done thoroughly elsewhere.[46] What I seek to do instead is elaborate on the ways in which the states were in agreement or discord over their objectives in the war. The differences between the Central Powers certainly were more pervasive than their shared goals. In fact, one of the most striking things about the allies' war aims is how frequently they came at the expense of the other. The conflict over war aims, as with the differences over coordination of military operations, stemmed from the fact that each state confronted different threats and different enemies and had vastly different priorities. Further, the differences derived from Austrian weakness and relative German strength. Austro-Hungarian aims diminished rapidly with the early defeats and the onset of war weariness; German war aims escalated with its numerous victories and successes.[47]

One of the first clashes Austria and Germany experienced in regard to their war aims was over the future of Russian Poland. From before the fighting even began in Galicia, the Central Powers disagreed over control of the territory. This debate persisted throughout the war. Germany sought to annex the industrial areas; Austria-Hungary sought Polish union with the Dual

Monarchy.[48] Austro-Hungarian foreign minister Count István Burián was afraid that if Poland attained sovereignty, the eight million Polish subjects of the Habsburg Empire might grow restless. His solution was a plan that would unify the areas with the Austrian Poles of Galicia in an independent kingdom under Habsburg authority. The Germans rejected this solution and proposed as an alternative an independent Poland with ties to Germany. These terms were accepted by Austria-Hungary only in the face of the disastrous defeat during the Brusilov offensive, at which time Germany once more had to bail out its weaker ally.[49]

The Poland issue became integral to the larger question of Germany's goal of Mitteleuropa. This central German war aim entailed the formation with Austria-Hungary of a customs union, to which all of the lesser states of the Continent would adhere.[50] Such a union would ensure the economic dependence of these states on Germany and secure German command of the Continent. In other words, Mitteleuropa was a plan for a "Greater Germany." It would entail the economic and, ultimately, political absorption of the Habsburg Empire.[51] The form and function of Mitteleuropa dominated conversations between Austria-Hungary and Germany throughout the war. Conflict between the Central Powers over Poland and over Mitteleuropa pervaded the relationship between the allies.[52]

The clash of war aims did not end with the Polish question or Mitteleuropa plans. In 1915, when Germany feared Italian intervention on the part of the Triple Entente, Germany repeatedly tried to prevent this outcome by promising Habsburg territory to Italy.[53] Germany believed it was necessary to satisfy, at least in part, Italian territorial aspirations in order to maintain Italian neutrality. Satisfying Italian irredentism, however, would require the cession of territory by Austria-Hungary. Germany made promises to Italy concerning the relinquishing of Trento by Austria-Hungary to it, despite the adamant refusal and indignation this aroused in the Dual Monarchy. "Basically," said Prussian war minister Wild von Hohenborn, "it does not matter a hoot to us whether Italy hacks another piece off the dying camel Austria."[54] Ultimately, the Austrians capitulated to German pressure, but it was too late, and Italy signed the Treaty of London on April 26, 1915.[55]

Germany and Austria-Hungary were at odds over Romania as well. It was unclear which side Romania would join, and Germany wanted to ensure Romanian allegiance to the Central Powers by making promises that would come, again, at Austria-Hungary's expense.[56] German and Austro-Hungarian differences extended to policy with Bulgaria and Greece as well as the Ottoman Empire. At every turn, it appeared that the Central Powers differed in their goals and strategy to attain them.[57]

The differences in German and Austrian goals became critical by the end of 1916 and beginning of 1917. Austria-Hungary was receptive to the idea of ending the war in compromise; Germany was not. In 1916, Austria wanted, together with its allies, to publish a joint and binding statement of the Central Powers' peace terms. Germany would not agree to do so—its aims were so ambitious in the west, there was no way the Entente would find a basis for negotiation.[58]

Ultimately, Germany did concede to Austrian wishes, yet Austria-Hungary itself believed that Germany's objectives in the west were overly ambitious and unrealistic. This was disappointing to Austria, as it was convinced that the expansionist objectives would prevent peace from being realized. Germany, for its part, was critical of Austrian aims in the Balkans, arguing that they, too, were overly aggressive.[59] Berlin pressured Vienna to agree on Balkan war aims and advocated giving the Serbs fairly easy peace terms. Austria-Hungary, for its part, tried similarly to contain German war aims in Belgium and the Baltic.[60]

The Germans continued to put off the Austrians in regard to a joint statement of war aims. They did, however, announce a peace offer at the end of 1916, though it was underscored by German certainty of victory and did not contain any explicit terms or conditions.[61] Not surprisingly, the Entente refused the offer. At the same time, the decision was made in Germany to begin the unrestricted U-boat campaign in January 1917, independent of the outcome of the German peace offer. This decision to employ unrestricted U-boat warfare was met with disapproval by the Habsburg monarchy.[62]

The widening gap between Germany's ambitious war aims and Austria-Hungary's desire for peace was manifest by April 1917 in Ottokar Czernin's memo to Emperor Karl, announcing the end of the military capability of the Habsburg Empire. In it, he anticipated that without peace, domestic instability and revolution would ultimately overwhelm the monarchy. He was critical of German policy regarding unrestricted submarine warfare and fearful of the consequences of the entry of the United States into the war. Karl supported Czernin's views, but Germany clung to its ambitious agenda and dismissed Austro-Hungarian anxiety.[63] This was neither the first nor the last Austrian plea with Germany to end the war.

Germany and Austria-Hungary diverged sharply from beginning to end over their principal objectives in the war. Frequently, in fact, they advocated policies that would come very directly at the expense of their ally. This was particularly true of Germany's desire to purchase the neutrality of Italy and Romania with Habsburg land. The Central Powers clashed over the future of Poland, over the form of Mitteleuropa, and over Belgium, Serbia, and the Balkans. Ultimately, they were divided, too, over peace. The German desire to win outright was at odds with Austro-Hungarian desperation to negotiate.[64] The divisions were so deep and the consequences so severe that, for Austria-Hungary, alliance with Germany ultimately culminated in the death of the Habsburg Empire.[65]

Resistance to Separate Peace

Despite the tremendous problems confronting the Central Powers' cohesion with regard to the coordination of their military operations and their war aims, the alliance did survive the duration of the war. However, even on this score the Central Powers' record is not completely clean. Although Austria-Hungary rejected separate peace initiatives by Britain, France, and the United States, it did come quite close to negotiating an agreement in 1917.

By late 1916, Austria-Hungary very much wanted out of the war. Upon the death of Emperor Franz Joseph, Karl acceded to the throne. Karl's wife, Empress Zita, was of French-Italian descent. Upon his accession, Karl summoned her brother, Prince Sixte of Bourbon-Parma, a French citizen serving in the Belgian army. Prince Sixte became the conduit of information, negotiating between Emperor Karl and the Entente in the search for a separate peace. From December 1916 to October 1917, Prince Sixte attempted to mediate in secret between the two sides. The first step was, after meeting with the emperor, to meet with the president of the French Republic, Raymond Poincaré, in early 1917. The emperor had communicated to Sixte that he was prepared to conclude peace based on four points—a secret agreement with Russia in which Constantinople would not be an issue; Alsace-Lorraine would revert to France; Belgian sovereignty would be restored; and a southern Slav monarchy comprised of Bosnia, Herzegovina, Serbia, Albania, and Montenegro would be formed.[66]

Sixte, after meeting with Poincaré, wrote to the emperor and asked that he put the points in a letter giving "definite and unambiguous assent" to the plan.[67] On March 24, 1917, the emperor replied with his notorious letter. Karl stated unequivocally that he would

> use all my personal influence and every other means in my power to exact from my Allies a settlement of her just claims in Alsace-Lorraine.
>
> As for Belgium, she must be restored in her entirety as a sovereign state, with the whole of her African possessions, and without prejudice to the compensations she may receive for the losses she has already suffered.[68]

Ultimately, the negotiations foundered, most particularly because of a failure to come to agreement over Italian demands. By late 1917, Karl's hopes for a general peace were dashed.

Not much else would have come of the Sixtus Affair, except that in April 1918 things came to a head between France and Austria-Hungary. Czernin hinted in a speech that Georges Clemenceau had desired to know under what conditions Austria-Hungary would negotiate peace. Czernin claimed that in response to the query, he had stipulated that France must renounce its claim to Alsace and Lorraine. Clemenceau, in retaliation, printed Emperor Karl's letter of the previous year.[69] The repercussions were far-reaching.[70] Yet the central point here is the wide differences between Germany and Austria. Austria was prepared to sell out its German ally; Germany was quite willing to do the same.[71] Austria simply did not want to continue fighting for "Germany's lust of conquest."[72]

In sum, although the Central Powers were able to survive the duration of the war, the difficulties the alliance members faced in doing so were grave. The problems that the two powers faced in wartime were far more complex and vital than they were during peacetime. The inability to agree on aims, or policy—diplomatic and military—to attain them, severely diminished the effectiveness of the alliance.

SUMMARY

Facing an adversarial coalition during wartime did not result in a unified threat that made the Central Powers cohesive. Theoretically, it would seem that the high level of external threat to the member states should guarantee some significant level of cohesion, particularly for an alliance that preexisted the war by thirty-five years.

During peacetime, a coalition that poses a common threat to another alliance will enhance the level of cohesion to the threatened alliance. Yet in this case, while the specificity of the threat during wartime appeared to become more salient, the sources of threat, though contained in one adversarial coalition, were different. This affected cohesion adversely. The implication is that ambiguous external threats during peacetime will not undermine cohesion in the same way they do during wartime. Further, during wartime the actual progress of the war was of vital importance; it was not solely the intentions of the threatening state or coalition that were crucial. Rather, it was how well the troops were holding up in battle.

Moreover, the different fronts of war in this case gave rise to a serious divergence in goals, means, and identification of threat. This was especially true for this alliance, which was between states of unequal strength. The Central Powers had divergent interests, but they also, counter to what would be supposed, had different enemies. It is true that Austria-Hungary did not sign a separate peace with the Entente, and Germany did support Austrian efforts in the east. Nevertheless, the persistent problems between the two states in coordinating goals and strategy indicate that the cohesion of the alliance was low.[73]

The Triple Entente

If the Central Powers were as divided during the war as they were united during the peace that preceded it, the opposite was true of the Triple Entente for the first years of the war. The most striking characteristic of the wartime Triple Entente was the members' commitment to the alliance, despite the lingering doubts, suspicion, and mistrust that came from the legacy of enmity prior to the war. Above all, it was the German threat that facilitated Entente unity. The overriding goal of the Triple Entente became to destroy the military prowess of Germany.[74]

The threat was amplified by consistent and persistent attempts on the part of Germany to divide the Triple Entente and conclude a separate peace with either Russia or France. Ultimately, the war became a test of durability, as the Central Powers tried repeatedly to divide the alliance; preserving the coalition became as significant a war aim as territorial ambitions such as Alsace-Lorraine.[75] German efforts to conclude a separate peace with either France or Russia meant compromises had to be made by their allies to provide continuous incentives to keep them in the war. Compromise within the Entente prevented compromise between the adversarial coalitions.[76]

Also in direct contrast to the Central Powers, the Entente was an alliance of relatively equal partners; no one state's goals prevailed over the others.[77] Instead, compromise among member states in their aims was necessary. The allies adopted each other's goals, despite the sacrifices pursuing them entailed. These were dramatic concessions, all made out of a desire to cement the alliance and ensure it prevailed, unified, in victory.

THREAT

The level of threat facing the Entente coalition was high. The most immediate source of threat did vary for the allies—for the French and British, it came from Germany; for Russia, primarily from Austria-Hungary. Russian military planning prior to the war focused on the Austrian theater of war. The traditional hostility between Austria-Hungary and Russia, as seen in the previous chapters, had not extended to Russia's relations with Germany. The final plans for war, which called for an offensive in East Prussia in accordance with French aims, underestimated the logistical difficulties of the attack. Further, the Russians had believed that France would be able to

deal a crippling blow to Germany in the beginning of the war.[78] As the realities of the war dawned, the Russians had to fight continuously against
Germany. Germany became the primary adversary to each member of the
Entente.[79] It was above all fear of Germany and its ambitious objectives that
served as the glue that sealed the Entente. In the absence of that threat, the
different and often inconsistent aims of the allies may have undermined the
alliance.[80]

The first year of the war was one full of disappointments for the Triple
Entente. For the French, Plan XVII failed, and stalemate soon emerged on
the western front.[81] The Russians failed to beat the Germans decisively, and
its casualties were staggering. Britain, too, experienced very heavy casualties—60 percent of its original force by November.[82] There were, however,
encouraging developments as well—Russia made significant gains against
Austria-Hungary, and Britain's call to arms was answered resoundingly.[83]

The second year of the war was one of significant setbacks for the Entente, heightening the threat the member states faced. The Russians confronted massive losses in 1915. In May alone, Russia lost 412,000 men; more
than 850,000 troops were captured by the Germans in their greatest victory
of the war.[84] When Russia started to lose heavily on the eastern front, it
appealed to its allies for diversionary activity. Its allies heeded the call. In
February 1915, the British decided on a naval attack at the Dardanelles. In
March, the British and the French advanced toward the Narrows but struck
mines and called off the naval attack. Later that year, the British and French
landed troops at Gallipoli. Under the Constantinople Agreement of March
1915, the British, and more reluctantly the French, provided territorial
promises in order to secure continued Russian support and participation in
the war. (The allies' withdrawal from the Dardanelles, however, did widen
the rift between them and Russia.)[85]

France also experienced significant military setbacks in 1915, with stale-
mates at Artois and Champagne and costly losses in the Battle of Loos.[86]
None of the allies could yield significant gains in 1915; on the contrary, serious losses marked the year above all for the Entente. In addition to the
losses at the Dardanelles, Britain experienced a string of other defeats. By
late in the year, following British troops being defeated at Ctesiphon and
under siege at Kut, morale in London was low.[87]

The heightened threat confronting the allies in 1915 culminated in an
important advance in the alliance's cohesion. In early December 1915, the
military leadership of the Entente members met at French headquarters in
Chantilly to discuss coordinating efforts for the coming year. It was the first
attempt to agree on some general framework to coordinate conduct in the

war. The meeting highlighted mutual interests as well as each country's specific ones. Overall, consensus on the issues prevailed, with the exception of
whether to retain Salonika.[88]

The next year, 1916, did not dawn promisingly for the Triple Entente. The
French faced early setbacks at Verdun and, fearful of exhausting their army,
called on Britain for help.[89] The situation did ultimately turn—by summer,
the Triple Entente was challenging the Central Powers on every front; by fall,
the allies anticipated victory.[90] The successes of 1916 led France and Britain
to agree in mid November of that year to apply the same strategy of coordination and simultaneous offensives in 1917. At that time, discussions about
a conference with Russia regarding strategy was raised. The Petrograd Conference, though significant in regard to the cohesion of the alliance, was rendered insignificant with the Russian Revolution that came only a couple of
weeks after it ended.[91]

The threats confronting the Triple Entente in 1917 came not only from
the Central Powers—in the form, for example, of unrestricted U-boat warfare—but also from the domestic crises that faced each member of the Entente in the summer of 1917.[92] The most acute of these was the revolution
early in the year in which the Russian tsar was forced to abdicate. A provisional government came to power in Russia, raising fears in Britain and
France that Russia would defect from the alliance.

Military threats to the Entente abounded in 1917. In addition to the grave
situation in the east, the consummate failure of the Nivelle offensive, the
lack of decisive victory at Passchendaele, and the costly and bloody defeat of
the Italian army at Caporetto, the hampered war effort in Russia following
the revolution and Russia's separate peace later in the year were all devastating blows to the Entente.[93] The only mitigating factor was American entry
into the war.

In all, the level of threat to the Entente emanated more uniformly from
a common enemy—though less for Russia (and Italy) than for Britain and
France—than was the case for the Central Powers. This helped the Entente
forge solidarity.

COHESION

It would seem the very nature of alliances during wartime to present dramatic challenges to cohesion. The tasks of coordinating goals and strategies
and agreeing on war aims all present major challenges for allies, no matter
how well suited they are to fight together. As General Sir William Robertson said of the French: "I believe they are as good allies as any country could

have. I merely wish to emphasize the great difficulty there has been and always will be in operations conducted by allied armies. It is only natural." [94] The Triple Entente held together remarkably well, especially in comparison to its peacetime years. There was extensive collaboration and consultation, and the allies made substantial concessions on war aims. There were also challenges to the alliance, inhibiting its cohesion. Yet the members effectively resisted German efforts to divide the alliance until 1917, after the second change of government in Russia in the aftermath of the revolution. In this section, I will address the three components of wartime cohesion—coordination of strategy, war aims, and separate peace—and provide an analysis of Entente cohesion. The war, in some ways, had a positive effect on the members' relations. As Herbert H. Asquith said at a dinner given to members of the Duma and Council of the Empire on May 9, 1916:

> One of the most gratifying results of our Alliance is the complete agreement which has been established between the British and Russian Governments in regard to Eastern affairs. . . . The days of misunderstanding are happily over, and whether it be in Turkey or in Persia or wherever British and Russian interests come into contact with one another, we have arrived at a common policy which we are both determined loyally and in concert to pursue. [95]

Coordination of Strategy

Military planning in Russia and France prior to the war had called for a simultaneous French offensive against the Germans in the west and Russian offensives against Austria-Hungary and Germany in the east. Once the war began, however, it was immediately clear that calling for Russian offensives against Germany in East Prussia and Austria in Galicia overcommitted Russian forces, which could not be quickly mobilized. [96]

France and Britain also consulted over military and naval affairs in the decade preceding the war. Steps to provide the French with military aid against Germany had been in the works since 1905, though specific details regarding strategic deployment and coordination remained unresolved when war broke out. [97] The plans called for the British to immediately send their Expeditionary Force to France in order to aid in the offensive against Germany in the west. [98] The military conversations between France and Britain comprehensively specified the military cooperation between the two allies, although there was no provision for command relations between the two armies. [99] As David Lloyd George recounted after the war:

> The real weakness of Allied strategy was that it never existed. Instead of one great war with a united front, there were at least six separate and distinct wars with a separate, distinct and independent strategy for each. There was some pretence at

timing the desperate blows with a rough approach to simultaneity. The calendar was the sole foundation of inter-Allied strategy. . . . There was no real unity of conception, co-ordination of effort or pooling of resources in such a way as to deal the enemy the hardest knocks at his weakest point. There were so many national armies, each with its own strategy and its own resources to carry it through.[100]

The failure of the French and British to coordinate their strategy and the resulting defeat in the first joint operation of the war resulted in anger and recriminations that hampered Anglo-French relations.[101] Still more problematic was the fact that there were no plans for Anglo-Russian cooperation.[102]

During the early days of the war, the British and French were unable to stop the German advance. France, believing Russia was not doing enough to take the pressure off the western front, urged more from its ally. Russia launched its campaign in East Prussia and sustained heavy losses, and the British and French were able to reverse the German tide in the west.[103] Yet the losses suffered by Russia in 1914 for the cause of its allies exacerbated the problems it faced both at home and on the ground during the following months. Further aggravating Russian woes was the failure of the Allied fleet to prevent the German warships *Goeben* and *Breslau* from entering the Sea of Marmora. This led to the entry of the Ottoman Empire into the war on the side of the Central Powers. Turkey prevented Russia's allies access to the Black Sea, which meant desperately needed supplies could not get through to Russia, supplies that were needed in no small part due to losses suffered in pursuing strategy in aid of Russia's allies. Further, the drawing of German forces to the east increased pressure on Russia, while the pressure subsided in the west.[104] By the end of 1915, Russia had diminished confidence in its allies. Russian advances against Austria-Hungary as well as its losses against Germany led Germany to focus on its operations against Russia. The Germans concentrated on trying to prop up their ally and to knock Russia out of the war. France and Britain were unsuccessful at preventing Germany from defeating Russia. Russia, as a consequence, became bitter and disillusioned.[105]

The French and British did try to support their ally. They struggled to supply Russia with munitions and food. In September 1915, the British and Russians signed a financial agreement.[106] Militarily, the French and British tried to relieve their ally's burden; the French launched an offensive in Lens and Arras, which was abandoned not long thereafter, and then planned an Anglo-French assault on La Bassée Canal at Loos. These efforts did not succeed in relieving the pressure on Russia, and resentment in Russia continued to grow.[107]

The divergent strategies of the Entente powers in 1914–15 created significant challenges to the alliance. Disagreement was rife over grand strategy and key goals in 1915. The siege of Antwerp revealed the deficiencies of

Anglo-French strategy in painful detail; General Joseph Joffre, French commander on the western front, and Lord Horatio Herbert Kitchener, British secretary of state for war, appeared to be working at cross purposes.[108]

By 1916, the situation appeared to improve somewhat. The allies more effectively coordinated their military plans and munitions policy.[109] In 1916, Russia again heeded the call of its allies to undertake offensive operations in Russia's northern and western fronts.[110] Meanwhile, British troops in France, which had totaled just under 1 million in January, by the beginning of the Somme battles reached over 1.4 million.[111] These Entente efforts succeeded in relieving the pressure on the French at Verdun.[112]

In another example of alliance cooperation, in the spring of 1916 the Russians intensified their fighting in Galicia in response to Italian pleas for help. Some fifteen Austro-Hungarian divisions were consequently transported from the Italian front; eighteen German divisions were transferred to the Russian front from the French theater of operations; and three and a half German divisions (and two Turkish divisions) were sent to the Russian front from Salonika.[113]

Cooperation extended into the economic aspects of the war. British support began with the coordination of armaments contracts, then moved to the arena of shipping and ultimately to finance. The British secured long-term shipping charters with its merchant fleet for cargoes of military importance for its allies and supplied them with necessary goods on credit. What emerged, in the second half of the war, was a comprehensive and complex system of interallied cooperation in credit and finance.[114]

The Entente also attempted to create various councils to provide forums for making decisions regarding different aspects of alliance policy. Creating these forums should have facilitated the coordination of Entente policy. However, most of them appeared in the latter half of the war. The Inter-Allied Shipping Committee was set up in 1917, the Allied Maritime Transport Council later that year; interallied economic conferences met in 1916 and throughout the rest of the war;[115] and moreover there was the creation of the Inter-Allied Supreme War Council in 1917.[116]

A hierarchical command structure for the Allied troops did not come about until after Russia's departure from the alliance. In March 1918, Allied forces on the western front came under Ferdinand Foch's command.[117] Earlier attempts to consolidate the command structure were largely ineffective. In many ways, the military failures that the Entente experienced in 1915 were a consequence of problems in executing plans, not in their conception. The Entente was, at times, its own worst enemy—the Dardanelles campaign foundered more because of problems with the naval command in the Mediterranean and in France, and because of the inability of involved ministers to agree on the mission's scope and nature or to provide sufficient support, than because of the adversary's stand.[118]

Additional crises in Entente relations came during the period of command of General Robert Nivelle, new commander in chief of the French army. In 1917, for example, the French commander proposed a joint offensive to the British War Cabinet in which he suggested that centralized command of the combined forces would rest with him. At the Calais Conference later that year, Nivelle presented a draft proposal regarding the course of command relationships of British and French headquarters. In essence, the document eliminated the right of the British headquarters to communicate with the British government. Not surprisingly, the proposal was viewed as too far-fetched, and instead a compromise was reached. Ultimately, the agreement forced the commander in chief of the British Expeditionary Force, Douglas Haig, to adjust his plans according to Nivelle's wishes through the end of the joint offensive.[119] When the content of this agreement became known, there was tremendous opposition in Britain, and the London Conference the following month nullified the original agreement. The Nivelle offensive became for all intents and purposes "two separate and uncoordinated major operations."[120] This attempt at unifying the command structure of the allies' forces ended in disaster.

The natural rivalry that existed among the Entente members as a consequence of their history of enmity prior to the war pervaded the Entente's attempts to coordinate strategy. It was only by the end of the war that unity in command emerged.[121] The Triple Entente worked hard to coordinate strategy by consulting frequently and creating bodies to address specific issues related to the war effort. Nevertheless, the case reveals the myriad problems associated with interallied operations and the difficulties associated with coordinating strategy in the absence of preestablished hierarchies and plans.

War Aims

The Entente members had very different aims in the First World War. Their individual hopes for territorial gains diverged, even though each member state shared the desire to win the war decisively and defeat Germany. The prewar rivalries and animosities among the states had not completely disappeared.[122] These sentiments shaped the war aims of the allies in significant ways. Each state hoped to enhance its country's postwar security vis à vis enemies and allies alike.[123]

Despite lingering distrust, however, what was remarkable about the Entente war aims was the degree to which the states were ultimately able to make concessions to their allies to sustain support and solidarity. Russian (and Italian) concerns were in the east, while French and British interests were in the west. However, by relatively early in the war, even Russia recognized the need to reduce German military power and, with it, its ambitions for military, political, and economic domination of the region. Russia, too, came to see Germany as the principal enemy.[124]

The British and French, for their part, understood that the war could not be won without Russia and accepted, therefore, Russian objectives that before would have been unthinkable. British policy had always aimed at keeping Russia out of the Straits. Yet once the war started, Britain promised both Constantinople and the Straits to Russia.[125] The French were alienated over these guarantees to Russia yet ultimately had to capitulate. Their concerns over Russian domination in Turkey and the possibility of Russia becoming a Mediterranean naval power had to be subordinated to the goal of defeating Germany. France resigned itself to the compromises necessary in coalition warfare.

This turnabout from traditional British and French policy was connected to the allies' desire to keep Russia in the war. This was crucial, given the repeated German attempts to divide the alliance and conclude a separate peace with Russia from the beginning of the war.[126] Defeating Germany was paramount; numerous compromises and concessions—many of them unpalatable—had to be made to ensure that outcome.[127]

The sacrifices and compromises made in order to attain the goal of defeating Germany were indeed significant. Britain adopted France's aim of reclaiming Alsace-Lorraine; Britain and France supported the Russian goal of claiming Constantinople and the Straits; the Entente members had to agree to fight for Italian unredeemed land in possession of Austria-Hungary. They were able to agree, despite the fact that they had very different priorities. The Entente could do so because their ambitions were not wholly mutually exclusive.[128]

As discussed in the previous section, the German aim to dominate the European continent, its Mitteleuropa plan, and Austria-Hungary's need for self-preservation worked against the cohesion of their alliance. In contrast, Great Britain deliberately constrained its aims in order to preserve the solidarity of its alliance. Because Britain was aware that its allies might have been antagonized by its own expansionist aims, it tried as best it could to limit the territorial gains it would make on account of the war.[129] Historians have argued that the goals of the Triple Entente were defensive, while the Central Powers had offensive aims. According to this view, "a purely defensive war lacked inspiration," though it may have enhanced the possibility of cooperation among the allies.[130] However, the Entente war aims were quite ambitious; it is difficult to view them as purely defensive.

The ambitious territorial aims of the Entente were manifest in promises made to the members to keep them in the war, as well as in the promises to other states, such as Italy, to bring them into the war. The member states bargained over how to divide up the spoils of war; they were more willing and able to negotiate and compromise to keep their partners satisfied than the Central Powers were. Britain and France negotiated the disposition of Ottoman territory and concluded secret agreements over their plans for the Middle East.[131] Many of the French and British war aims were, in fact, outside of Europe.[132]

By fall of 1918, the threat to the alliance ultimately receded as Germany came to an exhausted halt. Interestingly, it is at this point that the Entente member states became increasingly concerned about the potential gains of the other members of the alliance.[133] This does support the idea that cohesion is more easily attained when an alliance is losing than winning, although there were indications that the Entente maintained cohesion when it was winning as well. France, for example, reaffirmed its solidarity with its allies in the euphoria following victory on the Marne.[134]

In sum, the Triple Entente struggled less with compromise on war aims than did its enemy coalition. The member states were able to negotiate among themselves and extend guarantees and promises to each other regarding the territorial spoils of war. Because, for the most part, the Entente members actually wanted different things, it was possible for them to come to agreement.

Resistance to Separate Peace

Throughout the war, Germany tried repeatedly to detach one or more members from the Triple Entente.[135] From the onset of the war, for example, Germany attempted to woo Russia. Feelers were extended to France as well. Germany's efforts to divide the Triple Entente, however, did not work. In the words of Walter Runciman, in a speech to the House of Commons on December 23, 1915: "Like the rest of my colleagues, I will be no party to a peace that in any way conflicts with the interests of the Allies. They stand together: they will not make peace separately and there will be no kind of hankering after peace before the main end has been attained."[136]

The Triple Entente, until 1917, held up in the face of German attempts to promote conflict and dissension within the alliance. As it turned out, German military success rendered those attempts failures; the threat posed by Germany compelled the allies to preserve their alliance above all in order to

defeat the Central Powers. The threat of German power and offensive intentions motivated each member to commit its "blood and treasure" to attain a decisive victory over Germany.[137] The Entente members would not,
as stipulated by the Treaty of London, conclude a separate peace.[138]

The situation changed dramatically in 1917, after revolution in Russia.
Once the Provisional Government came to power in early March, it tried
hard to signal strong continued support of the alliance. In a declaration some
five days after assuming power, the government declared that it would "sa-
credly observe the alliances which bind us to other powers and will unswerv-
ingly carry out the agreements entered into with the allies."[139] Paul Miliukov, the new foreign minister, went even further. He sent a statement to the
Allied governments that read,

> shoulder to shoulder with [our allies] we shall fight our common foe to the end,
> unswervingly and indefatigably. The Government, of which I am a member, will
> devote all its energy to the achievement of victory and will make every effort to
> correct as rapidly as possible the errors of the past, which may have paralyzed up
> to now the enthusiasm and spirit of sacrifice of the Russian people.[140]

Yet the approach of Miliukov and the Provisional Government to the war
effort was unrealistic; the Russian army was disintegrating, and war weariness was pervasive. This made continuing the war effort nearly impossible.
In March 1917, General Mikhail Alexeev, commander in chief of the Russian forces, wrote to the Russian war minister, Alexander Guchkov:

> It is too late to speak now of the coördinated operations planned by the Allies
> and myself. We had decided on them in Chantilly in November, 1916, and in
> Petrograd, in February, 1917. And in those conferences Russia had assumed cer-
> tain obligations. But the present situation is such that, despite our efforts to pre-
> serve our standing in the eyes of the Allies, we must either postpone the fulfill-
> ment of those obligations or wholly abandon them.
>
> The above obligations were these: The Russian army guaranteed to launch a
> decisive attack on the enemy not later than three weeks after the beginning of the
> offensive of the Allies. We have already given notice that, owing to disorganiza-
> tion, bad conditions of transport, and lack of supplies, we are not in a position to
> begin action before the early part of May. But, according to your letter, we can
> not fulfil even that modified obligation. To engage in any serious operation with-
> out reinforcements is out of the question. The Allies must be informed that we
> cannot be counted upon for any action before June, and our reasons for that must
> be made clear. Thus, by force of circumstances we are coming to the conclusion
> that during the next four months our army must remain quiet and avoid ex-
> tended and decisive operations.[141]

Worse than being unrealistic, Miliukov's policy approach was very un-
popular with the soviets and the population as a whole. This came to a head

in April, over a note he sent to the Allied governments. This note communicated Russian fidelity to its allies and said that Russia would fight to a conclusive victory. Once published, there was a popular outcry that culminated in Miliukov's resignation.[142] The political wranglings were worsened by the deteriorating situation on the ground. In one final Russian campaign, the prime minister, Alexander Kerensky, called for an offensive against Austria-Hungary and Germany to signal Russian integrity of intentions vis à vis the allies. The offensive began on July 1 and culminated in a dramatic failure for Russia. The Central Powers advanced in Galicia and captured Riga.[143]

The failure of the Kerensky offensive, combined with domestic turmoil, war weariness, and mounting hostility toward the allies as consequence of Allied reaction to Russian disorder, all culminated in the Bolshevik coup in November. The Bolsheviks, who had promised the population peace, withdrew from the war after signing an agreement at Brest Litovsk in December 1917.

The Russian Revolution and subsequent armistice with the Central Powers in late 1917 signified the end of the Triple Entente. One central aim of the alliance had been to avoid the conclusion of a separate peace by any member. The abrupt rupture of the alliance was a consequence of the revolution and the complete transformation of the political system and structure in Russia. Attempts by Germany to conclude a separate peace with Russia throughout the course of the war prior to the revolution had been wholly unsuccessful. The fundamental diplomatic objective of German policy in 1915 was to lure Russia away from the Triple Entente. Given the military failures of Russia in Poland at the time, given the traditional friendliness that characterized Russo-German relations, given the similarities in their political systems, one might have believed Russia would be seduced. German attempts were comprehensive and appealing. Yet everything the Germans tried—be it conjuring images of the Three Emperors' Leagues, parading a commitment to the dynastic principle, threatening Russia's defeat in war, threatening the loss of Poland, offering the Straits, defeating Serbia, illuminating the inability of France and Britain to make significant headway, playing up the entry of Bulgaria into the war—failed to move the Russians.[144]

The interplay between domestic and international forces was dramatic in the Russian case. Once more we see the complex forces at work that profoundly alter alliance cohesion during wartime. In the case of the Triple Entente, the war affected domestic politics in important ways, which in turn influenced the course of events at the international level. For the Russians, this process was clear. The war was instrumental in contributing to domestic unrest, one of several factors that culminated in not one but two changes in government and ultimately the withdrawal of Russia from the war. Both the role of the war in bringing about the revolution and the revolution's role in bringing about an end to the war are important.

The Triple Entente, like the Central Powers, until 1917 was able to withstand efforts by the adversarial coalition to divide it, despite the traditional enmities. Great Britain especially believed that it could not possibly win the war without France and Russia. When it uncovered Germany's repeated attempts throughout 1914, 1915, and 1916 to divide the alliance, Britain made the preservation of the cohesion of the Entente its most important objective.[145] From the beginning to the end of the war, Great Britain in particular worked very hard to cement relations among the allies. In the words of Lord Kitchener: "Even at considerable military risk we must convince France . . . that we are ready and willing to do our utmost to cooperate with her, and even if France agrees to maintain a defensive attitude for the present, then she and ourselves must convince Russia that it is wise to do so in the interest of all." [146] These efforts were not in vain. As Lord Curzon remarked in a speech at Montagu House on France's Day, July 7, 1915:

> Had we been meeting a year ago, who would have prophesied that the friendship between ourselves and France, steadily growing as it has been during the past 50 years and blossoming as it did into fresh life under the fostering hand of the late King Edward, would have expanded into an alliance which rests not merely upon the necessities, but upon the deep emotions and convictions of both peoples, and which has now been cemented, as all know by twelve months of suffering, sacrifice, and tears? [147]

Although there were residual suspicions and resentments, nevertheless a profound transformation in the relationships among the allies during the war did occur. Until the domestic events in Russia during 1917 shattered the alliance, the Entente member states proved remarkably cohesive and withstood the repeated efforts on the part of Germany to divide them.

SUMMARY

The Triple Entente faced a number of the same problems as its adversarial counterpart did. It had difficulties in coordinating strategy, differences in priorities of front. It also experienced conflicts over Allied war aims. Despite the military planning prior to the war, the Entente members had difficulty coordinating their strategies. The members of the Entente managed nevertheless to maintain their alliance until the Russian Revolution and subsequent armistice. The glue of the alliance largely came from the threat of the adversarial coalition. Because the power capabilities of the states were relatively equal and because of the traditional enmity between the member states, conscious efforts were made to maintain the effectiveness of the fighting coalition. The alliance broke down only following the revolution in Russia and Russia's withdrawal from the war; domestic forces overrode the systemic constraints that had operated until that time.

Although formed partially as a tethering alliance, the Triple Entente was transformed in the years prior to war. During wartime, it served as a balancing alliance. It acted to contain a growing dominance of a geographically, economically, and militarily threatening state with belligerent intentions. The member states committed to negotiation and compromise in order to attain the goal of defeating Germany. These conscious efforts meant that the war would continue until there was a clear winner and loser—a negotiated or compromise peace with the adversary was not possible.

The vulnerability of the Entente to potentially divisive forces—the traditional friendliness between Britain and Germany, Russia and Germany, France and Austria-Hungary, and Britain and Austria-Hungary; the wariness and suspicion, historically and at that time, between Britain and Russia and Britain and France—produced the intra-alliance negotiating and bargaining that in turn produced cohesion and solidarity among the members.

Conclusion

The Central Powers and the Triple Entente are a study in contrasts. The Central Powers were fairly cohesive during the peacetime years yet during wartime became an incredibly divisive alliance. The Entente, in comparison, grew more cohesive as the threat from Germany came to trump its internal conflicts. In contrast to the Central Powers, the threat emanated to the member states from the same source. This further benefited cohesion. In addition, because the Entente was more informal than the Central Powers, fears of abandonment were heightened, which compelled the member states to pull together all the more.[148] The divergence in the war aims between Austria-Hungary and Germany also had a pernicious effect on the workings of the alliance. Once war began, Austria's war aims became more defensive while Germany's became increasingly offensive. In comparison, the member states of the Triple Entente, a tethering alliance during peacetime with traditional adversaries, had relatively similar goals and became a fairly cohesive force once war came. The alliance certainly had its challenges in trying to coordinate policy and agree on war aims. Yet it managed more effectively than the Central Powers to conduct the war in a unified way. Disproportionate burden sharing appeared to have a more telling influence on alliance cohesion during the war than did the rise and fall of threats coming with defeats and victories. This illustrates the transforming effect of a wartime environment on the dynamics of alliance.

One observation that is worth emphasizing is the fact that the level of threat internal to the Central Powers was higher in wartime than it was during peacetime. Austria was certainly threatened by Germany, particularly by the end of the war. Germany considered Austria-Hungary the possible target of the next war it would fight. In contrast, the level of threat internal to the Triple Entente during its peacetime years was eclipsed by the external threat represented most especially by Germany. It is absolutely essential to examine the levels of threat internal to the alliances and the effect on cohesion, even during wartime. The effect is very important, although other forces play crucial roles in affecting wartime alliance cohesion as well.

The Triple Entente and the Central Powers during wartime are cases that reveal the interplay between domestic and international factors. The duration of a war and the effect it has on the domestic political conditions have a tremendous influence on the course of international events. This linkage between domestic and international politics is perhaps more marked during wartime than peacetime, since the effects of war are so pervasive and far-reaching. Another important insight is that the distribution of power within the alliances affected cohesion. The asymmetrical Central Powers struggled far more than the more balanced Triple Entente.

Above all, the experiences of the Triple Entente and the Central Powers during the Great War reveal that we cannot wholly generalize about the workings of alliances during peacetime to their workings during wartime. We cannot completely extrapolate how an alliance will function during wartime from its peacetime practices. The background conditions are dramatically different; divergent forces come into play that affect the cohesion of alliances during peacetime in contrast to wartime. Wartime alliance cohesion depends greatly on the agreed-upon hierarchies and chains of command, the symmetry of power politics within the alliance, the duration and intensity of the war, and the extent to which sacrifices are made by one ally for the other. It appears that the balance of interests may play an even greater role during wartime than peacetime. The motivations of warring states have a tremendous effect on wartime alliance cohesion. In peacetime, cohesion is more directly influenced by threat levels—both internal and external to the alliance. Once war ends, these factors come back to life and affect which wartime alliances persist after wars end and which crumble.

CHAPTER 7

Conclusion

THE ARGUMENT throughout this book has been that different levels of threat produce different alliance behaviors. A central implication of this study is that to understand alliance formation and cohesion, it is necessary to examine the levels of threat inside as well as outside the alliance. Looking exclusively at the level of external threat, as is suggested by the traditional view of alliances, is not enough.[1] This chapter reviews and synthesizes the findings of the project and discusses the extent to which the argument has currency in the contemporary era.

Alliance Formation under Conditions of Threat

but how are these "alliances"?

States have different motivations for forming alliances; these motivations vary with the level of threat they confront from another state. The case studies here have illustrated how at low levels of threat, states try to hedge their bets by forging low or moderate commitment level agreements with potential friends and enemies. This was precisely what Germany attempted with both Three Emperors' Leagues as well as with the Dual Alliance. The cases also reveal that under conditions of moderate threat, states actually seek to form alliances to tether and contain their enemies. This was evident in Russian and Austrian motivations when they forged the Three Emperors' Leagues, Austrian and Italian motives embodied in the Triple Alliance, as well as the French, British, and Russian reasons for creating the Triple Entente. These tethering alliances were forged to enhance cooperation among the signatories; their external missions were secondary. The cases also show that as the level of threat grows to high levels, states seek to balance against threats. This was manifest in Austrian motivations for concluding the Dual Alliance and the impetus for both signatories in the Franco-Russian Alliance.

The argument I present in this book regarding alliance formation also suggests that[at extremely high levels of threat, states seek to bandwagon.]This proposition remains untested, however, as there were no such cases during the period under review. There is some evidence that at exceedingly high levels of threat during the wartime period, states did seek to conclude a separate peace—Austria-Hungary in 1916/17 and Russia in 1917. These represented defections from existing alliances but not attempts to forge new ones.

The cases demonstrate that the relationship between threat and alliance motivation is curvilinear. They also reveal that[under conditions of moderate threat, alliances are not merely tools for capability aggregation as they are at higher levels of threat. Instead, they serve as devices to manage and constrain partners; their internal dynamics thus become central.]

Alliance Cohesion as a Consequence of Internal and External Threat

The characteristics of the alliances were affected by the member states' motives for joining them—in terms of commitment levels and in terms of cohesion. My argument regarding alliance cohesion has been that it is a function not only of the level of external threat but also the level of threat within an alliance. This argument was borne out by the evidence presented in the cases. In tethering alliances with significant levels of internal threat and low levels of external threat—both Leagues of the Three Emperors, the Triple Alliance, and the Triple Entente—cohesion was low. The balancing alliances in which the level of internal threat was low and the level external threat moderate, namely the Dual Alliance and the Franco-Russian Alliance, had high cohesion. When the level of external and internal threat was high, the latter years of the Triple Entente, for example, cohesion was difficult but not impossible to attain. These findings illustrate that[it is indeed important to evaluate the dynamics that take place within alliances and not to assume that alliance cohesion is derivative of external threats alone.]

When looking at the summary of results in Table 7.1, note that in all but the wartime cases, there is a direct relationship between external threat and cohesion and an inverse relationship between internal threat and cohesion. The in-depth case studies reveal in more detail how the relationships played out. Direct conflicts of interest between allied adversaries frustrated the cohesion of those alliances, and, without the aid of a unifying external threat, their cohesion was very low. Higher levels of external threat had an important effect on getting states to resolve their conflicts of interest, which in turn had a positive effect on cohesion.

[The commitment level of the alliances examined in the book did indeed

TABLE 7.1
Summary of Findings: Threat and Alliance Characteristics

Case	Level of uniform or complementary external threat	Level of internal threat	Commitment level	Cohesion
First League of the Three Emperors	Low/Absent	High	Low (2)	Low
Second League of the Three Emperors	Low/Absent	High	Low (1)	Low
Dual Alliance	Moderate	Low	Moderate (4)	High
Triple Alliance	Low/Absent	High	Moderate (4)	Low
Franco-Russian Alliance	Moderate/High	Low	Moderate/High (5)	Moderate
Triple Entente (peacetime)	Low/Moderate	High	Low (0)	Low
Central Powers	Moderate	Moderate/High	Moderate (4)	Low
Triple Entente (wartime)	High	Moderate	Low (0)	Moderate

appear to be a function of threat. With one peacetime exception, the Triple Alliance, the commitment levels were a direct function of the level of external threat, and all but the wartime alliances had commitment levels that were inversely related to the degree of internal threat. This makes sense since allied adversaries will not necessarily want to be bound to an agreement that stipulates their close involvement in war on the part of their enemy. States that forge capability aggregation alliances, however, will want exactly that—a commitment from their allies to intervene on their behalf and accord the same promise in kind. In other words, commitment levels depend on whether an alliance serves as a capability aggregation device or as a vehicle for managing partners. There are certainly exceptions to this, witness the Triple Alliance, and there may be times when tethering partners want to bind their allies as much as they possibly can. Promises are made when alliances are forged, although they certainly are not always honored. A further caveat in this regard is that alliances of more than three states may fulfill more than two motivations; as such, the alliance is a balancing alliance for some dyads, hedging or tethering for others. In these cases, it is more difficult to anticipate the commitment level, except to establish which motivations were most prevalent in forging the alliance. For example, within the NATO alliance, multiple motivations exist among the different dyads that comprise it. However, most of the dyads, though certainly not all, were formed for balancing purposes. It is not, then, surprising that the commitment level of the alliance is the highest possible (6).[2]

It is important to note in this context that there is a substantial "stickiness" once alliances are formed. Altering treaties of alliance once they are negotiated and ratified generally occurs with added articles; it is rare for the original treaty text to be altered. As a consequence, once formed, alliance commitment levels rarely change—even as their motivations do. For example, the Triple Entente was forged with barely a whisper of a commitment to any party (other than the Franco-Russian component). However, as the level of external threat grew and the level of internal threat diminished, the commitment level never changed in the context of the agreements, though it did de facto in the terms of the actual military planning for war on the part of the signatories. It was only after war began that the allies signed the Treaty of London promising each other they would not conclude a separate peace.[3] Yet the Entente never had an agreement that stipulated they would come to one another's aid.

The promises that states make to their allies are a function of the threats they experience at the time they forge the agreement. In general, the commitments will be higher for those seeking capability aggregation and lower for those seeking to tether or hedge. This may be a function of the alliance security dilemma; states confronting higher levels of external threat may care more about being abandoned than entrapped, while states that are allying with their adversaries may fear entrapment more than abandonment.[4] The promises allies make may indeed change, but they are not always altered with the motivations that underpin the alliance.

Peacetime versus Wartime Alliance Dynamics

The alliance dynamics that hold during conditions of peacetime are disrupted once wars begin. This is so for a number of reasons. During wartime, alliances serve above all as capability aggregating devices; tethering alliances that have not undergone a transformation prior to war will disintegrate once wars begin, since the threat level rises. Although the internal dynamics still matter—the level of threat within an alliance may still be high and may still inhibit cohesion and prevent the duration of the alliance beyond the war's end—it is the external mission that motivates wartime alliances. Second, alliances that are cohesive during peacetime may become divisive during wartime and vice versa. This reversal has to do with the similarities or differences in war aims and principal enemies or targets during wartime. During peacetime, states may face complementary threats that may not exist during wartime. For example, since Germany was threatened by France and Austria-Hungary by Russia, the Franco-Russian Alliance became a natural enemy for the Dual Alliance. However, during wartime, the fact that Austria had no

quarrel with France and Germany less with Russia than France actually became a grave source of friction within the Central Powers' alliance. In other
words, during wartime, merely complementary interests may collapse into
divergent ones.[5]

Wars also have a tremendous impact on the domestic political conditions
of participating states. The developments at the domestic level have a substantial influence on the course of international events. These events in turn
have profound effects on alliance politics during wartime. While domestic
populations may find certain alliance obligations wearying during peacetime, the consequences are not nearly so grave as they are during wartime.
Heavy fatalities incurred for the sake of an ally may have far-reaching effects
on the political governance of a state and on alliance decisions as a consequence. This was certainly true in the Russian case during the First World
War but was quite marked in the Austrian case as well.

During wartime, a multitude of forces come into play that may not be
significant during peacetime. The allies' capacity to agree on chains of command, hierarchies, disposition of troops, and so forth becomes critical during wartime. Even in the absence of such agreement, during peacetime an
alliance may be cohesive; not so during wartime. Issues of wartime logistics
can be extremely difficult to navigate. States nearly always resist placing their
troops under another state's command.

For these reasons, it is difficult to project from peacetime what the wartime dynamics of an alliance will be. In the cases examined in the previous
chapter, we saw that in many ways, the dynamics of the alliances reversed
themselves during wartime. The Triple Entente was a loosely constructed
alliance that was initially forged for tethering purposes. Once war began, the
states worked hard to preserve the cohesion of the alliance, and though not
always effective, the signatories did have impressive successes. In fact, the cohesion of this alliance inhibited the ability of the warring parties to end the
war. States seek to purchase their allies' continued contributions to the war
effort by enlarging the purposes for which they fight. As war aims expand, it
becomes increasingly difficult to negotiate an end to the war.[6] Compounding this are the intra-alliance negotiations necessary to agree on terms to end
a war, even if they are to conclude a separate peace with a state in an opposing coalition. For example, Austria-Hungary's attempt to forge a separate peace with the Entente was frustrated by Italy. Britain and France, despite their desire to accept Austria's terms, ultimately refused Emperor Karl
because their ally would not agree. Coalitional dynamics frustrated attempts
to terminate the war and thus perpetuated it.

One important observation that therefore emerges from this study is that
the dynamics of alliances during wartime have an important effect on war

termination. It may be easier to find a bargaining space for warring states that have no allies. The intra-alliance bargaining that takes place during wartime—particularly among states of symmetrical capabilities—makes inter-alliance bargaining very difficult. Asymmetries within alliances undermine cohesion, especially during wartime.

A Unifying Theory of Alliance Formation and Cohesion

The theoretical framework presented here unifies ideas incorporated in both realism and liberalism. It helps us understand the conditions under which each argument holds. Realist perspectives suggest that alliance formation and cohesion will be derivative of common external threats. Liberalist or institutionalist ideas imply that the dynamics within alliances are worth exploring. Indeed, by looking at both, a more nuanced understanding of alliance politics is generated.

Realist ideas are fundamental to an understanding of how alliances function under conditions of shared threats. Yet they cannot help us comprehend how or why alliances operate effectively under conditions of low or even moderate levels of threat. In this regard, institutionalist ideas are central. Alliances, like other institutions, provide opportunities for improved communication and transparency, thereby offering the potential for deepening trust and cooperation among the signatories. This insight seems intuitively obvious when we examine long-lived contemporary alliances such as NATO; yet alliance theory could not previously account for this aspect of military cooperation while simultaneously explaining the more traditional aspects of alliance politics.

In addition to offering an argument that explains both alliance formation and cohesion, the theory presented here helps us understand why certain wartime alliances dissolve and others persist, or why some alliances, such as NATO, endure while others, such as the Warsaw Pact, dissolve once their external missions are fulfilled. Without attending to both the levels of internal and external threat, a significant portion of alliance behavior is missed. Fluctuations in both the levels of internal and external threat determine when alliances will form, their cohesion, and their dissolution.

The argument unifies different explanations of alliance politics and in so doing clears up important puzzles regarding alliance behavior. As discussed at the start of the book, allies frequently do not fulfill their alliance obligations and in fact frequently fight each other.[7] Once we understand that alliances sometimes involve adversaries coming together to try to manage their conflicts of interest, it is no surprise that if the level of threat between them grows, they will defect from their agreements and may even find themselves at war on opposite sides not long thereafter.

The Alliance Paradox

Alliances that are forged to keep the peace may improve relations among the signatories and facilitate a diminution in the threat that exists between or among them. During the pre–World War I period, tethering alliances were concluded by Russia and Austria-Hungary in the two Leagues of the Three Emperors, Austria-Hungary and Italy in the Triple Alliance, and Britain and France and Britain and Russia in the Triple Entente. Although only these latter agreements succeeded in facilitating cooperation among signatories, in so doing they heightened uncertainty and insecurity in the system. The Triple Entente ultimately threatened the Triple Alliance, despite the fact that the agreements that comprised it—with the exception of the Franco-Russian Alliance—never committed the signatories to the others' defense. Germany, despite the fact that it was kept apprised of the negotiations that culminated in the Entente, came to feel encircled. Further, despite the fact that Britain very nearly joined the Triple Alliance and was closely associated with Germany for decades prior to the First World War, it ultimately came to be threatened by Germany. Although it was the growth of German power, not only the alliance commitments, that began to threaten the Entente Powers, the alignments of the system played a significant role in heightening security.

Paradoxically, the more effective the alliances were at keeping the peace among their signatories, the more threatening they appeared to nonmembers. This spiral of insecurity in the system, coupled with the web of alliances and the belief by most military strategists of the period that it was preferable to attack than defend, ultimately culminated in war. Alliances used to manage other countries appear especially dangerous to those excluded by the arrangements.

The Historical and Contemporary Relevance of Dangerous Alliances

The insights generated by this study are not exclusively linked to the pre–World War I era. Although additional scholarship is necessary to test the theory in other regions and other time periods, it is worth noting that tethering has occurred repeatedly throughout history. The European alliances in the post-Napoleonic period; the Quadruple Alliance of 1814 between Great

Britain, Prussia, Russia, and Austria; the Holy Alliance of 1815 concluded by Prussia, Russia, and Austria; and the Quintuple Alliance of 1818, in which France joined the Quadruple Alliance, all contained important elements of tethering. The signatories were more interested in the ways in which the agreements offered transparency and management of the other members than they were in capability aggregation.

Similarly, the Treaty of Nonaggression between Germany and the Union of Soviet Socialist Republics signed in 1939 was a straightforward tethering arrangement. The threat between the two states led them to form an alliance to keep the peace between them. As the reciprocal level of threat grew in the period immediately following the treaty's conclusion, the agreement broke down, and two years later the states were at war with one another. The Sino Soviet Treaty of Friendship, Alliance, and Mutual Assistance, concluded in 1950, was also a tethering device. The threat level between the Soviet Union and China was significant; both were great powers, and they were experiencing substantial tension in regard to their long common border. The response of the countries was to forge an alliance. To the outside world, this appeared to be a capability aggregation alliance that was very threatening; yet the Soviet Union and China concluded the agreement largely out of concerns regarding each other.

There are important insights from this study for contemporary international politics as well. Although the Europe of 1873–1918 bears little resemblance to the region today, there are still a number of lessons we can glean from the past and generalize to the present and future. I made the point at the start of this book that NATO was formed for external and internal reasons. Although its principal mission was to counter the Soviet Union, it was an important device for enhancing cooperation among the signatories as well. Since the demise of the Soviet Union, the alliance has endured, although its role in international affairs has been transformed with the reduction in external threat. It is the internal mission of the alliance that has brought it into the twenty-first century and will likely motivate the alliance's continued active role in international affairs well into the future. NATO has been and continues to be an important mechanism to keep the peace among signatories, to serve as a facilitator of transparency, and to promote the consolidation of democracy in Europe. As such, its future viability depends on maintaining low levels of internal threat in the absence of a uniform external threat.

The alliance behaviors I have analyzed in this book have taken place in the context of a multipolar world. Structure does certainly affect alliance decisions, even if it is not always determinant.[8] While it is difficult to assess the extent to which these behaviors would hold in a different context such as a bipolar world, there are similarities in the strategic environment of the past to the one that exists today. In 1873, Great Britain possessed nearly a quarter of the world's power capabilities, not unlike the United States in the contemporary age. Further, although the world has changed dramatically since the turn of the previous century, the United States confronts a situation in which it can create a "hub and spokes" system of alliances not unlike those of the late nineteenth century.[9]

There are two important challenges to confront from the vantage point of the arguments presented here. First, as NATO continues to enlarge in the contemporary era, the level of threat within the alliance may ultimately eclipse any uniform external threat. An alliance of twenty-six member states may lead to increasing divergence over the principal mission of the organization. The internal mission remains paramount—to consolidate democracy, resolve any border disputes or minority rights issues, and reform civil-military relations in newly acceding members—even if the external purpose of the alliance is in question. If the level of internal threat comes to equal or exceed the level of external threat, it will be more and more difficult over time to sustain the cohesion of the alliance, in terms of solidarity as well as in terms of joint goals and strategies to attain those goals. This possibility could be exacerbated by forceful American policies, such as unilateral pursuit of a ballistic missile defense or an aggressive stance in regard to the "war on terrorism." American actions may culminate in heightened threat to others, potentially even within the NATO alliance itself.

A second challenge also arises from the altered strategic environment and the transformed NATO. As NATO facilitates the solidification of democracy in an ever-expanding geographic area, there may be dangerous unanticipated consequences. Alliances look different from the outside looking in than from the inside looking out. There are two important points to make in this context. First, tethering Russia in the form of Partnership for Peace arrangements, the Founding Act of 1997, and the NATO-Russia Council established in 2002 has gone a long way toward allaying Russian antagonism toward continued NATO expansion. The agreements give Russia special status; Council deliberations take place at NATO monthly, and the alliance members do not coordinate their positions in advance. This tethering arrangement facilitates transparency, allows the states to constrain their hostility, and serves as a management device for all signatories. The agreements seek to reduce conflicts and prevent the deployment of capabilities against each other. These understandings have worked toward managing the threat levels between Russia and its adversaries.

In essence, even without full membership status, a significant amount of tethering has taken place between Russia and NATO, and it has, thus far, been successful at keeping the peace. Yet if the level of threat from the United States or other NATO member states increases to Russia, the arrangements may break down and culminate in heightened levels of threat in the system. Further, the issue of Russia's accession to the alliance may ultimately become a source of friction, depending on the extent to which the current arrangements remain sufficient in the face of an ever-enlarging NATO. It makes sense, however, that the tethering arrangements at this point are embodied in lower commitment level agreements.

Russia is not the only other state in the system that is relevant to an analysis of dangerous alliances in the contemporary age. Other great powers in the system, such as China, may ultimately be alienated by a growing and influential NATO. This danger highlights the need to develop further tethering arrangements as the alliance continues to adapt to the changing security environment. Alliances must be inclusive or they are likely ultimately to trigger heightened insecurity in the system.

A final point that the arguments of this book highlight for the contemporary age is that wartime alliance cohesion is far more complex to attain and sustain than the cohesion of peacetime alliances. Since NATO member states have become increasingly engaged in military operations in the aftermath of the Cold War, the lessons regarding wartime alliance cohesion may become increasingly salient. First, given the tight and binding structure of the NATO alliance, member states may increasingly face fears of entrapment, rather than abandonment, which will undermine the cohesion of the alliance, as we saw in the case of the Central Powers. Further, the fact that complementary interests during peacetime deteriorate into divergent interests during wartime suggests that any extended NATO operation may undermine cohesion. Certainly the sophisticated and intricate decision-making structure of the Atlantic Alliance will facilitate cohesion during its wartime operations. Yet we know we cannot simply project how cohesive the alliance will be during wartime from its peacetime experience. Asymmetry within the alliance could debilitate it during wartime.[10] Extended wartime operations may ultimately do to the alliance what the system structure could not—undermine its future viability. In sum, the future of NATO depends not only on the external threats that its signatories perceive but on the level of threat within the organization as well, during the times of war and peace ahead.

The current international system is one that offers both opportunities and constraints, not unlike the period that preceded the First World War. Just as in the pre–World War I period, today it is supremely possible for states to seek to de-escalate tension with historic enemies. It is also a moment in which certain historic enmities may ultimately prevail, just as we saw in the period of history that preceded the Great War. In addition, just as in the pre–World War I period, the consequences of alignments and realignments will have a profound effect on the course of events that follow. One central truth that continues to hold today is that military alliances are perpetually used as tools of statecraft—to manifest relations of enmity and amity, to manage and constrain alliance partners, to counter threats, to promote desirable behavior, and to deter and threaten aggressors. It is equally vital today as it was in the past not to underestimate the range of alliance behavior that may emerge under varying circumstances or to underestimate the dramatic impact those alliances have on the workings of the international system.

Ultimately, alliances are not mere reflections of the constellations of the states in the system; they motivate, drive, and transform those constellations as well. The most well intentioned and effective alliances in keeping the peace among signatories may heighten insecurity and uncertainty in the system, bringing with them a heightened prospect for war. As we continue to learn more about alliances and as policy continues to evolve, we need to be attentive to these dynamics. We need to bear in mind the power alliances have in shaping our world.

REFERENCE MATTER

Great Power Capabilities and Proximity Data

TABLE A.1
Great Power Capabilities and Proximity Data, 1873–1918

CCODE	YEAR	CAP	MILEX	ENERGY	IRST	UPOP	TPOP
UK	1873	.23	20,867	116,230	6,670	7,688	32,176
FR	1873	.11	24,975	24,780	1,380	3,369	36,340
GER	1873	.10	14,234	37,582	1,980	2,122	41,564
AH	1873	.05	9,762	8,800	530	1,299	36,322
IT	1873	.03	8,055	991	30	2,108	26,962
RUS	1873	.10	26,407	1,883	380	2,159	88,940
UK	1874	.23	20,839	112,894	6,090	7,892	32,500
FR	1874	.10	24,764	23,632	1,410	3,442	36,490
GER	1874	.10	16,972	37,610	1,660	2,290	42,004
AH	1874	.05	9,818	8,569	490	1,333	36,222
IT	1874	.03	7,198	1,062	30	2,143	27,124
RUS	1874	.10	26,287	2,191	380	2,273	90,447
UK	1875	.23	21,098	119,198	6,470	8,100	32,838
FR	1875	.11	25,528	24,452	1,450	3,517	36,664
GER	1875	.10	18,262	38,900	1,760	2,471	42,518
AH	1875	.05	9,723	9,965	460	1,369	36,436
IT	1875	.03	7,677	1,092	30	2,179	27,287
RUS	1875	.10	26,943	2,562	430	2,394	91,978
UK	1876	.23	22,307	118,918	6,660	8,315	33,200
FR	1876	.10	27,541	24,806	1,440	3,594	36,830
GER	1876	.10	18,168	39,684	1,610	2,667	42,726
AH	1876	.05	10,838	9,381	400	1,405	36,708
IT	1876	.03	8,066	1,487	20	2,216	27,452
RUS	1876	.10	34,424	3,129	440	2,521	93,536
UK	1877	.23	25,051	121,098	6,710	8,534	33,576
FR	1877	.10	29,114	24,156	1,510	3,510	37,000
GER	1877	.10	20,482	38,820	1,720	2,778	43,610
AH	1877	.04	9,838	9,344	390	1,442	36,950
IT	1877	.03	8,933	1,362	20	2,253	27,617
RUS	1877	.13	77,022	3,079	400	2,655	95,120

CCODE	YEAR	CAP	MILEX	ENERGY	IRST	UPOP	TPOP
UK	1878	.23	25,926	118,986	6,480	8,760	33,942
FR	1878	.10	29,956	24,552	1,520	3,596	37,180
GER	1878	.10	19,727	40,042	1,900	2,894	44,128
AH	1878	.05	14,821	9,670	430	1,480	37,166
IT	1878	.03	8,909	1,358	20	2,290	27,783
RUS	1878	.13	59,952	4,078	420	2,796	96,731
UK	1879	.22	25,121	119,446	6,090	8,992	34,304
FR	1879	.10	29,391	25,372	1,400	3,678	37,320
GER	1879	.11	19,656	42,524	1,970	3,016	44,640
AH	1879	.05	14,045	10,713	400	1,520	38,620
IT	1879	.03	8,073	1,558	10	2,329	27,951
RUS	1879	.10	32,091	4,099	430	2,944	98,368
UK	1880	.22	21,448	125,270	7,870	9,229	34,622
FR	1880	.11	32,816	29,082	1,730	3,761	37,450
GER	1880	.11	19,397	47,144	2,470	3,142	45,094
AH	1880	.05	10,314	11,364	460	1,560	38,960
IT	1880	.03	8,872	1,870	20	2,368	28,119
RUS	1880	.10	30,408	5,430	450	3,101	100,035
UK	1881	.21	22,350	131,878	8,270	9,474	34,934
FR	1881	.11	36,993	28,976	1,890	3,829	37,590
GER	1881	.11	20,892	48,996	2,620	3,274	45,428
AH	1881	.04	10,460	12,232	540	1,602	39,224
IT	1881	.03	9,633	2,207	30	2,407	28,289
RUS	1881	.10	30,187	5,531	470	3,265	101,728
UK	1882	.21	24,028	132,468	8,720	9,652	35,206
FR	1882	.11	39,695	30,488	2,040	3,891	37,730
GER	1882	.11	19,531	52,530	3,000	3,480	45,718
AH	1882	.05	12,668	12,646	610	1,677	39,524
IT	1882	.03	10,690	2,327	20	2,448	28,460
RUS	1882	.10	27,617	5,828	480	3,439	103,452
UK	1883	.21	24,410	138,112	8,670	9,834	35,450
FR	1883	.11	38,423	32,020	2,070	3,937	37,860
GER	1883	.11	20,054	55,860	3,140	3,700	46,016
AH	1883	.05	10,807	13,712	700	1,757	39,862
IT	1883	.03	12,290	2,524	20	2,483	28,658
RUS	1883	.09	22,196	6,704	480	3,539	105,203
UK	1884	.20	27,051	134,634	7,930	10,019	35,724
FR	1884	.10	35,795	30,580	1,870	3,981	38,010
GER	1884	.11	20,634	57,356	3,240	3,933	46,336
AH	1884	.05	11,097	14,023	730	1,840	40,268
IT	1884	.04	12,708	2,790	20	2,518	28,857
RUS	1884	.09	22,500	6,570	510	3,643	106,985
UK	1885	.21	38,021	132,024	7,530	10,208	36,014
FR	1885	.10	35,721	29,450	1,630	4,018	38,110
GER	1885	.11	19,973	58,710	3,270	4,182	46,706
AH	1885	.05	10,426	14,820	710	1,927	40,672
IT	1885	.04	12,898	3,159	20	2,554	29,058
RUS	1885	.09	25,140	7,369	530	3,750	108,798

CCODE	YEAR	CAP	MILEX	ENERGY	IRST	UPOP	TPOP
UK	1886	.20	29,412	130,710	7,120	10,400	36,312
FR	1886	.10	34,895	29,236	1,520	4,046	38,230
GER	1886	.11	20,838	52,828	3,130	4,446	47,134
AH	1886	.05	10,227	15,174	720	2,019	41,062
IT	1886	.04	13,001	3,115	10	2,591	29,261
RUS	1886	.10	24,932	8,331	530	3,860	110,368
UK	1887	.19	27,740	133,728	7,680	10,597	36,598
FR	1887	.10	35,359	30,804	1,570	4,111	38,260
GER	1887	.12	30,038	60,828	3,530	4,719	47,153
AH	1887	.05	13,574	16,035	700	2,114	41,454
IT	1887	.04	16,384	3,804	10	2,628	29,465
RUS	1887	.09	23,279	8,773	610	3,973	111,960
UK	1888	.19	27,136	138,900	8,130	10,796	36,880
FR	1888	.09	35,068	32,008	1,680	4,256	38,290
GER	1888	.13	38,013	64,188	3,810	5,009	48,168
AH	1888	.05	13,484	16,940	790	2,215	41,836
IT	1888	.04	21,137	4,099	10	2,666	29,670
RUS	1888	.09	21,482	9,221	670	4,090	113,576
UK	1889	.19	28,990	143,732	8,460	11,000	37,178
FR	1889	.10	36,677	33,316	1,730	4,328	38,370
GER	1889	.12	25,670	68,562	3,960	5,317	48,716
AH	1889	.05	12,947	17,954	860	2,319	42,266
IT	1889	.04	16,296	4,235	10	2,704	29,877
RUS	1889	.09	27,233	11,175	740	4,210	115,215
UK	1890	.18	29,602	145,138	8,030	11,207	37,484
FR	1890	.10	36,771	36,500	1,960	4,489	38,380
GER	1890	.12	37,454	71,398	4,100	5,644	49,240
AH	1890	.05	12,801	19,700	970	2,429	42,650
IT	1890	.04	15,198	4,587	10	2,743	30,085
RUS	1890	.10	30,191	10,967	930	4,333	116,878
UK	1891	.18	29,742	149,040	7,520	11,419	37,802
FR	1891	.10	37,244	36,618	1,900	4,575	38,350
GER	1891	.12	28,276	77,190	4,100	5,991	49,762
AH	1891	.05	13,455	19,836	920	2,545	43,006
IT	1891	.04	13,827	4,123	10	2,782	30,295
RUS	1891	.10	34,531	11,844	1010	4,461	118,565
UK	1892	.17	31,871	146,158	6,820	11,634	38,134
FR	1892	.09	36,900	36,624	2,060	3,829	38,360
GER	1892	.12	32,984	72,778	4,350	6,228	50,266
AH	1892	.05	13,116	19,688	940	2,608	43,308
IT	1892	.03	13,133	4,091	10	2,822	30,506
RUS	1892	.10	30,053	13,547	1070	4,592	120,276
UK	1893	.17	29,824	130,784	7,090	11,854	38,490
FR	1893	.09	35,917	35,932	2,000	4,660	38,380
GER	1893	.13	35,890	75,806	4,430	6,475	50,756
AH	1893	.05	13,477	21,338	980	2,673	43,640
IT	1893	.03	13,174	3,945	10	2,862	30,719
RUS	1893	.10	32,131	14,632	1150	4,907	122,011

CCODE	YEAR	CAP	MILEX	ENERGY	IRST	UPOP	TPOP
UK	1894	.17	33,168	149,956	7,550	12,078	38,858
FR	1894	.09	36,617	35,022	2,070	4,704	38,420
GER	1894	.13	33,328	77,594	4,700	6,731	51,338
AH	1894	.05	13,319	22,246	1,070	2,739	44,044
IT	1894	.03	11,218	4,901	10	2,903	30,933
RUS	1894	.11	35,039	17,066	1,330	5,244	123,772
UK	1895	.17	35,743	150,482	7,830	12,306	39,220
FR	1895	.09	35,936	38,364	2,000	4,748	38,460
GER	1895	.12	30,885	80,540	4,770	6,998	52,000
AH	1895	.05	13,719	23,316	1,130	2,808	44,454
IT	1895	.03	16,677	4,514	10	2,945	31,148
RUS	1895	.11	36,019	17,348	1,450	5,604	125,558
UK	1896	.17	35,253	154,616	8,800	12,538	39,598
FR	1896	.09	36,062	39,126	2,340	4,793	38,550
GER	1896	.13	30,902	86,918	5,560	7,276	52,734
AH	1896	.05	14,144	25,132	1,220	2,878	44,908
IT	1896	.03	13,452	4,281	10	2,987	31,365
RUS	1896	.11	36,679	18,896	1,620	5,989	127,370
UK	1897	.16	35,187	158,090	8,940	12,775	39,986
FR	1897	.09	37,421	41,430	2,480	4,899	38,700
GER	1897	.13	39,222	92,992	6,010	7,612	53,514
AH	1897	.05	16,042	25,600	1,310	2,949	45,378
IT	1897	.03	13,849	4,470	10	3,030	31,584
RUS	1897	.11	39,486	20,890	1,870	6,401	129,208
UK	1898	.16	38,741	157,884	8,750	13,017	40,380
FR	1898	.08	37,337	42,972	2530	5,008	38,810
GER	1898	.12	35,428	97,112	6,370	7,965	54,282
AH	1898	.05	16,755	28,448	1,430	3,023	45,836
IT	1898	.03	13,716	4,653	10	3,073	31,804
RUS	1898	.10	38,697	23,698	2,230	6,488	131,325
UK	1899	.17	63,547	168,502	9,570	13,263	40,774
FR	1899	.08	38,813	45,030	2,580	5,119	38,900
GER	1899	.12	37,508	103,660	7,160	8,333	55,052
AH	1899	.05	16,462	27,472	1,470	3,098	46,298
IT	1899	.03	12,506	5,129	20	3,117	32,026
RUS	1899	.11	43,240	27,580	2,710	6,576	133,477
UK	1900	.18	119,587	171,420	4,979	13,513	41,154
FR	1900	.08	40,569	47,988	1,565	5,233	38,900
GER	1900	.13	39,681	112,998	6,461	8,719	56,046
AH	1900	.04	16,242	29,096	1,170	3,175	46,798
IT	1900	.03	14,112	5,118	116	3,162	32,249
RUS	1900	.11	43,104	30,376	2,201	6,666	135,664
UK	1901	.17	116,896	165,652	4,975	13,769	41,538
FR	1901	.07	41,993	46,240	1,425	5,350	38,962
GER	1901	.13	42,008	112,484	6,137	9,123	56,870
AH	1901	.04	16,948	29,854	1,099	3,255	47,326
IT	1901	.03	13,573	5,087	129	3,208	32,474
RUS	1901	.11	44,270	31,988	2,212	6,990	137,886

CCODE	YEAR	CAP	MILEX	ENERGY	IRST	UPOP	TPOP
UK	1902	.16	93,419	173,274	4,988	13,932	41,892
FR	1902	.07	40,335	43,648	1,568	5,373	39,060
GER	1902	.13	42,770	110,254	7,466	9,556	57,746
AH	1902	.04	17,147	30,936	1,167	3,355	47,878
IT	1902	.03	13,638	5,650	135	3,277	32,687
RUS	1902	.11	46,085	33,812	2,166	7,331	140,145
UK	1903	.14	66,400	170,042	5,115	14,098	42,246
FR	1903	.07	39,552	48,356	1,840	5,398	39,140
GER	1903	.13	42,263	119,896	8,430	10,011	58,576
AH	1903	.04	17,630	29,802	1,162	3,460	48,374
IT	1903	.03	14,385	5,768	187	3,348	32,902
RUS	1903	.11	48,301	34,016	2,434	7,689	142,441
UK	1904	.13	59,715	171,922	5,107	14,266	42,610
FR	1904	.07	38,956	47,308	2,088	5,422	39,210
GER	1904	.13	42,420	125,510	8,564	10,487	59,390
AH	1904	.04	19,241	30,884	1,257	3,567	48,626
IT	1904	.03	14,580	6,134	201	3,420	33,118
RUS	1904	.11	50,305	34,830	2,755	8,064	144,775
UK	1905	.12	55,604	173,640	5,905	14,435	42,980
FR	1905	.06	41,947	51,444	2,240	5,446	39,240
GER	1905	.12	46,167	126,952	9,669	10,986	60,246
AH	1905	.04	20,591	32,164	1,459	3,678	48,880
IT	1905	.03	14,844	6,684	270	3,494	33,335
RUS	1905	.16	170,006	37,238	2,266	8,457	147,147
UK	1906	.12	53,899	179,022	6,565	14,607	43,360
FR	1906	.07	45,662	51,434	2,451	5,471	39,252
GER	1906	.13	48,721	142,248	10,700	11,509	61,152
AH	1906	.04	20,252	34,844	1,608	3,792	49,136
IT	1906	.03	15,766	7,938	391	3,570	33,554
RUS	1906	.12	90,733	34,802	2,496	8,869	149,558
UK	1907	.12	53,207	187,620	6,626	14,781	43,736
FR	1907	.07	44,152	54,704	2,767	5,531	39,321
GER	1907	.14	51,965	153,886	11,619	11,849	62,012
AH	1907	.04	20,297	39,218	1,731	3,909	49,568
IT	1907	.03	16,452	8,580	430	3,647	33,774
RUS	1907	.12	68,797	39,110	2,671	9,301	152,008
UK	1908	.12	51,755	181,228	5,381	14,957	44,124
FR	1908	.07	45,054	56,634	2,723	5,592	39,390
GER	1908	.15	57,865	156,992	10,726	12,200	62,862
AH	1908	.05	22,296	40,958	2,018	4,031	50,000
IT	1908	.03	18,265	8,758	537	3,726	33,996
RUS	1908	.12	58,887	40,550	2,698	9,755	155,639
UK	1909	.12	56,532	183,074	5,976	15,135	44,520
FR	1909	.07	47,412	55,294	3,039	5,654	39,461
GER	1909	.13	58,567	156,818	11,515	12,561	63,716
AH	1909	.05	26,217	41,902	1,963	4,156	50,438
IT	1909	.03	19,573	9,596	662	3,806	34,219
RUS	1909	.12	60,029	42,484	2,940	10,230	159,359

CCODE	YEAR	CAP	MILEX	ENERGY	IRST	UPOP	TPOP
UK	1910	.11	61,417	185,026	6,476	15,315	44,916
FR	1910	.07	49,539	55,054	3,413	5,716	39,531
GER	1910	.14	60,416	158,650	13,100	12,932	64,568
AH	1910	.04	23,208	40,686	2,174	4,285	50,894
IT	1910	.03	22,016	9,696	732	3,888	34,444
RUS	1910	.12	62,099	41,398	3,314	10,729	163,165
UK	1911	.12	65,309	192,220	6,566	17,502	45,286
FR	1911	.07	55,441	57,726	3,837	5,780	39,602
GER	1911	.14	61,652	163,974	14,303	13,316	65,358
AH	1911	.04	22,227	42,468	2,348	4,418	51,308
IT	1911	.03	29,379	9,969	736	3,973	34,670
RUS	1911	.12	64,291	43,802	3,933	11,253	167,065
UK	1912	.12	67,957	180,212	6,905	17,618	45,436
FR	1912	.07	61,367	59,416	4,429	5,843	39,671
GER	1912	.14	63,926	173,946	16,355	13,709	66,146
AH	1912	.05	27,376	45,752	2,708	4,555	51,728
IT	1912	.04	38,849	10,474	918	4,058	34,897
RUS	1912	.12	73,512	47,480	4,490	11,801	171,060
UK	1913	.11	67,734	195,282	7,787	17,768	45,648
FR	1913	.07	66,706	62,828	4,687	5,908	39,742
GER	1913	.14	88,418	187,800	17,600	14,115	66,978
AH	1913	.05	37,513	49,406	2,611	4,696	52,166
IT	1913	.03	40,379	11,224	934	4,146	35,127
RUS	1913	.12	85,391	54,532	4,925	12,376	175,145
UK	1914	.14	1,678,843	196,015	7,971	17,852	45,801
FR	1914	.08	1,235,000	60,324	2,802	5,906	39,581
GER	1914	.16	1,785,000	186,734	13,810	14,279	66,109
AH	1914	.07	1,042,000	20,154	2,162	4,405	52,580
IT	1914	.03	87,453	11,845	909	4,097	35,571
RUS	1914	.11	857,000	48,654	4,466	10,479	169,843
UK	1915	.15	4,651,398	196,788	8,687	17,967	45,973
FR	1915	.08	3,525,000	58,421	1,111	5,903	39,246
GER	1915	.15	5,014,000	173,401	12,278	14,402	65,924
AH	1915	.06	2,013,000	12,641	2,667	4,126	53,011
IT	1915	.03	105,871	12,136	1,009	4,014	35,902
RUS	1915	.12	4,524,000	45,206	4,120	8,943	164,528
UK	1916	.15	6,213,396	197,254	9,136	18,084	46,040
FR	1916	.09	4,604,000	55,739	1,784	5,901	39,194
GER	1916	.15	4,974,000	187,564	14,871	14,576	65,006
AH	1916	.04	2,445,000	10,071	2,781	3,954	53,445
IT	1916	.04	164,207	12,742	1,269	3,963	36,427
RUS	1916	.14	4,343,000	48,978	4,276	7,548	158,974
UK	1917	.15	7,600,458	198,941	9,873	18,196	46,229
FR	1917	.09	5,825,000	53,678	1,991	5,897	39,087
GER	1917	.16	7,150,000	196,520	15,501	14,643	63,294
AH	1917	.04	2,862,000	9,846	2,896	3,257	53,883
IT	1917	.03	197,412	12,983	1,332	3,906	36,994
RUS	1917	.11	4,040,000	43,638	3,080	6,471	147,841

CCODE	YEAR	CAP	MILEX	ENERGY	IRST	UPOP	TPOP
UK	1918	.15	8,104,264	199,756	9,692	18,271	46,410
FR	1918	.09	7,708,000	51,267	1,800	5,893	38,843
GER	1918	.18	8,779,000	188,472	14,092	14,737	58,451
AH	1918	.03	2,133,000	7,933	2,642	54,325	—
IT	1918	.03	228,943	13,549	933	4,351	37,203

SOURCE: National Material Capabilities Data, 1816–1985, ICPSR 9903, Principal Investigators J. David Singer and Melvin Small.

CAP is national power capabilities. It reflects a state's proportion of total system capabilities in military expenditure, military personnel, energy consumption, iron and steel production, urban population, and total population.

MILEX is military expenditures. For 1870–1913 in thousands of current year British pounds; for 1914–1917 in thousands of current year US dollars.

ENERGY is energy consumption in thousands of coal-ton equivalents.

IRST is thousands of tons of iron and steel production.

UPOP is urban population in thousands.

TPOP is total population in thousands.

TABLE A.2

Summary of Great Power Capabilities by Decade, 1873–1913

YEAR	CCODE	CAP	YEAR	CCODE	CAP
1873	AH	0.05	1893	IT	0.03
1873	FR	0.11	1893	RUS	0.10
1873	GER	0.10	1893	UK	0.17
1873	IT	0.03			
1873	RUS	0.10	1903	AH	0.04
1873	UK	0.23	1903	FR	0.07
			1903	GER	0.13
1883	AH	0.05	1903	IT	0.03
1883	FR	0.11	1903	RUS	0.11
1883	GER	0.11	1903	UK	0.14
1883	IT	0.03			
1883	RUS	0.09	1913	AH	0.05
1883	UK	0.21	1913	FR	0.07
			1913	GER	0.14
1893	AH	0.05	1913	IT	0.03
1893	FR	0.09	1913	RUS	0.12
1893	GER	0.13	1913	UK	0.11

TABLE A.3

Great Power Borders, 1873–1917

	UK	FR	GER	AH	IT	RUS
UK		2, 3	0	0	3 ('90)	3
FR	2, 3		1, 3 ('84)	0	1,3 ('90)	0
GER	0	1, 3 ('84)		1	0	1
AH	0	0	1		1	1
IT	3 ('90)	1, 3('90)	0	1		0
RUS	3	0	1	1	0	

SOURCE: Randolph M. Siverson and Harvey Starr, *The Diffusion of War* (Ann Arbor: University of Michigan Press, 1991).

0 = no border
1 = contiguous border
2 = water border
3 = colonial border
Parentheses indicate year of border change, if not from beginning of time period.

Abbreviations

AIB	Ambasciata d'Italia a Berlino
ASDMAE	Archivio Storico Diplomatico, Ministero degli Affari Esteri, Rome
ASG	Archivio Segreto di Gabinetto
CP	Correspondance Politique
CV	Cassette Verdi
DDF	Documents Diplomatiques Français
FO	Foreign Office
GDD	German Diplomatic Documents
KA	Krasnyi Arkhiv
MAE	Archives du Ministère des Affaires Étrangères, Paris
PRO	Public Record Office, Kew, U.K.

CHAPTER 1 *Introduction*

1. NATO, "Defence Expenditures of NATO Countries 1975–1999," D13–D16. See Krebs, "Perverse Institutionalism," 343–77.

2. I do not mean to imply that Greece and Turkey joined NATO to tether one another, although there are alliances that are forged for such purposes. As I will discuss in the next chapter, certain alliances, such as NATO, have member states whose motivations for joining the alliance differ vis à vis the various other member states of the alliance.

3. Bueno de Mesquita, *The War Trap*, 160; see also Sabrosky, "Interstate Alliances"; Conybeare, "A Portfolio Diversification Model of Alliances."

4. Schroeder, "Alliances, 1815–1945."

5. Cf. Schweller, "Bandwagoning for Profit," who argues that balancing and bandwagoning may both be viewed from a realist perspective.

6. This is especially true for democracies. See Lake, "Powerful Pacifists: Democratic States and War." See also Weitsman and Shambaugh, "International Systems, Domestic Structures, and Risk."

7. This is what Kenneth N. Waltz refers to when he writes that flexibility in alignment makes "for rigidity of strategy or the limitation of freedom of decision." Waltz, *Theory of International Politics*, 169. For an excellent discussion of intra-alliance negotiation and management during peacetime, see Snyder, *Alliance Politics*.

8. See the classic Robert Jervis, *Perception and Misperception in International Politics*.

9. As Jervis observes in *System Effects*, 177, when relations between two adversaries improve, third parties will almost certainly be affected. Further, he notes, loose agreements may have the effect of menacing third parties, even if that is not the intention (178). Jervis refers to the alliance paradox when he describes Britain's decision to form the Entente Cordiale with France in 1904. He writes, "Intended as a substitute for a firm alignment with one side, the Entente of 1904 became a prelude to it; designed to increase British diplomatic flexibility, it had the opposite effect; agreed to with little thought to its implications for relations with Germany, it set in motion forces that greatly increased Anglo-German tensions, which in turn generated much stronger ties to France" (245–46).

10. See, for example, Snyder, *Alliance Politics*.

CHAPTER 2 *Theory of Alliance Formation and Cohesion*

1. I define an alliance as any formal or informal agreement between two or more states intended to further (militarily) the national security of the participating states. It is a continuing security association among member states with an element of forward planning and understanding to aid member states militarily or through benevolent neutrality.

2. This is a behavioral conceptualization of cohesion: the ability of member states "to agree on goals, strategy, and tactics, and coordinate activity directed toward those ends." Holsti, Hopmann, and Sullivan, *Unity and Disintegration in International Alliances*, 16. I discuss this in more detail later in the chapter.

3. Lakatos, "Falsification and the Methodology of Scientific Research Programmes," 134–38. This is a brief application of Lakatos's Methodology of Scientific Research Programs. For a recipe on how to apply his ideas more comprehensively, see Elman and Elman, "How Not to Be Lakatos Intolerant."

4. Bueno de Mesquita, *The War Trap*, 160; see also Sabrosky, "Interstate Alliances"; Conybeare, "A Portfolio Diversification Model of Alliances"; and Gaubatz, "Democratic States and Commitment in International Relations," who argues that state type has an important effect on the duration of alliance commitments. See also Bennett's extension of this argument in "Testing Alternative Models of Alliance Duration." Cf. Ray, "Friends as Foes," who argues that empirically the situation is more ambiguous.

5. Arguments within the realist school of thought have been classified in a variety of ways. See Rose, "Neoclassical Realism and Theories of Foreign Policy."

6. The distribution of capabilities can also function as an indicator of potential threat. The distinction between threat and capabilities is fine. For a discussion of balance of threat and balance of power, see Walt, *The Origins of Alliances*, esp. ch. 8.

7. On the difference between "offensive" and "defensive" realism, see Snyder, *Myths of Empire*. For a review, see Rose, "Neoclassical Realism and Theories of Foreign Policy."

8. Waltz, in his *Theory of International Politics*, argues that states ally in order to maintain their relative power position in the system, not for power aggrandizement. He argues that states are concerned with maximizing security, not power. "If states wished to maximize power, they would join the stronger side, and we would see not balances forming but a world hegemony forged. This does not happen because balancing, not bandwagoning, is the behavior induced by the system" (126). States are concerned with relative, not absolute gains.

Balance of power has a number of different meanings. For a review of the different uses of the term, see Haas, "The Balance of Power"; Claude, *Power and International Relations*, esp. 11–39; Zinnes, "An Analytical Study of Balance of Power Theories." See also Zinnes, "Coalition Theories and the Balance of Power."

9. Waltz, *Theory of International Politics*, 168.

10. Ibid. See also Liska, *Nations in Alliance*, 93.

11. For works within this tradition, see Mueller, "Patterns of Alliance"; Axelrod and Bennett, "A Landscape Theory of Aggregation." See also "structural balance theory" discussed and described by Healy and Stein, "The Balance of Power in International History"; and McDonald and Rosecrance, "Alliance and Structural Balance in the International System."

12. See, for example, Walt, *The Origins of Alliances*; Christensen and Snyder, "Chain Gangs and Passed Bucks"; Christensen, "Perceptions and Alliances in Europe"; Schweller, *Deadly Imbalances*; Cha, *Alignment Despite Antagonism*. See also Niou, Ordeshook, and Rose, *The Balance of Power*; Niou and Ordeshook, "Alliances in Anarchic International Systems"; Mueller, "Patterns of Alliance"; Axelrod and Bennett, "A Landscape Theory of Aggregation."

13. See Walt, *The Origins of Alliances*, 148–53.

14. As I will describe later in the chapter, tethering is actually more the behavioral opposite to balancing than bandwagoning, since it not only involves allying with, rather than against, one's ally, but also the motivation is opposite. Tethering is undertaken to conciliate one's adversary; balancing is motivated by a desire to resist the enemy. Bandwagoning, since it involves asymmetry, is not quite the precise opposite of balancing, even though the behavior involved, allying with, rather than against, one's enemy is still contrary to balancing. I am grateful to Glenn Snyder for making this point.

15. Walt, *The Origins of Alliances*, 125–26, 173–78. See also Walt, "Alliance Formation in Southwest Asia"; Larson, "Bandwagon Images in American Foreign Policy," 102–3. David, *Choosing Sides*, similarly argues that leaders of Third World states make alliance choices based on how such choices can best assure their political survival. See especially chapter 1. See also Harknett and VanDenBerg's extension to this argument in "Alignment Theory and Interrelated Threats."

It is important to note that Walt describes bandwagoning as behavior undertaken by the weak to survive but also in order to reap the fruits of victory or to share the spoils of war. I focus in this book on the first type of bandwagoning. See Walt, *The Origins of Alliance*, 19–21. Healy and Stein, "The Balance of Power in International History," refer to this as an "ingratiating effect" and argue that it served as the stabilizing mechanism in Europe, 1870–81: whenever states proved their strength in some capacity, other states attempted to ingratiate themselves with that strong power.

16. Schweller, "Bandwagoning for Profit." This is an extremely important argument in the context of bandwagoning behavior but is a departure from examining alliance behavior under conditions of threat. See Waltz, "Evaluating Theories," 915; Schweller, "New Realist Research on Alliances," 928.

17. See the contributions by John A. Vasquez, Kenneth N. Waltz, Stephen M. Walt, Randall Schweller, Thomas J. Christensen, Jack Snyder, and Colin Elman and Miriam Fendius Elman in the forum section of the *American Political Science Review* 51.4 (December 1997): 899–935.

18. See, for example, Sorokin, "Alliance Formation and General Deterrence"; Conybeare, "The Portfolio Benefits of Free Riding in Military Alliances"; Conybeare, "Arms versus Alliances"; Altfeld, "The Decision to Ally"; Morrow, "Alliances and Asymmetry"; Morrow, "Arms versus Allies"; and Morrow, "Alliances, Credibility, and Peacetime Costs."

19. Snyder, *Alliance Politics*. Snyder develops two models, one to explain alliance formation, the other to better understand alliance management.

20. Ibid., 44.

21. See, for example, Risse-Kappen, "A Liberal Interpretation of the Transatlantic Security Community"; see also Risse-Kappen, *Cooperation among Democracies*; Hellmann and Wolf, "Neorealism, Neoliberal Institutionalism, and the Future of NATO"; Duffield, "International Regimes and Alliance Behavior"; McCalla, "NATO's Persistence after the Cold War."

22. Duffield, "International Regimes and Alliance Behavior"; Duffield, *Power Rules*; Duffield, "NATO's Functions after the Cold War."

23. Wallander and Keohane, "Why Does NATO Persist?"; Wallander, "Institutional Assets and Adaptability."

24. Wallander, Haftendorn, and Keohane, "Introduction."

25. Krebs, "Perverse Institutionalism."

26. Gelpi, "Alliances as Instruments of Intra-Allied Control."

27. See also Lake, *Entangling Relations*; Lake, "Beyond Anarchy."

28. See Schroeder's exceptional piece, "Alliances, 1815–1945."

29. One additional avenue of inquiry that has attracted limited attention is the idea that states with similar ideological backgrounds tend to ally together. Walt, in *The Origins of Alliances*, found this hypothesis to be weak as compared with the realist propositions concerning external threats. Siverson and Emmons found support for it, however. See their "Birds of a Feather."

30. Jervis, "From Balance to Concert." See also Jervis, "Security Regimes," 362–68.

31. Keohane, *International Institutions and State Power*, 163.

32. As I noted earlier, Walt describes two types of bandwagoning—capitulation to a stronger state and allying in order to reap the fruits of victory. See Walt, *The Origins of Alliances*. Schweller describes how bandwagoning may be undertaken as a response to threats but also because of states' opportunities for gain. See Schweller, *Deadly Imbalances*, esp. 67–70 and 76–82. Since the focus of this book is alliance behavior under conditions of threat, I focus on bandwagoning behavior that is motivated by states' responses to threats.

33. See Walt, *The Origins of Alliances*; Waltz, *Theory of International Politics*, 126.

34. Walt, "Alliance Formation in Southwest Asia," 55, writes that "bandwagoning involves *unequal exchange*; the vulnerable state makes asymmetrical concessions to the dominant power and accepts a subordinate role."

35. Both Walt and Schweller view bandwagoning as "siding with the stronger state or coalition." Schweller, "New Realist Research on Alliances," 928.

36. I am grateful to Glenn Snyder for pointing this out and for his input in the following sections.

37. Jervis, *System Effects*, 181–91. As he notes on 193, "a state will be in a strong bargaining position vis à vis a potential ally if it can turn elsewhere with little difficulty."

38. Preempting a state from allying elsewhere has usually been considered balancing behavior. As Hans Morgenthau wrote, states ally in order to "add to their power the power of other nations, or withhold the power of other nations from the adversary." Morgenthau, "Alliances," 80. Yet balancing occurs when a state's primary motivation is to enhance its security against another. In tethering, a principal enemy is the state with which one is allying. As I discuss later in the chapter, tethering and balancing motivations are compatible. One shortcoming in the alliance literature is that scholars frequently neglect to discuss the fact that since alliances are formed between or among two or more states, each state may have different motivations for forming the alliance. A "balancing" alliance may actually be a balancing alliance for one state and a tethering alliance for another. The literature is problematic because of its failure to examine the dyadic nature of alliance relationships. Since alliances have more than one member state and not all members are compelled by the same motivations, each member state's motivation for acceding to an alliance should be specified. This in turn will allow us to characterize the alliances themselves more precisely.

39. Again, see Jervis's excellent discussion of triangular relations and the pivot position in *System Effects*, 177–209. As he notes on 185, "What is important is the relative conflict of interest and antagonism among the states. That is, a state that has sharp conflicts with two others may still be well positioned if the other two are divided by differences even less bridgeable."

40. As Jervis summarizes his discussion of the pre–World War I alliances in *System Effects*: "While the results of the diplomacy of the pre–World War I years were unusual, the dynamics were not. . . . [T]he most important determinant of a state's relations with another often lies in the relations each has with third parties. In other words, the underlying or intrinsic interests do not dictate the course of international history. States alter and establish their orientations toward some actors through the effect of ties made or sought with others. . . . Alignments are more than passive reflectors of interests. They set in motion forces that create and ameliorate conflicts, sometimes as statesmen foresee, but often as they do not" (252).

41. Ibid., 179.

42. Jervis queries, what determines whether a state has to choose between two potential allies or be forced to rely on one? This is similar to the question of whether a state will hedge or tether. Jervis argues that the answer in part is geography—the closer two states are the more likely they are to have greater conflicts. This is true—the difference between a state that hedges and one that tethers is the level

of threat it confronts. That threat level will be driven by geography, as well as the other factors that heighten threat level, i.e., capabilities and intentions. See ibid., 183–84.

43. Grieco, "Understanding the Problem of International Cooperation," 331–34; Grieco, "The Maastricht Treaty"; Grieco, "State Interests and Institutional Rule Trajectories"; Deudney, "The Philadelphian System"; Deudney, "Binding Sovereigns," esp. 213–16. See also Schweller's discussion in *Deadly Imbalances*, 70–71.

44. Grieco, "The Maastricht Treaty."

45. Ikenberry, *After Victory*, esp. 50–79.

46. Ibid., 258–59.

47. Deudney, "Binding Sovereigns," 214.

48. See the text of the agreements at the NATO website, www.nato.int/issues/nato-russia/nato-russia.htm

49. Numerous authors make reference to alliance cohesion, but the arguments are not developed nearly as effectively as the arguments concerning alliance formation. See the following section.

50. See Snyder, *Alliance Politics*, 165–200.

51. Chernoff, "Stability and Alliance Cohesion."

52. Richardson, *When Allies Differ*.

53. Walt, "Why Alliances Endure or Collapse."

54. O'Leary, "Economic Relationships among the Allies"; Ravenal, "Extended Deterrence and Alliance Cohesion."

55. Holsti, Hopmann, and Sullivan, *Unity and Disintegration in International Alliances*.

56. The dynamic I describe here is confined to peacetime alliances; wartime conditions are different, and the difference in context of interaction will alter the resulting alliance behavior.

57. I employ a behavioral conceptualization of cohesion: the ability of member states "to agree on goals, strategy, and tactics, and coordinate activity directed toward those ends." Holsti, Hopmann, and Sullivan, *Unity and Disintegration in International Alliances*, 16. This is in contrast to Liska, who distinguishes between cohesion and efficacy. See Liska, *Nations in Alliance*, chs. 2–3. In my view, cohesion is *not* analytically the same as duration. It might be preferable to discuss cohesion as a "we feeling," but assessing it as such would be inherently impressionistic. Adopting a behavioral conception is a suitable alternative.

58. See, for example, Deutsch, *Political Community and the North Atlantic Area*; Risse-Kappen, *Cooperation among Democracies*; Adler, "Europe's New Security Order."

59. Risse-Kappen, *Cooperation among Democracies*, 30–31.

60. Ibid., 32.

61. See Snyder, "Richness, Relevance, and Rigor."

62. George, "Case Studies and Theory Development."

63. These data can be found in *www.icpsr.umich.edu*.

64. Siverson and Starr, *The Diffusion of War*.

65. For a comprehensive review of the various definitions and conceptualizations of alliance, see Schweller, "The Concept of Alliance."

66. Weitsman and Young, "Alliance Dynamics in the Old Europe." Cf. Weber, "Hierarchy Amidst Anarchy," whose distinctions are somewhat different from this

one. See also Singer and Small, "Formal Alliances, 1815–1939," and Singer and Small, "Formal Alliances, 1816–1965," who distinguish between defense pacts, neutrality pacts, and ententes.

67. One might argue that an alliance that is not honored is no alliance at all. Yet one cannot construct a definition post hoc. The promise levels in an agreement are important, even if they are not honored. They signify the degree to which states are seeking to commit themselves. The agreement itself, at the time it is concluded, serves as a signal to the member states as well as to the rest of the states in the system. Even if the terms are not fulfilled, no state is necessarily aware that will occur at the time the agreement is signed. Germany and Austria-Hungary had doubts regarding Italy's intentions to fulfill its alliance obligations in the Triple Alliance. They sought higher and higher promise levels from Italy as a consequence. This offers interesting insight into the nature of tethering alliances.

68. Holsti, Hopmann, and Sullivan, *Unity and Disintegration in International Alliances*, 16.

69. See Liska, *Nations in Alliance*, chs. 2–3.

CHAPTER 3 *The Two Leagues of the Three Emperors*

1. See Langer, *European Alliances and Alignments*, 21; Craig, *Germany*, 104; Fay, *The Origins of the World War*, 56.

2. Quoted in Bagdasarian, *The Austro-German Rapprochement*, 98.

3. Ibid.

4. Ibid., 86.

5. Andrássy, *Bismarck, Andrássy, and Their Successors*, 17; see also 18, 27.

6. Simpson, *The Saburov Memoirs*, 170.

7. Quoted in Bagdasarian, *The Austro-German Rapprochement*, 116–17.

8. Langer, *European Alliances and Alignments*, 212, 217.

9. Gauld, "The 'Dreikaiserbund' and the Eastern Question 1871–1876," 215.

10. Bagdasarian, *The Austro-German Rapprochement*, 77.

11. Bismarck to Bülow, August 14, 1876, *German Diplomatic Documents, 1871–1914* (GDD), vol. 1, 23–24.

12. Memo by Bismarck, August 30, 1876, GDD, vol. 1, 26.

13. Langer, *European Alliances and Alignments*, 370.

14. Bülow to Count Münster, November 27, 1876, GDD, vol. 1, 43.

15. See the Appendix for more detailed data on geographic proximity and power.

16. The Italian threat to Austria-Hungary is discussed in detail in the next chapter.

17. The reciprocal threat between Great Britain and Russia is discussed in detail in Chapter 5.

18. Additional historical background of the Leagues can be found in Rupp, *A Wavering Friendship*; Gauld, "The 'Dreikaiserbund' and the Eastern Question 1871–1876"; Gauld, "The 'Dreikasierbündnis' and the Eastern Question, 1877–1878"; Gorianiov, "The End of the Alliance of the Emperors"; Medlicott, "Bismarck and the Three Emperors' Alliance"; Medlicott, *The Congress of Berlin and After*; Langer, *European Alliances and Alignments*; Craig, *Germany*; Fay, *The Origins of the World War*; Birch, *Britain and Europe*; Albrecht-Carrié, *Britain and France*. This is not nearly an exhaustive list; diplomatic histories that discuss the Leagues are numerous. While

there are differences in the historical accounts of some of the diplomatic incidents taking place, there is general agreement on the sources of conflict among the members and the motivations on the part of the members to participate in the Leagues.

19. Craig, *Germany*, 113–14. See the next chapter for an in-depth discussion of the Dual Alliance.

20. Pribram, *The Secret Treaties of Austria-Hungary*, vol. 1, 185–87.

21. For the text of the Schönbrunn Convention, see ibid.

22. Craig, *Germany*, 107.

23. For more details on the war scare of 1875, see Langer, *European Alliances and Alignments*, 42–55; Craig, *Germany*, 107–10; Seymour, *The Diplomatic Background of the War*, 21–26; Fay, *The Origins of the World War*, 57–58.

24. Birch, *Britain and Europe*, 35–40; Albrecht-Carrié, *Britain and France*, 186–92; Craig, *Germany*, 110–13; Langer, *European Alliances and Alignments*, 59–86; Coolidge, *Origins of the Triple Alliance*, 84–98; Fay, *The Origins of the World War*, 59–67. The literature on the uprisings in Bosnia and Herzegovina, pan-Slavism, and great power interest in the Balkans is substantial. For further citations, see MacKenzie, *The Serbs and Russian Pan-Slavism*, and Sumner, *Russia and the Balkans*, who focus on Russian-Serb relations; see also Rupp, *A Wavering Friendship*, and Harris, *A Diplomatic History of the Balkan Crisis*, who pay more attention to the great power relations during this period.

25. Albrecht-Carrié, *Britain and France*, 186–87.

26. Birch, *Britain and Europe*, 38–40; Albrecht-Carrié, *Britain and France*, 194–96; Langer, *European Alliances and Alignments*, 121–40; Fay, *The Origins of the World War*, 65–67. See also MacKenzie, *The Serbs and Russian Pan-Slavism*; Sumner, *Russia and the Balkans*; Rupp, *A Wavering Friendship*; Medlicott, *The Congress of Berlin and After*.

27. Corti, *The Downfall of Three Dynasties*, 248–49. See also Langer, *European Alliances and Alignments*, 141–66.

28. Simpson, *The Saburov Memoirs*, 129–30. Cf. Taylor, *The Struggle for Mastery in Europe*, who writes that the threat of revolutionary socialism was used only as an excuse for the emperors since their interests were so different and this stance was the only thing on which they could agree. He further suggests that "it is difficult to think of a time when Europe was more remote from revolution than between 1871 and 1875." (219).

29. For more details on the social pressures in Germany 1871–90, see ch. 1, "Social Forces under Bismarck," in Rosenberg, *Imperial Germany*. This volume was first published in English in 1931 under the title *The Birth of the German Republic, 1871–1918*. See also ch. 2, "The Fruition of Liberalism," in Hayes, *A Generation of Materialism*.

30. Clearly Kulturkampf was undertaken in Germany for domestic reasons. This analysis, however, focuses only on the international implications.

31. Langer, *European Alliances and Alignments*, 36–44; see also Craig, *Germany*, 69–78.

32. See *Krasnyi Arkhiv* (KA), vol. I, 64–90, 92–126; Simpson, *The Saburov Memoirs*.

33. Simpson, *The Saburov Memoirs*, 119. Russia was unaware of the substance of the Dual Alliance at this point.

34. Goriainov, "The End of the Alliance," 330.
35. Medlicott, "Bismarck and the Three Emperors' Alliance," 78.
36. The figure is given in 1990 British pounds since the data colleted by J. David Singer and Melvin Small, National Material Capabilities Data, 1816–1985 (ICPSR Code 9903), was collected in July 1990 and tabulated in current year pounds. See the Appendix for more information.
37. Simpson, *The Saburov Memoirs*, 131.
38. Goriainov, "The End of the Alliance," 330.
39. Medlicott, "Bismarck and the Three Emperors' Alliance," 65–67.
40. Ibid., 78.
41. Quoted in Simpson, *The Saburov Memoirs*, 186.
42. Medlicott, "Bismarck and the Three Emperors' Alliance," 71–72, 76.
43. Ibid., 69.
44. Quoted in Simpson, *The Saburov Memoirs*, 121.
45. Ibid., 232.
46. Bismarck, *Bismarck*, vol. 2, 234.
47. Langer, *European Alliances and Alignments*, 211.
48. Goriainov, "The End of the Alliance," 325.
49. Quoted in Bagdasarian, *The Austro-German Rapprochement*, 116.
50. Bismarck, *Bismarck*, vol. 2, 246.
51. Ibid., 249.
52. Ibid., 250. See also Langer, *European Alliances and Alignments*, 198.
53. Langer, *European Alliances and Alignments*, 196.
54. In 1881, power shares were as follows: Austria 4 percent, France 11 percent, Germany 11 percent, Italy 3 percent, Russia 10 percent, and the United Kingdom 21 percent. Percentages refer to a state's proportion of total system capabilities in military expenditure, military personnel, energy consumption, iron and steel production, urban population, and total population.
55. Medlicott, "Bismarck and the Three Emperors' Alliance," 65.
56. Simpson, *The Saburov Memoirs*, 131.
57. Langer, *European Alliances and Alignments*, 198.
58. A frequently cited quotation of Bismarck's is: "'All politics reduces itself to this formula: Try to be *à trois* as long as the world is governed by the unstable equilibrium of five Great Powers.'" Bismarck to Saburov in 1878; drawn here from Joll, *The Origins of the First World War*, 37. There were, of course, six great powers in Europe at this time, although as the power data in the Appendix reveals, Italy was the weakest of the great powers. Their rank order in terms of capability are Great Britain 23 percent, France 11 percent, Russia 10 percent, Germany 10 percent, Austria-Hungary 5 percent, Italy 3 percent.
59. Fay, *The Origins of the World War*, 71–77.
60. Ibid., 203–4.
61. Pribram, *The Secret Treaties of Austria-Hungary*, vol. 2, 37–41.
62. Craig, *Germany*, 124–28.
63. Langer, *European Alliances and Alignments*, 208.
64. Medlicott, "Bismarck and the Three Emperors' Alliance," 68.
65. Goriainov, "The End of the Alliance," 328–29.

66. Corti, *The Downfall of Three Dynasties*, 292–94; Langer, *European Alliances and Alignments*, 340–42.

67. Langer, *European Alliances and Alignments*, 344–45; Medlicott, "Bismarck and the Three Emperors' Alliance," 77.

68. Corti, *The Downfall of Three Dynasties*, 308–17; for more details on Bulgaria, see 279–329. See also Medlicott, *The Congress of Berlin and After*; Jelavich, *The Habsburg Empire*, 132–34.

CHAPTER 4 *The Dual and Triple Alliances*

1. The term "Dual Alliance" is sometimes used to refer to the alliance between Germany and Austria-Hungary and sometimes to refer to the Franco-Russian Alliance. For the purposes of this book, Dual Alliance refers to the alliance between Germany and Austria-Hungary concluded in 1879; the alliance between France and Russia will be referred to as the Franco-Russian Alliance.

2. Germany at first intended to keep the contents of the treaty secret. However, only a month after the treaty was signed, it was published. See Langer, *European Alliances and Alignments*, 173.

3. The conclusion of the Dual Alliance is considered to be a fundamental turning point in German foreign policy. The alliance decision is viewed as Germany ultimately deciding to side with Austria against Russia. The German decision in 1890 not to renew the Reinsurance Treaty with Russia, combined with its alliance agreement with Austria, is said to have made the Franco-Russian Alliance inescapable. Not all historians agree, however. See Fay, *The Origins of the World War*, 68–71, 77–80, 95–96. Fay writes that "historians have generally exaggerated the importance of the non-renewal of the Re-insurance Treaty as a factor in the formation of the Franco-Russian Alliance" (93). He claims this is true partly because of Bismarck, who was bitter about his successor and his successor's policies and wrote numerous articles criticizing those policies. Fay maintains that there were a number of reasons why the French and the Russians came together, aside from nonrenewal of the Reinsurance Treaty. Despite these other factors, however, it is true that once Germany made a choice between Austria-Hungary and Russia, and such a choice became inevitable, the ground was paved for the Franco-Russian Alliance. See ibid., 93–96.

4. KA, vol. I, Saburov's conversations with Bismarck, 1879, 72; Langer, *European Alliances and Alignments*, 180.

5. Count Herbert Bismarck to Radowitz, August 9, 1879, GDD, vol. 1, 101; Langer, *European Alliances and Alignments*, 179; Bagdasarian, *The Austro-German Rapprochement*, 286–87.

6. See Craig, *The Politics of the Prussian Army*, 288–89; Ritter, *The Sword and the Sceptre*, vol. 2, 239–40.

7. Herbert Bismarck to Radowitz, August 9, 1879, GDD, vol. 1, 102.

8. Langer, *European Alliances and Alignments*, 176–77; Bagdasarian, *The Austro-German Rapprochement*, 295.

9. Report by Saburov, August 13, 1879, KA, vol. I, 64.

10. Langer, *European Alliances and Alignments*, 178.

11. Ibid., 180.

12. Waller, *Bismarck at the Crossroads*, 92–95.

13. Ibid., 136–37.

14. Bagdasarian, *The Austro-German Rapprochement*, 291; Sumner, *Russia and the Balkans*, 558; Schmitt, *Triple Alliance and Triple Entente*, 14; Langer, *European Alliances and Alignments*, 176; see also Tunstall, *Planning for War*, 15–16.

15. Simpson, *The Saburov Memoirs*, 100.

16. Ibid., 103–4.

17. Waller, *Bismarck at the Crossroads*, 142; Tunstall, *Planning for War*, 17.

18. Tunstall, *Planning for War*, 17.

19. Bismarck to Foreign Office, November 10, 1879, GDD, vol. 1, 105; Langer, *European Alliances and Alignments*, 176–77, 180, 186–87; Bagdasarian, *The Austro-German Rapprochement*, 295.

20. GDD, vol. 1, 107.

21. Bismarck, *Bismarck*, vol. 2, 258–60.

22. Ibid., 262–63. For the text of the letter, see 261–66. Lewis's reply is on 266–67.

23. Ibid., 276–77.

24. Ibid., 281.

25. See KA, vol. I, Saburov's conversations with Bismarck.

26. See Shuvalov's first report to Alexander III, April 29, 1887, of his discussions with Bismarck regarding the secret convention. KA, vol. I, 92.

27. Other scholars have argued that the exaggeration and exacerbation of the Russian-German quarrel was a tactic Bismarck employed in order to convince Emperor Wilhelm (a friend of Russia and Tsar Alexander's uncle) to sanction the alliance with Austria-Hungary. See, for example, Taylor, *The Struggle for Mastery in Europe*, 260–61.

28. Coolidge, *Origins of the Triple Alliance*, 172–73; Schmitt, *Triple Alliance and Triple Entente*, 6.

29. Jelavich, *The Habsburg Empire*, 114.

30. January 29, 1880, GDD, vol. 1, 107.

31. GDD, vol. 1, 9–10.

32. Andrássy, *Diplomacy and the War*, 3.

33. Bagdasarian, *The Austro-German Rapprochement*, 222–23.

34. Quoted in ibid., 289. See also Andrássy, *Bismarck, Andrássy, and Their Successors*, 38–39.

35. The relative power of the states in question in 1879 were as follows: Austria-Hungary 5 percent, France 10 percent, Germany 11 percent, Italy 3 percent, Russia 10 percent, and the United Kingdom 22 percent. See the Appendix for additional power data.

36. Coolidge, *Origins of the Triple Alliance*, 172–73.

37. Ibid., 163–64.

38. Carroll, *Germany and the Great Powers*, 165.

39. Ibid., 156. Waller, in *Bismarck at the Crossroads*, argues that Bismarck justified the alliance on the grounds of historical and racial ties, yet these factors did not enter his reasoning in forming the alliance. However, there is little doubt that the his-

torical and sentimental ties contributed to the domestic popularity of the alliance. See 195.

40. May, *The Hapsburg Monarchy*, 142.

41. Schmitt, *Triple Alliance and Triple Entente*, 16; Fay, *The Origins of the World War*, 69. May, in *The Hapsburg Monarchy*, 434–35, writes that Austro-Germans totaled some 35.58 percent of the Austrian Empire (according to a 1910 census) and that "German culture still held first place, however much its absolute importance had been impaired by the cultural progress of other nationalities. And Germans . . . were more prominent in the intellectual and economic affairs of the empire than all other nationalities taken together."

42. Benedetti, *Studies in Diplomacy*, 32.

43. Pribram, *The Secret Treaties of Austria-Hungary*, vol. 1, 26.

44. Ibid., 25.

45. Ibid., 25–31. The fifth and final article of the alliance simply gives the terms of ratification and validity.

46. Ibid., 217–19.

47. Germany and Russia had conflicts beyond Germany's alliance with Austria-Hungary (e.g., over Bulgaria and Constantinople and over grain tariffs). There was also a negative newspaper campaign against Russia in Germany. See, for a brief overview, Fay, *The Origins of the World War*, 90–110. In fact, even after signing the Reinsurance Treaty in 1887, there were statesmen in the upper echelons of Germany, particularly in the military, who believed war with Russia was inevitable. They favored the launching of a preventive war with Austria against Russia and encouraged Austrian provocation against Russia to this end. This was not the predominant view in Berlin, yet it indicates that, divorced from Austrian interests, Germany had its own problems with Russia. Nevertheless, those conflicts were not deep seated or unresolvable. And although counterfactuals are difficult to argue, it seems that those conflicts could well have been resolved but for Germany's commitment to Austria, widening the differences between Russia and Germany. See Craig, *Germany*, 131–34.

48. The unintended consequence of this was that the member states' relationships with others in the system deteriorated.

49. Taylor, *The Struggle for Mastery in Europe*, 327.

50. See, for example, ibid., 263.

51. Ibid., 318. Taylor also writes that the Russians would have been shocked if they had learned that, just before the signing of the Reinsurance Treaty, Germany had "engineered the Mediterranean coalition against them or that Moltke was constantly advising the Austrians, with Bismarck's encouragement, how to improve their striking power in Galicia" (319).

52. Ibid., 239. Fay, in *The Origins of the World War*, writes that the growth of pan-Slavism and the determination of Russia to dominate in the Balkans offended Austria so much that Germany had to abandon the Reinsurance Treaty, and thereafter Russia became the "the enemy of the Central Powers" (95).

53. Craig, *The Politics of the Prussian Army*, 276.

54. See Fay, *The Origins of the World War*, 378–406. Fay writes that, despite the full-fledged German support for Austria during this crisis and despite the good understanding between the two states' heads of army staffs, "there was more friction

between the two allies than has generally been supposed" (405). He goes on to note, however, that "occasionally, Bethmann felt it necessary to renew promises to support policies which Austria deemed essential for her vital interests in the Balkans, because he would otherwise have caused such dissatisfaction at the Ballplatz as to have seriously weakened the alliance which still remained the corner-stone of German foreign policy" (405−6).

55. Craig, *The Politics of the Prussian Army*, 289.

56. See Waller, *Bismarck at the Crossroads*, for more on the argument that the Dual Alliance was devised by Bismarck in order to impress on Russia the need to come to terms and return to the League of the Three Emperors.

57. Craig, *Europe*, 15−18, 187.

58. Salvatorelli, *La triplice alleanza*, 38−42, 47−53; Langer, *European Alliances and Alignments*, 219−21; Jelavich, *The Habsburg Empire*, 128.

59. Ironically, it is Sonnino who was principally responsible for Italy's rupture of the alliance thirty-four years later.

60. The article is reproduced in almost its entirety in Chiala, *La triplice e la duplice alleanza*, 20−24.

61. Ibid., 21.

62. Ibid., 24.

63. Launay to Rudini, March 22, 1891, Archivio Segreto di Gabinetto (ASG), cassette verdi (CV), cassetta (C) 1, Archivio Storico Diplomatico, Ministero degli Affari Esteri (ASDMAE).

64. Pribram, *The Secret Treaties of Austria-Hungary*, vol. 1, 12.

65. Salvatorelli, *La triplice alleanza*, 46.

66. Launay to Rudini, March 22, 1891, ASG, CV, C1, ASDMAE.

67. Launay to Rudini, March 8, 1891, ASG, CV, C1, ASDMAE.

68. Nigra to Prinetti, April 2, 1902, Lanza to Prinetti, April 12, 1902, ASG, CV, C3, ASDMAE.

69. Lanza to Prinetti, April 12, 1902, ASG, CV, C3, ASDMAE.

70. Tittoni to Lanza, February 16, 1904, ASG, CV, C3, ASDMAE.

71. Lanza to Tittoni, July 25, 1904, ASG, CV, C3, ASDMAE.

72. Lanza to Tittoni, February 5, 1905, ASG, CV, C3, ASDMAE.

73. Tittoni to Avarna, February 10, 1905, ASG, CV, C3, ASDMAE.

74. Colonnello del Mastro to Avarna, March 6, 1905, ASG, CV, C3, ASDMAE. From 1887 to 1905, Austrian military expenditures jumped over 7 million 1972 British pounds.

75. March 6, 1905, ASG, CV, C3, ASDMAE.

76. Avarna to Tittoni, May 22, 1907, Avarna to Tittoni, July 6, 1907, ASG, CV, C3, ASDMAE.

77. Avarna to Sangiuliano, August 12, 1911, ASG, CV, C4, ASDMAE.

78. See Sangiuliano to Avarna, December 6, 1911, Avarna to Sangiuliano, December 7, 1911, Sangiuliano to Avarna, December 9, 1911, ASG, CV, C4, ASDMAE.

79. Martin Franklin, Italian ambassador in Berlin, to Sangiuliano, December 29, 1911, ASG, CV, C4, ASDMAE.

80. Pansa to Sangiuliano, December 11, 1912, AIB, busta n. 114, ASDMAE.

81. ASG, CV, C4, ASDMAE.

82. See Sangiuliano's memo regarding a conversation with Mérey (the Austro-Hungarian ambassador in Rome), November 1, 1912, 1731 Gabinetto Riservatissimo, AIB, busta n. 114, ASDMAE.

83. Avarna to Tittoni, March 6, 1905, ASG, CV, C3, ASDMAE.

84. Coolidge, *Origins of the Triple Alliance*, 215–16.

85. Pribram, *The Secret Treaties of Austria-Hungary*, vol. 1, 5; see also vol. 2, 41.

86. Jelavich, *The Habsburg Empire*, 128; Schmitt, *Triple Alliance and Triple Entente*, 19.

87. Andrássy, *Bismarck, Andrássy, and Their Successors*, 97.

88. Pribram, *The Secret Treaties of Austria-Hungary*, vol. 2, 3–4.

89. Tunstall, *Planning for War*, 21.

90. Ibid., 24.

91. Pribram, *The Secret Treaties of Austria-Hungary*, vol. 2, 95.

92. Tunstall, *Planning for War*, 87–93.

93. Ibid., 87.

94. Quoted in Pribram, *The Secret Treaties of Austria-Hungary*, vol. 2, 6.

95. GDD, vol. 1, 114–15.

96. Pribram, *The Secret Treaties of Austria-Hungary*, vol. 2, 41.

97. Launay to Mancini, January 31, 1882, Inventario delle Rappresentanze Diplomatiche Berlino, 1867–1947, Legazione d'Italia a Berlino, busta n. 44, ASDMAE.

98. GDD, vol. 1, 113.

99. GDD, vol. 1, 117.

100. Reuss to Bismarck, March 24, 1882, GDD, vol. 1, 119; Pribram, *The Secret Treaties of Austria-Hungary*, vol. 2, 65.

101. GDD, vol. 2, 53–57.

102. Pribram, *The Secret Treaties of Austria-Hungary*, vol. 2, 60.

103. Andrássy, *Bismarck, Andrássy, and Their Successors*, 314.

104. French military spending jumped in 1880–81 some 4 million 1972 British pounds. In 1882, power shares were as follows: Austria 5 percent, France 11 percent, Germany 11 percent, Italy 3 percent, Russia 10 percent, and the United Kingdom 21 percent. In 1887, power shares were the same; in 1891, Austria maintained 5 percent, France fell to 10 percent, Germany increased to 12 percent, Italy was up to 4 percent, Russia maintained 10 percent, and the United Kingdom fell to 18 percent. At the time of the fourth renewal in 1902, Austria had 4 percent, France dropped to 7 percent, Germany was up a percentage point to 13 percent, Italy fell back to 3 percent, Russia was up a point to 11 percent, and the United Kingdom was down to 16 percent. By 1912, at the final renewal of the Triple Alliance, Austria was at 5 percent, France was still at 7 percent, Germany was up a percentage point to 14 percent, Italy was up at 4 percent again, Russia was up to 12 percent, and the United Kingdom was down to 12 percent. In sum, Italy and Austria-Hungary maintained approximately the same power share for the time period, while France dropped in its ranking, as did the United Kingdom. Russia increased a bit in its share, and Germany's share grew the most dramatically.

105. Taylor, *The Struggle for Mastery in Europe*, 273. Bosworth, in *Italy and the Approach of the First World War*, writes that there were 11,000 Italians in Tunis.

106. Coolidge, *Origins of the Triple Alliance*, 191–206.

107. Seymour, *The Diplomatic Background of the War*, 33.

108. Fay, *The Origins of the World War*, 142–51.

109. It is true, however, that the period 1875–85 saw warmer relations between Germany and France. This came to an end with the appointment of General Boulanger as minister of War in France. See ibid., 96–104.

110. Pribram, *The Secret Treaties of Austria-Hungary*, vol. 2, 40.

111. Craig, *Germany*, 116; Pribram, *The Secret Treaties of Austria-Hungary*, vol. 2, 41; Fay, *The Origins of the World War*, 84–85.

112. *Die Grosse Politik der Europäischen Kabinette (1871–1914). Sammlung der Diplomatischen Akten des Auswärtigen Amtes* (Berlin), vol. 18, 5780, as cited in Albertini, *The Origins of the War of 1914*, 135.

113. Albertini, *The Origins of the War of 1914*, 182; Pribram, *The Secret Treaties of Austria-Hungary*, vol. 2, 138 43; Fay, *The Origins of the World War*, 150–51.

114. As cited in Pribram, *The Secret Treaties of Austria-Hungary*, vol. 2, 138. See also Albertini, *The Origins of the War of 1914*, 162–84.

115. Conrad von Hötzendorf to Aehrenthal, September 24, 1911, quoted and cited in Pribram, *The Secret Treaties of Austria-Hungary*, vol. 2, 157.

116. Tunstall, *Planning for War*, 92–93.

117. Pribram, *The Secret Treaties of Austria-Hungary*, vol. 2, 143, 145.

118. Herwig, *The First World War*, 151.

119. Salandra, *Italy and the Great War*, 25–26.

120. Pribram, *The Secret Treaties of Austria-Hungary*, vol. 1, 65–73.

121. Fay, *The Origins of the World War*, 142–43.

122. Pribram, *The Secret Treaties of Austria-Hungary*, vol. 1, 156–57. For the full text of the second treaty of the Triple Alliance, see ibid., 105–15; for the full text of the third treaty, see 151–63.

123. For the full text of the fourth treaty of the Triple Alliance, see ibid., 221–33; the fifth treaty is also in ibid., 245–59.

124. Ibid., vol. 2, 45; Albertini, *The Origins of the War of 1914*, 51, 84; Fay, *The Origins of the World War*, 86–87.

125. Sangiuliano to Pansa, January 5, 1912, Ambasciata d'Italia a Berlino (AIB), busta n. 114, ASDMAE.

126. As cited in Pribram, *The Secret Treaties of Austria-Hungary*, vol. 2, 67–68.

127. Luigi Chiala, *Tunisi* (Torino, 1895), 58, as cited in Albertini, *The Origins of the War of 1914*, 31.

128. Albertini, *The Origins of the War of 1914*, 31.

129. Pribram, *The Secret Treaties of Austria-Hungary*, vol. 2, 82–84.

130. Askew, "Austro-Italian Antagonism," 176–220. Askew sees the sources of antagonism between Italy and Austria as popular opinion, Albanian rivalry, the Balkans outside the Adriatic, irredentism, pressures from the military, and economic rivalry between the two allied adversaries.

131. See, for example, Fay, *The Origins of the World War*, 396–97, on the effects of the Bosnian crisis of 1908 on the cohesion of the Triple Alliance.

132. Fay writes in *The Origins of the World War* that the Balkan Wars "increased the internal friction within the Triple Alliance and Triple Entente. . . . This internal friction, however, was more than counter-balanced by the feeling in each group that

it must do everything possible to preserve unity and solidarity among its members. Allies must stand together and support one another's policies, consenting to policies which were unpalatable, or even consenting to acts which might involve dangers to the peace of Europe" (346–47).

133. The text of this agreement can be found in Pribram, *The Secret Treaties of Austria-Hungary*, vol. 1, 283–305.

134. See Williamson, *Austria-Hungary*, 88.

135. Bosworth, *Italy, the Least of the Great Powers*, 247.

136. Ibid., 46.

137. Ibid., 46–56; Askew, "Austro-Italian Antagonism," 212–17.

138. Crispi, *The Memoirs of Francesco Crispi*, 346–47.

139. Ibid., 347.

140. See Seymour, *The Diplomatic Background of the War*, 32.

141. See Crispi, *The Memoirs of Francesco Crispi*, 61.

142. Doyle, "Liberalism and World Politics," 1156.

143. Pribram, *The Secret Treaties of Austria-Hungary*, vol. 2, 39.

CHAPTER 5   *The Franco-Russian Alliance and the Triple Entente*

1. For the text of the Reinsurance Treaty, see Hurst, *Key Treaties*, 645–47.

2. Shuvalov's first report to Alexander III, April 29, 1887, of his discussions with Bismarck regarding the secret convention, KA, vol. I, 92. These reports are published in their original French with a Russian translation.

3. KA, vol. I, 98–100. See also Goriainov, "The End of the Alliance," 335–36. As Goriainov was the former archivist of the Russian Foreign Office, this article has an abundance of archival material, only some of which has been published, principally in the Krasnyi Arkhiv. This article contains information, including the text of the Reinsurance Treaty, that had not been publicly available until the publication of Goriainov's piece.

4. Shuvalov's fourth report to Alexander III of his discussions with Bismarck, KA, vol. I, 118.

5. KA, vol. I, 120. See also Goriainov, "The End of the Alliance," 337–38.

6. Langer, *The Franco-Russian Alliance*, 28; Kennan, *The Decline of Bismarck's European Order*, 366–67; Taylor, *Bismarck*, 328; Goriainov, "The End of the Alliance," 343.

7. Langer, *The Franco-Russian Alliance*, 34.

8. Quoted in ibid., 34.

9. Ibid., 39–44; Taylor, *Bismarck*, 243–49.

10. Archives du Ministère des Affaires Étrangères, Paris (MAE), Correspondance Politique, 1871–96 (CP), Russie, vol. 288, April–June 1890, Vauvineux to Ribot, April 9, 1890, dispatch nos. 34 and 35.

11. See the conversations between Shuvalov and the kaiser, reported in Langer, *The Franco-Russian Alliance*, 47–48.

12. Langer, *The Franco-Russian Alliance*, 65–67.

13. Goriainov, "The End of the Alliance," 348–49.

14. MAE CP, Russie, vol. 288, April–June 1890.

15. Langer, *The Diplomacy of Imperialism*, 6–8, 118–19.

16. MAE Livres Jaunes, 262, "L'alliance franco-russe. Origines de l'alliance, 1890–1893, convention militaire, 1892–1899 et convention navale, 1912," document no. 10. See also Michon, *The Franco-Russian Alliance*, 34, who writes that Russia was solely concerned with Britain at the time the Franco-Russian Alliance was concluded.

17. The colonial disputes between England and Russia will be discussed in detail later in the chapter in the section on the Anglo-Russian Convention of 1907.

18. White, *Transition to Global Rivalry*, 7.

19. MAE CP, Russie, vol. 287, January–March 1890, dispatch no. 5, January 10, 1890.

20. MAE CP, Angleterre, vol. 863, July 1891, annexe to dispatch no. XV, Waddington to Ribot, July 27, 1891.

21. MAE Livres Jaunes, 262, annexe to document no. 17, August 19/21, 1891. This then became the basis of the understanding between France and Russia. Giers continues on in his letter to spell out the formula for the understanding with France.

22. Niou, Ordeshook, and Rose, *The Balance of Power*, 236, summarize the historical consensus on this point well. As they write in their discussion of the possible combination of powers in this period, "examining the potential coalitions and alliances for Germany from 1871 to 1887, in light of French *revanchist* ambitions arising from the Franco-Prussian War—for example, the demand for return of Alsace-Lorraine as a condition of negotiation—and the role of Franco-German rivalry in the emergence of the German state, we eliminate as infeasible any coalitions that include France." They go on to note that "scholarly opinion is virtually unanimous in identifying the same impediments to such a [Franco-German] coalition" (236–37, n. 13).

23. France confronted a sufficiently high level of threat from Germany to make balancing desirable, yet, as we can see from Chapter 2, one state's desire to ally is not enough. Two or more states need to have compatible motivations in order for an alliance to emerge. Until this time, Russia was unavailable as an ally.

24. As an interesting anecdote in this context, the Imperial War Museum in London portrays the Franco-Russian Alliance as being a necessary counterpoint to the hostile Central Powers. Further, the British decision to join that alliance is portrayed as similarly being driven by the aggressive and expansionist Central Powers. Yet the lag time of almost thirty years between the conclusion of the Dual Alliance between Germany and Austria and the fact that Britain was, until at least 1904 and even beyond, more associated with that alliance than the Franco-Russian Alliance seem to offer compelling contrary evidence. In fact, Britain drove the French and Russians together in the first place. To characterize the interests among France, Russia, and Britain as congruent in the pre–World War I period is to ignore the most important facets and dynamics of interstate relations at this time. It is worthwhile remembering that all six great powers had ambitious imperial designs and policies and that Germany, Russia, France, and Britain were all involved in serious endeavors to strengthen their military capacities. Russia was completely preoccupied by the desire to maintain cordial relations with Germany. Its principal fear was that it would be dragged into a war of revenge by France against Germany. This concern actually

led the tsar to briefly suspend negotiations toward an agreement with France in August 1891. Ribot speculates in a letter to Carnot, president of the Republic, that the suspension was because the tsar was not directly menaced by Germany (MAE Livre Jaune, 262, document no. 15, August 11, 1891). Even the negotiations between General Boisdeffre and General Obroutcheff that culminated in the military convention between France and Russia were peppered by debates regarding Germany. Boisdeffre was compelled to counter Obroutcheff's claims that Germany was not the principal enemy that they faced. See MAE Livre Jaune, 262, document no. 53, August 10, 1892. German militarism is certainly important in the pre–World War I context. Yet this particular turning point in the diplomatic relations of the great powers was driven by the British, not German, threat.

25. Fay, in *The Origins of the World War*, 24–25, writes that the fact that Poincaré viewed war as inevitable made a European war inevitable. Although accounts differ on the level of hostility between Germany and France, and in fact the level of hostility varied over the years 1871–1914, there is historical consensus that "the major obstacle to any lasting improvement in Franco-German relations was the treaty of Frankfurt, by which Germany annexed Alsace and Lorraine." Keiger, *France and the Origins of the First World War*, 68. See Keiger on the ups and downs of Franco-German relations prior to the Great War. See also Carroll, *French Public Opinion and Foreign Affairs*.

26. Langer, *The Diplomacy of Imperialism*, 43–50.

27. Documents Diplomatiques Français (DDF), 1871–1914, 1st Series (1871–1901), vol. VIII, March 20, 1890–August 28, 1891, dispatch no. XX, document no. 371, June 6, 1891.

28. On the implications of the *flirt anglo-triplicien* for the emergence of the Franco-Russian Alliance, see Langer, *The Franco-Russian Alliance*, 183; Langer, "The Franco-Russian Alliance," 574.

29. MAE CP, Angleterre, vol. 862, June 1891, Waddington to Ribot, June 5, 1891, dispatch no. 171.

30. MAE CP, Angleterre, vol. 862, June 1891, dispatch no. 188.

31. MAE CP, Angleterre, vol. 862, June 1891, Waddington to Ribot, June 3, 1891, June 4, 1891, June 5, 1891, June 23, 1891, a second dispatch June 23, 1891, June 25, 1891; MAE CP, Angleterre, vol. 863, July 1891, Waddington to Ribot, July 3, 1891.

32. MAE CP, Angleterre, vol. 862, June 1891, Waddington to Ribot, June 25, 1891, dispatch no. XII.

33. MAE CP, Angleterre, vol. 862, June 1891, Waddington to Ribot, dispatch no. 170. In this dispatch Waddington also attaches an article of the same date from the *Daily News* that described the king of Italy's admission of a "formal assurance" of support from Lord Salisbury that Fergusson did not deny in the House of Commons when the issue was raised, again, by Labouchère.

34. MAE CP, Angleterre, vol. 863, July 1891, Waddington to Ribot, July 2, 1891, dispatch no. XIII.

35. Ibid.

36. MAE CP, Angleterre, vol. 863, July 1891, Waddington to Ribot, July 12, 1891, dispatch no. 206.

37. MAE CP, Angleterre, vol. 863, July 1891, Waddington to Ribot, July 16, 1891, dispatch no. 209.

38. MAE CP, Allemagne, vol. 102, May–June 1891, Herbette to Ribot, June 6, 1891, dispatch no. 20. On July 3, 1891, Herbette reported to Ribot that the sense in Germany was that Britain was a "confidant" or "an honorary member" of the Triple Alliance. MAE CP, Allemagne, vol. 103, July–September 1891, dispatch no. 165.

39. MAE CP, Allemagne, vol. 102, May–June 1891, Herbette to Ribot, June 18, 1891, dispatch no. 162.

40. MAE Livres Jaunes, 262, Laboulaye to Ribot, July 18, 1891, document no. 3.

41. MAE Livres Jaunes, 262, Ribot to Laboulaye, July 24, 1891, document no. 4.

42. MAE Livres Jaunes, 262, Ribot to Laboulaye, July 24, 1891, document no. 5. See also MAE Livres Jaunes, 262, Ribot to Freycinet August 6, 1891, document no. 10, and document no. 17, August 15/27, 1891, Mohrenheim to Ribot, regarding the renewal of the Triple Alliance, the adhesion of Britain, and the need for an alliance between the two states.

43. MAE Livres Jaunes, 262, Mohrenheim to Ribot, August 15/27, 1891, and September 21, 1891, document nos. 17 and 18. See a translation of the agreement in Hurst, *Key Treaties*, 662–65.

44. Pribram, *The Secret Treaties of Austria-Hungary*, vol. 2, 209.

45. Ibid., 209–11.

46. Langer, *The Franco-Russian Alliance*, 68. The relative power shares at the time the alliance was forged in 1891 were as follows: Austria-Hungary 5 percent, France 10 percent, Germany 12 percent, Italy 4 percent, Russia 10 percent, and the United Kingdom 18 percent. The French and Russians were not surprisingly threatened by the coming together of the two most powerful states in the system. A German-British agreement would bring together 30 percent of the power capabilities. This, combined with the 9 percent of Austria and Italy, sharply increased the threat level to France and Russia in 1891. They believed they faced an alliance that totaled nearly 40 percent of the power capabilities of the system.

47. Kennan, *The Fateful Alliance*, 155.

48. Schmitt, *Triple Alliance and Triple Entente*, 42.

49. Gooch, *History of Modern Europe*, 510–11.

50. Ibid., 514–17.

51. See, for example, Michon, *The Franco-Russian Alliance*, 63–64; Tardieu, *France and the Alliances*, 10.

52. Pribram, *The Secret Treaties of Austria-Hungary*, vol. 2, 223–25.

53. Langer, *The Franco-Russian Alliance*, 90.

54. Michon, *The Franco-Russian Alliance*, 109, 160–61.

55. Taylor, *The Struggle for Mastery in Europe*, 434.

56. Kennan, *The Fateful Alliance*, 151.

57. Michon, *The Franco-Russian Alliance*, 74.

58. Pribram, *The Secret Treaties of Austria-Hungary*, vol. 2, 215.

59. Ibid., emphasis added.

60. Kennan, *The Fateful Alliance*, 181–83.

61. Langer, *The Franco-Russian Alliance*, 240.

62. Ibid., 261–63.

63. Ibid., 268–69.

64. Michon, *The Franco-Russian Alliance*, 80–81. French foreign minister Hano-taux wanted to refuse the German invitation to Kiel and wrote to the tsar asking whether Russia would be sending representatives to Kiel. Nicholas II responded by writing that he did not understand French hesitation and that as allies, given that the Russians were sending warships to Kiel, he expected the French to do so as well. See ibid., 81, n. 1. Cf. Carroll, *French Public Opinion and Foreign Affairs*, 162–63.

65. Parr, *Théophile Delcassé*, 56–61. See also Kennan, *The Fateful Alliance*, 35, about the diverse aims and goals of France and Russia.

66. Schmitt, *Triple Alliance and Triple Entente*, 74.

67. Michon, *The Franco-Russian Alliance*, 231.

68. This is a natural effect of systems dynamics. As Jervis describes in *Systems Effects*, "Because systems are interconnected, the relations between two actors are often determined less by their common and conflicting bilateral interests than by their relations with other actors, which means that a shift in stance sets off a chain of consequences." See 211–18.

69. Sazonov, *Fateful Years, 1909–1916* (London: 1928), 128, as cited in Albertini, *The Origins of the War of 1914*, 571.

70. Monger, *The End of Isolation*, 62, 66.

71. Williamson, *The Politics of Grand Strategy*, 201–2, 250–51.

72. Andrew, "The Entente Cordiale," 17.

73. Monger, *The End of Isolation*, 168.

74. Williamson, *The Politics of Grand Strategy*, 22.

75. Schmitt, *Triple Alliance and Triple Entente*, 59.

76. See Andrew, "The Entente Cordiale," 33.

77. MAE Les Papiers Delcassé, Angleterre II, 1899–1905, vol. 14, Barrère to Delcassé, April 11, 1904.

78. *British Documents on Foreign Affairs*, Part I, Series F Europe, vol. 11, France 1891–1904, dispatch no. 59, document no. 52, Dawson to Monson, November 20, 1898.

79. See Albertini, *The Origins of the War of 1914*, 111–12.

80. As cited in ibid., 112.

81. Rolo, "Lansdowne," 159–60.

82. Brandenburg, 176–81, cited in Albertini, *The Origins of the War of 1914*, 116; see also 112–13, 115.

83. Neilson, *Britain and the Last Tsar*, 367.

84. Again, this is not to say that German militarism did not play an important role in the pre–World War I period, but it was not determinant at this point. British-German relations were warm in the early part of the new century.

85. Monger, *The End of Isolation*, 12–13.

86. William II, *The Kaiser's Letters to the Tsar*, 54–55.

87. Quoted in Wilson, *The Policy of the Entente*, 5.

88. See Rolo, "Lansdowne," 159.

89. Andrew, *Théophile Delcassé*, 125. See also Albertini, *The Origins of the War of 1914*, 187.

90. Monger, *The End of Isolation*, 114.

91. Public Record Office (PRO) Foreign Office (FO) 633 6, Cromer Papers, Letters to Secretaries of State, 1883–1905.

92. October 28, 1903, to Brodrick, quoted in James Tomes, *Balfour and Foreign Policy*, 121.

93. PRO FO 800 126, Lansdowne Correspondence, France 1903–5.

94. PRO FO 181 801, Cecil Spring Rice to Lansdowne, April 27, 1904. See also April 28, 1904, and May 18–27, 1904.

95. Rolo, *Entente Cordiale*, 274; Albertini, *The Origins of the War of 1914*, 152. Taylor, in *The Struggle for Mastery in Europe*, writes that perhaps French efforts to defuse this crisis were of consequence, but the main reason the crisis was defused was that the British did not want a conflict, nor did the Russians (424). Yet this argument is not very compelling, first because one can always say a crisis was averted because the two parties wanted to avoid it, and second, according to the British documents, French intervention was welcomed and effective. See document nos. 5–31, esp. no. 21, Gooch and Temperley, *British Documents on the Origins of the War*. See Lansdowne's note to Paul Cambon where he thanks Cambon and Delcassé profusely, MAE, Delcassé Papers, July 23, 1904.

96. Andrew, *Théophile Delcassé*, 118.

97. See ibid., 124–26.

98. Cambon, *Correspondance*, 49–50.

99. See Cambon to his sons of December 1903, ibid., 101–4.

100. See MAE, Papiers Delcassé, Angleterre II, 1899–1905, vol. 14, télégramme no. 134, May 23, 1903, and Paul Cambon to Delcassé, July 9, 1904. See also PRO FO 633 6, Cromer Papers, Cromer to Lansdowne November 27, 1903; PRO FO 633 6, Cromer to Lansdowne December 12, 1903. The French wanted, above all, to secure an Anglo-Russian agreement. See also PRO FO 800 176, Bertie Papers, Bertie to Lansdowne, January 17, 1905.

101. PRO FO 800 176, Bertie Papers, Russia 1898–1905, November 23, 1902.

102. See his note to Paul Cambon, July 23, 1904, MAE Papiers Delcassé, Angleterre II, 1899–1905, vol. 14.

103. PRO FO 181 823, no. 88, October 31, 1904, from the Admiralty to Channel Fleet Gibraltar. See telegrams from October 31, 1904, no. 385, and PRO FO 181 823, October 5–November 5, 1904, to Hardinge.

104. PRO FO 181 823, telegram no. 232, November 1, 1904.

105. In fact, one important characteristic of the negotiations between Britain and Russia was the degree to which Russia consulted Germany as the process of rapprochement unfolded. The popular view, that Germany was the catalyst in all major alignment decisions during this period, can be seen, for example, in Taylor, *The Struggle for Mastery in Europe*, 427, who argues that the revolution in European affairs was caused by Germany. He does admit, to the contrary, a chapter or so later, that the "Anglo-Russian entente had little to do with Germany" (442). Williams, "Great Britain and Russia," says that the British decision had much to do with Germany but later illuminates the tethering motives between Britain and Russia in "Strategic Background." The archival materials are unequivocal on the point, however. British decision makers were completely preoccupied with how to reduce tension between their nation and Russia.

106. PRO FO 800 176.

107. PRO FO 181 801, Cecil Spring Rice to Lansdowne, April 27, 1904.

108. Ibid.

109. Chamberlain memo, September 10, 1900, cited in Neilson, *Britain and the Last Tsar*, 211.

110. Neilson, *Britain and the Last Tsar*, 216.

111. Williams, "The Strategic Background," 371.

112. Ibid. See also Neilson, *Britain and the Last Tsar*, 268.

113. PRO FO 800 72, November 16, 1906, Grey to Nicholson.

114. PRO FO 899, January 2, 1907, Nicholson to Grey.

115. Ibid.

116. There is extensive evidence of this in the archives. See PRO FO 800 72, Sir Edward Grey's private papers on Russia 1905–7; PRO FO 181 863, Correspondence from Sir Arthur Nicholson, October 18–December 1906, especially November 17, 1906, no. 745, from Nicholson to Grey. See also Churchill, *The Anglo-Russian Convention of 1907*, 125, who makes this point from looking at Nicholson's son's memoirs of his father. More regarding Nicholson is hard to come by, as the only copy of the journal he kept throughout the period that he negotiated the agreement as British ambassador to Russia is missing from the PRO. Only his correspondence is available.

117. McDonald, *United Government*, 76–79.

118. Churchill, *The Anglo-Russian Convention*, 87–89.

119. KA, vol. V, 25. The text of the treaty is in French, followed by a Russian translation.

120. Churchill, *The Anglo-Russian Convention*, 98–100; MacDonald, *United Government*, 80–81. See also Lamsdorff's letter to Nelidov (the Russian ambassador to France) of September 16, 1905, in which he expresses his anger over the agreement. KA, vol. V, 1924, 5–49.

121. This suggests that once alliances are formed, they factor into decision making regarding agreements with other states. This is not a startling insight, but it does imply that the relationship between threat and probability of seeking an alliance is, to some degree, influenced by those existing agreements. It also highlights how those alliances function as institutions that affect the behavior and expectations of states. In this case, we see that Russia was flirting with the idea of a hedging arrangement of some kind with Germany and vice versa. Yet no formal agreement emerged, in large part due to their respective obligations. What is important to note is that the alliance-seeking behavior between the two powers did change significantly as the level of threat between them changed. The status quo prevailed with the other great powers at this time, due to the fact that the threat level between them was not substantially altered. France still balanced Germany and vice versa; Russia still balanced Austria and vice versa; Italy continued to tether Austria and vice versa; and so forth. We do see a threat reduction between Italy and France; the consequence is a series of negotiations, declarations, exchanges of letters, and agreements. These developments are consistent with the theoretical argument, though describing them in any detail is beyond the scope of this project. To see copies of the agreements, see Pribram, *The Secret Treaties of Austria-Hungary*, vol. 2, app. C, 226–59.

122. For evidence of the rumors regarding a reconstituted Dreikaiserbund, see PRO 181 863, November 15, 1906, Nicholson to Grey, no. 762. PRO FO 800 72, Spring Rice to Grey of May 5, 1906, discusses the intimacy of the emperors, which did not bode well for Britain or France. PRO FO 181 906, June 18, 1907, Nicholson to Grey no. 328, raises questions of "counter" agreements between Germany and Russia.

123. MacDonald, *United Government*, 104–8.

124. Vitte, *The Memoirs of Count Witte*, 699.

125. PRO FO 181 865, October 15, 1906, Nicholson to Grey, no. 694.

126. PRO FO 181 863, November 7, 1906, Nicholson to Grey, no. 745. PRO FO 181 899, January 27, 1907, no. 53, Nicholson to Grey, reports again that Germany is fine with the negotiations between Britain and Russia.

127. PRO FO 800 72.

128. See PRO FO 181 899, Correspondence from Sir Arthur Nicholson January–February 20, 1907, January 13, 1907, Nicholson to Grey, no. 28, January 19, 1907, Nicholson to Grey, no. 50, January 27, 1907, Nicholson to Grey, no. 54. See also PRO FO 181 893, Correspondence from Sir Arthur Nicholson, February 20–May 6, 1907, especially Nicholson to Grey, March 26, 1907, no. 160, in which Nicholson speculates that Germany's influence over Russian policy has eclipsed the French.

129. PRO FO 181 893, no. 160.

130. Ibid.

131. PRO FO 418 39, August 10, 1907, O'Beirne to Grey, no. 139. That Izvolsky attended this meeting raised questions in Britain over what had been reported to the German court. Grey stated, however, that he "understood perfectly that, Russia and Germany being neighbours, it was natural for them to have discussions and communications with each other." PRO FO 418 39, Grey to O'Beirne, August 10, 1907, no. 300.

132. PRO FO 418 39, O'Beirne to Grey, August 10, 1907, no. 407.

133. PRO FO 418 39, Lascelles to Grey, October 1, 1907, no. 427.

134. In 1904, the relative power shares were the United Kingdom 13 percent, France 7 percent, Germany 13 percent, Austria-Hungary 4 percent, Italy 3 percent, Russia 11 percent. In 1907, they were the United Kingdom 12 percent, France 7 percent, Germany 14 percent, Austria-Hungary 4 percent, Italy 3 percent, and Russia 12 percent.

135. Monger, *The End of Isolation*, 134.

136. See GDD, vol. 3, 268–98, 326–62.

137. It certainly is not true that by 1908–9 Anglo-German rivalry had reached the point of no return. On the contrary, there was still hope that an agreement between them would ensure misunderstandings would be laid to rest. See the documents in GDD, vol. 3, 326–62.

138. Albertini, *The Origins of the War of 1914*, 550. By 1913, relative power shares were the United Kingdom 11 percent, France 7 percent, Germany 14 percent, Austria-Hungary 5 percent, Italy 3 percent, and Russia 12 percent.

139. Schmitt, *Triple Alliance and Triple Entente*, 78–81.

140. Telegram, February 14–27, 1909, no. 251, in Schreiner, *Entente Diplomacy*, 235–36.

141. Schmitt, *Triple Alliance and Triple Entente*, 94.

142. See Williamson, *The Politics of Grand Strategy*, 135–37; Schmitt, *Triple Alliance and Triple Entente*, 85; document nos. 598–619 in Schreiner, *Entente Diplomacy*, 524–44. Especially of note are document nos. 605 and 606, in which Russia is adamant in divorcing its policy choices from its allies, and no. 614, which discusses the blow the Triple Entente sustained from the Potsdam agreement.

143. Fay, *The Origins of the World War*, 293.

144. Albertini, *The Origins of the War of 1914*, 339. See also Fay, *The Origins of the World War*, 291; Schmitt, *Triple Alliance and Triple Entente*, 74–75.

145. Williamson, *The Politics of Grand Strategy*, 299.

146. Ibid., 317.

147. Ibid., 339. See also Schreiner, *Entente Diplomacy*, 724–34, document nos. 850–56.

CHAPTER 6 *Alliances and the Great War*

1. Österreichisches Staatsarchiv-Kriegsarchiv, Vienna, Conrad Archiv, B Flügel-adjutant, vol. 1, as cited in Herwig, *The First World War*, 9.

2. Herwig, *The First World War*, 8–33.

3. Cf. Goemans, *War and Punishment*.

4. Asprey, *The German High Command at War*, 99–106, 122–24.

5. Herwig, *The First World War*, 87–96.

6. See Stone, *The Eastern Front*, 165–93; Silberstein, *The Troubled Alliance*, 177.

7. Deák, *Beyond Nationalism*, 192.

8. Silberstein, *The Troubled Alliance*, 302.

9. Herwig, *The First World War*, 204.

10. Ibid., 209–17.

11. French, *The Strategy of the Lloyd George Coalition*, 31.

12. Ludendorff, *My War Memories*, vol. 1, 312.

13. Herwig, *The First World War*, 335.

14. Ibid., 352–61, 364–65.

15. Ibid., 376–79.

16. Ludendorff, *My War Memories*, vol. 2, 680–81, 684.

17. French, *The Strategy of the Lloyd George Coalition*, 223.

18. Silberstein, *The Troubled Alliance*, 263.

19. Ritter, *The Sword and the Sceptre*, vol. 3, 45.

20. Gottlieb, *Studies in Secret Diplomacy*, 264–65; Silberstein, *The Troubled Alliance*, 275. The irony, of course, is that the dismemberment that did occur was far worse.

21. See Rothenberg, "The Habsburg Army in the First World War," 73–86. Cf. Luvaas, "A Unique Army." See also Deák, *Beyond Nationalism*, who describes challenges presented by the multilingual and multinational character of the army of the Habsburg Empire.

22. Tunstall, *Planning for War*, 21–23. On the evolution of German war planning prior to the war, see Ritter, *The Sword and the Sceptre*, especially vols. 1 and 2; Craig, *The Politics of the Prussian Army*; and Snyder, *The Ideology of the Offensive*, for more

information on the evolution of German military strategy. See also Stone, "Moltke and Conrad."

23. Tunstall, *Planning for War*, 33–40.

24. Quoted in Herwig, "Disjointed Allies," 273.

25. Snyder, *The Ideology of the Offensive*, 109.

26. Stone, "Moltke and Conrad," 224.

27. Quoted in ibid., 229.

28. Ritter, *The Sword and the Sceptre*, vol. 3, 58–59.

29. Herwig, "Disjointed Allies," 265; Asprey, *The German High Command*, 90; Ritter, *The Sword and the Sceptre*, vol. 3, 58–59.

30. Herwig, *The First World War*, 108.

31. Ibid., 89.

32. Ibid., 91.

33. Quoted in Herwig, "Disjointed Allies," 266; see also Herwig, *The First World War*, 96.

34. Asprey, *The German High Command*, 432–33; Fischer, *Germany's Aims*, 206.

35. Herwig, *The First World War*, 135, 186.

36. Ritter, *The Sword and Sceptre*, vol. 3, 78. For an easy and comprehensible geographic guide to the First World War, see Gilbert and Banks, *First World War Atlas*.

37. Ritter, *The Sword and Sceptre*, vol. 3, 66–80. The need for unified command in the east was illuminated in the spring of 1916 when Austria-Hungary, against repeated warnings by Germany, launched an offensive against Italy from Tyrol. Having removed the best German-Austrian forces from the Russian front to launch this offensive, the Russian offensive in June was met with inadequate defense. The concurrent failure at Verdun exacerbated the problems. Germany had wanted unified command under Hindenburg, but Austria-Hungary had resisted relinquishing control. By July, however, Austrian losses were so heavy they finally accepted that Hindenburg would take over the command of the eastern front from the Baltic to Tarnopol, and command would be shared on the groups further south. See ibid., 185–200.

38. Ibid., 89.

39. Stone, *The Eastern Front*, 282.

40. Stevenson, *The First World War*, 216.

41. Deák, *Beyond Nationalism*, 200.

42. Silberstein, *The Troubled Alliance*, 65. See also Craig, "The World War I Alliance of the Central Powers."

43. Gottlieb, *Studies in Secret Diplomacy*, 265.

44. Ibid., 258–63; May, *The Passing of the Hapsburg Monarchy*, vol. 1, 96.

45. Pribram, *Austrian Foreign Policy*, 100.

46. See, for example, Fischer, *Germany's Aims*; Fischer, "German War Aims"; Dahlin, *French and German Public Opinion on Declared War Aims*. For an excellent recent overview, see Goemans, *War and Punishment*.

47. Cf. Goemans, *War and Punishment*, who argues that German war aims escalated as the situation on the ground deteriorated. He asserts that because oligarchs will pay dearly if they lose a war, in the face of bad news they will actually increase their war aims in order to purchase acquiescence from the domestic population.

212 Notes to Chapter 6

They have little to lose and everything to gain. His argument is persuasive, yet it does not explain the difference between Austria-Hungary's and Germany's behavior in regard to their aims.

They have little to lose and everything to gain. His argument is persuasive, yet it does not explain the difference between Austria-Hungary's and Germany's behavior in regard to their aims.

48. See Herwig, *The First World War*, 90, 109.

49. Stevenson, *The First World War*, 95–97.

50. Fischer, *Germany's Aims*, 247.

51. Gottlieb, *Studies in Secret Diplomacy*, 260. See also Fischer, *Germany's Aims*, 211.

52. See Shanafelt, *The Secret Enemy*, 72–80. See also Gottlieb, *Studies in Secret Diplomacy*, 272–77; Fischer, *Germany's Aims*, 523–33.

53. May, *The Passing of the Hapsburg Monarchy*, vol. 1, 144.

54. Quoted in Herwig, *The First World War*, 153.

55. See May, *The Passing of the Hapsburg Monarchy*, vol. 1, 194–202; Silberstein, *The Troubled Alliance*, 278–79.

56. See Silberstein, *The Troubled Alliance*, 184–87, 192–204, 213.

57. See Weber, *Eagles on the Crescent*, 242, 260–61; Pribram, *Austrian Foreign Policy*, 98–99.

58. Fischer, *Germany's Aims*, 293.

59. Ibid., 315, 343.

60. Shanafelt, *The Secret Enemy*, 84.

61. Fischer, *Germany's Aims*, 296.

62. See ibid., 300–309, 313–15. See also May, *The Passing of the Hapsburg Monarchy*, vol. 1, 480.

63. Fischer, *Germany's Aims*, 351–52.

64. Stone, *The Eastern Front*, 243.

65. Shanafelt, *The Secret Enemy*, 208.

66. de Manteyer, *Austria's Peace Offer*, 37. This is by far the most detailed and comprehensive account of the Sixtus Affair.

67. Quoted in de Manteyer, *Austria's Peace Offer*, 65.

68. de Manteyer, *Austria's Peace Offer*, 83–84.

69. Stevenson, *The First World War*, 216–17.

70. See May, *The Passing of the Hapsburg Monarchy*, vol. 2, 635–36.

71. Fischer, *Germany's Aims*, 316.

72. Ibid., 498–99. Fischer is citing the "Vienna Document" of March 27, 1917, that Czernin and Bethmann Hollweg drew up regarding their respective aims.

73. What Schweller calls the "balance of interests" may offer a powerful alternative explanation for the unraveling of the Central Powers. In Schweller's typology, Germany may have been a wolf, Austria-Hungary a lamb. The divergence in their motivations and interests had an adverse effect on the cohesion of their alliance. Combining interests with threats may help us better understand the lack of cohesion of the alliance. See Schweller, *Deadly Imbalances*, esp. 83–91. My thanks to Tim Lomperis for raising this point.

74. Malone, "War Aims toward Germany," 136.

75. Stevenson, *French War Aims*, 12–13.

76. Cf. Goemans, *War and Punishment*.

77. In 1914, the United Kingdom possessed 14 percent of the world's capabilities, Russia 11 percent, and France 8 percent, while Austria-Hungary possessed

7 percent to Germany's 16 percent. By 1916, the United Kingdom had 15 percent, Russia 12 percent, and France 9 percent, while Germany had 15 percent to Austria's 4 percent.

78. See Snyder, *The Ideology of the Offensive*, 177–94.

79. See Smith, *The Russian Struggle for Power*, 47–48, again, where Russia recognizes Germany as its principal enemy.

80. Albrecht-Carrié, *France, Europe and the Two World Wars*, 51. See also Farrar, *Divide and Conquer*, 40.

81. Farrar, *The Short War Illusion*, 126–27.

82. French, *British Strategy and War Aims*, 58, 65.

83. Ibid., 25.

84. Herwig, *The First World War*, 144.

85. Guinn, *British Strategy and Politics*, 116–17; Gottlieb, *Studies in Secret Diplomacy*, 106–31.

86. See Joffre, *The Memoirs of Marshall Joffre*, 411, 461, who argued that problems arose because each ally had a separate front and separate rules governing their behavior. See 409–10.

87. French, *British Strategy and War Aims*, 150.

88. Neilson, *Strategy and Supply*, 122–24.

89. Philpott, *Anglo-French Relations*, 120–21.

90. Prete, "French Military War Aims," 893–94.

91. Neilson, *Strategy and Supply*, 225–48.

92. French, *The Strategy of the Lloyd George Coalition*, 67.

93. Philpott, *Anglo-French Relations*, 135–49.

94. Quoted in ibid., 161.

95. Hoover Archives, British Foreign Office, *Britain's Share in the War*.

96. See Snyder, *The Ideology of the Offensive*, 157–98; Rutherford, *The Russian Army*, 34–35; Liddell Hart, *Strategy: The Indirect Approach*, 181.

97. Philpott, *Anglo-French Relations*, 1.

98. Guinn, *British Strategy and Politics*, 16–22.

99. Williamson, *The Politics of Grand Strategy*, 316.

100. Lloyd George, *War Memoirs*, vol. 4, 2347–48.

101. Philpott, *Anglo-French Relations*, 18.

102. Neilson, "Managing the War," 97.

103. Rutherford, *The Russian Army*, 49–61; Liddell Hart, *Strategy*, 182; Golovine, *The Russian Army in the World War*, 212–14.

104. Golovine, *The Russian Army in the World War*, 218–20.

105. Ibid., 238–39.

106. Neilson, "Managing the War," 108; Neilson, *Strategy and Supply*, 112.

107. Rutherford, *The Russian Army*, 162–67.

108. Philpott, *Anglo-French Relations*, 19–21, 29, 36–45, 53–81.

109. Neilson, *Strategy and Supply*, 134.

110. Golovine, *The Russian Army in the World War*, 240.

111. Guinn, *British Strategy and Politics*, 131, 133.

112. See ibid., 146; Golovine, *The Russian Army in the World War*, 240.

113. Golovine, *The Russian Army in the World War*, 241–42.

114. Hardach, *The First World War*, 100–102, 145–46.

115. Ibid., 102–3; Rothwell, *British War Aims*, 268–69.

116. David Lloyd George, *War Memoirs* (Odhams Press, 1938), vol. 2, 1438, cited in Guinn, *British Strategy and Politics*, 266.

117. Possony and Mantoux, "Du Picq and Foch," 230.

118. Guinn, *British Strategy and Politics*, 178.

119. Ibid., 214–15.

120. Ibid., 216.

121. See also De Weerd, "Churchill, Lloyd George, Clemenceau," 297.

122. French, *The Strategy of the Lloyd George Coalition*, 3–4. See also Abrash, "War Aims toward Austria Hungary," 113–14.

123. French, *The Strategy of the Lloyd George Coalition*, 260.

124. Smith, *The Russian Struggle for Power*, 46–48.

125. Zeman, *A Diplomatic History of the First World War*, 69; Malone, "War Aims Toward Germany," 136. For an extremely thorough and comprehensive discussion of Entente war aims, see Goemans, *War and Punishment*.

126. Farrar, *The Short War Illusion*, 85.

127. Stevenson, *French War Aims*, 29. See also Smith, *The Russian Struggle for Power*, 216; Farrar, *Divide and Conquer*, 40; French, *British Strategy and War Aims*, 81.

128. Here again we see the salience of the "balance of interests" to an assessment of wartime alliance cohesion. See Schweller, *Deadly Imbalances*, 83–91.

129. Rothwell, *British War Aims*, 282.

130. Taylor, "The War Aims of the Allies," 475.

131. See Gottlieb, *Studies in Secret Diplomacy*, 88–105; Prete, "French Military War Aims," argues that the French peace plans were remarkably aggressive. See 898.

132. Fest, "British War Aims and German Peace Feelers," 286.

133. Goemans, *War and Punishment*, 291. This, too, has implications for the "balance of interests." State classifications (e.g., wolves, foxes, ostriches, doves, and lions) may change as the strategic environment changes, which in turn will affect state behavior. See Schweller, *Deadly Imbalances*, 84–91.

134. Stevenson, *French War Aims*, 13.

135. See Farrar, *Divide and Conquer*.

136. Hoover Archives, British Foreign Office, *Britain's Share in the War*.

137. Stevenson, *French War Aims*, 35. Stevenson is speaking of the French here.

138. Farrar, *Divide and Conquer*, 4.

139. Quoted in Wade, *The Russian Search for Peace*, 9.

140. Quoted in ibid., 13.

141. Golovine, *The Russian Army in the World War*, 265.

142. Wade, *The Russian Search for Peace*, 38–47.

143. Herwig, *The First World War*, 334; Stone, *The Eastern Front*, 282.

144. Farrar, *Divide and Conquer*, 26.

145. French, *British Strategy and War Aims*, 56.

146. Kitchener Papers, January 1915, WO 159/3, quoted in Neilson, *Strategy and Supply*, 63.

147. Hoover Archives, British Foreign Office, *Britain's Share in the War*.

148. My thanks to Glenn Snyder for making this point.

CHAPTER 7 *Conclusion*

1. See Walt, "Why Alliances Endure or Collapse," 156–79.

2. See the commitment level gradations in Chapter 2.

3. Hoover Archives, Nicolas de Bazili papers, accession number 65017-9.23, Box no. 11, folder, "WWI: Miscellaneous Documents."

4. See Snyder, "The Security Dilemma and Alliance Politics"; Snyder, *Alliance Politics*. See also Cha's elaboration on Snyder's argument in *Alignment Despite Antagonism*.

5. My thanks to Glenn Snyder for his comments summarizing this so succinctly.

6. Cf. Goemans, *War and Punishment*, who argues that regime type determines the degree of ease or difficulty of war termination.

7. Bueno de Mesquita, *The War Trap*, 160; see Sabrosky, "Interstate Alliances"; Conybeare, "A Portfolio Diversification Model of Alliances."

8. See Jervis, *Systems Effects*, 201–9.

9. Joffe, " 'Bismarck' or 'Britain'?" 94–117.

10. For an elaboration on this argument, see Weitsman, "Alliance Cohesion and Coalition Warfare."

ARCHIVES

Public Record Office, Kew, United Kingdom

  Private Papers

   Lord Balfour

   PRO 1 364 (General Correspondence)

   Sir Francis Bertie

   FO 800 159 (Index Correspondence Series A)

   FO 800 164 (Correspondence 1904–1907, France)

   FO 800 176 (Correspondence 1897–1905, Russia)

   FO 800 177 (Correspondence 1905–1915, Russia)

   Cromer

   FO 633 6 (Correspondence on Entente Cordiale, 1883–1905)

   Sir Edward Grey

   FO 800 49 (Correspondence France, 1905–1906)

   FO 800 72 (Correspondence Russia, 1905–1907)

   Lord Kitchener

   PRO 30/57 34 (War Office Reform April 1905)

   PRO 30/57 31 (India 1902–1914, Afghanistan July 1905)

   PRO 30/57 32

   PRO 30/57 36 (Egypt 1900–1911, Misc.)

   PRO 30/57 37 (Russo-Japanese War 1903–1905)

   Landsdowne

   FO 800 141 (Correspondence Russia, 1904–1905)

   FO 800 125 (Correspondence France, 1900–1905)

   Sir Arthur Nicholson

   FO 800 338 (February–December 1906)

   FO 800 339 (Misc. Corr., Vol. I, 1–8/1907)

   FO 800 340 (Misc. Corr., Vol. II, 8–12/1907)

   Roberts

   WO 105 44 (1903–1908)

Embassy and Consular Archives: Russia Correspondence

Hardinge
FO 181 803 to CH (Charles Hardinge) May 16–18, 1904
FO 181 805 to CH May 18–June 29, 1904
FO 181 819 to CH June 29–August 10, 1904
FO 181 813 to CH August 10–October 5, 1904
FO 181 823 to CH October 5–November 5, 1904
FO 181 799 to CH November 8–December 12, 1904
FO 181 802/1 to CH December 13–31, 1904
FO 181 801 from CH May 18–27, 1904
FO 181 810 from CH May 28–August 16, 1904
FO 181 815 from CH August 17–October 12, 1904
FO 181 807 from CH October 13–November 10, 1904
FO 181 811 from CH November 12–December 1904
FO 181 851 from CH January–February 7, 1905
FO 181 857/4 from CH February 8–April 18, May 29–June 1905
FO 181 831 from CH June 22–August 15, 1905
FO 181 857/5 from CH August 18–October 7, 1905
FO 181 841 from CH October 7–25, 1905, from SR (Spring-Rice) October 27–November 28, 1905

Spring Rice (Cecil)
FO 181 856/1 November 29–December 14, 1905
FO 181 828 December 14–31, 1905
FO 181 866 January–February 22, 1906
FO 181 869 from SR (Spring Rice) February 23–May 5, 1906

Nicholson (Sir Arthur):
FO 181 871 from SR May 7–28, 1906; from N (Nicholson) May 29–July 6, 1906
FO 181 888/1 from N July 6–August 30, 1906
FO 181 865 from N August 30–October 17, 1906
FO 181 863 from N October 18–December 1906
FO 181 899 from N January–February 20, 1907
FO 181 893 from N February 20–May 6, 1907
FO 181 906 from N May 7–August 1907

General Correspondence, France/Diplomatic Dispatches from Embassy
FO 27 3579 July–September 18, 1902
FO 27 3580 September 19–October 1902
FO 27 3581 November–December 1902
FO 27 3618 January–February 24, 1903
FO 27 3619 February 25–April 4, 1903
FO 27 3620 April 7–May 1903
FO 27 3621 June–July 10, 1903
FO 27 3622 July 11–September 17, 1903
FO 27 3623 September 18–November 15, 1903

FO 27 3624 November 16–December 1903
FO 27 3664 January–March 1904
FO 27 3665 March 7–May 12, 1904
FO 27 3666 May 13–July 18, 1904
FO 27 3667 July 20–October 1904
FO 27 3668 November–December 1904

General Correspondence, Russia
FO 418 38 January–June 1907
FO 418 39 July–December 1907

Other
Cab 21, Minutes of the CID, September 18, 1902–November 24, 1905, meetings 1–82;
Cab 4, 1 Imperial Defence Misc., 2/28/1903–11/4/1905;
Cab 4, vol. II 51b–100b, 1905–1906
FO 881 9130 Russia, Select Correspondence, Memo Respecting Anglo-Russian Convention, 1/29/1908

Archives Diplomatiques, Ministère des Affaires Étrangères, Paris, France

Correspondance Politique, 1871–1896: Russie
vol. 287 January–March 1890 (Laboulaye, Le Cte de Vauvineux)
vol. 288 April–June 1890 (Laboulaye, Le Cte de Vauvineux)
vol. 289 July–September 1890 (Laboulaye, Le Cte de Vauvineux)
vol. 290 October–December 1890 (Laboulaye, Le Cte de Vauvineux)
vol. 291 January–March 1891 (Laboulaye, Le Cte de Vauvineux)
vol. 292 April–June 1891 (Laboulaye, Le Cte de Vauvineux)

Livres Jaunes 262
L'alliance franco-russe: Origines de l'alliance 1890–1893, Convention militaire, 1892–1899 et convention navale 1912

Correspondance Politique et Commerciale, 1897–1918: Grande-Bretagne
NS 14 Relations avec France July–December 1903
NS 15 Relations avec France January–March 24, 1904
NS 16 Relations avec France March 25–April 8, 1904
NS 17 Relations avec France April 9–26, 1904

Papiers Delcassé
Carton 8: D. France-Angleterre, t. 14.

Archivio Storico Diplomatico, Ministèro degli Affari Èsteri, Rome, Italy

Inventario delle Rappresentanze Diplomatiche
Parte Prima: Rappresentanza Italiana a Berlino, 1867–1943
Legazione d'Italia a Berlino
Legazione d'Italia a Stoccarda
Busta n. 44 (1882) (Negotiations for the Triple Alliance)

Busta n. 57 (1886) (Launay's reports and private correspondence)
Busta n. 60 (1887) (Launay's correspondence and reports)
Busta n. 75 (1892) (Correspondence Launay-Rudini; reaction of the press to the Triple Alliance)
Busta n. 100 (1901–1902) (Renewal of the Triple Alliance)
Busta n. 114 (1913) (The Triple Alliance)
Parte Seconda: Rappresentanza Italiana a Vienna (1862–1938)
Legazione d'Italia a Vienna
Ambasciata d'Italia a Vienna
Busta n. 118 (1882) (Affairs in General, January–December)
Busta n. 197 (1908) (Correspondence on the succession of Italian subjects in Trieste)
Busta n. 215 (1911) (Incidents to the King's Italian subjects in Austria; emigres in Austria)

Indice dell'archivio segreto di gabinetto (1869–1914)

Cassette Verdi
Cassetta 1: Triple Alliance, 1887–1900
Cassetta 2: Triple Alliance and Relations with England, 1893–1896
Cassetta 3: Triple Alliance and General Policy, 1901–1907
Cassetta 4: Triple Alliance, 1906–1913
Cassetta 5: Miscellaneous, 1890–1914
Cassetta 8: Secret Accords, 1888–1891

Hoover Institution Archives

Nikolai Aleksandrovich Bazili Papers, 1881–1959, Boxes 1, 2, 11, 12
Bertram Cadwalader Papers, 1918–1929
Great Britain, Foreign Office, *Britain's Share in the War*, 1916
Louis, Loucheur Papers, 1872–1931, Boxes 2, 9–12
Antonio Salandra Speech, 1914
William II, Correspondence, 1925

PUBLISHED PRIMARY SOURCES

Andrássy, Count Julius. *Diplomacy and the War*. Translated by J. Holroyd Reece. London: John Bale, Sons and Danielsson, 1921.
———. *Bismarck, Andrássy, and Their Successors*. Boston: Houghton Mifflin, 1927.
Bismarck, Otto von. *Bismarck: The Man and the Statesman*. Vol. 2. New York: Harper and Brothers, 1898.
Cambon, Paul. *Correspondance 1870–1924*. Vol. 2, *1898–1911*. Paris: B. Grasset, c. 1940–46.
Crispi, Francesco. *The Memoirs of Francesco Crispi*. Vol. 2, *The Triple Alliance*. New York: Hodder and Stoughton, 1912.
France. *Documents Diplomatiques Français, 1871–1914*. Paris: Impr. Nationale, 1929–59.
George, David Lloyd. *War Memoirs*. Vol. 4. Boston: Little Brown, 1933–37.
Germany. *German Diplomatic Documents, 1871–1914*. London: Methuen, 1928.
Gooch, G. P., and Harold Temperley. *British Documents on the Origins of the War, 1898–*

1914. Vol. 4, *The Anglo-Russian Rapprochement, 1903–1907*. London: His Majesty's Government Printing Office, 1928.

Hurst, Michael, ed. *Key Treaties for the Great Powers, 1814–1914*. Vol. 2, *1871–1914*. New York: St. Martin's Press, 1972.

Joffre, Joseph Jacques C. *The Memoirs of Marshal Joffre*. Translated by T. Bentley Mott. London: Geoffrey Bles, 1932.

Krasnyi Arkhiv. Moscow: Gospolitizdat, 1922–41.

Ludendorff, Erich. *My War Memories*. Vols. 1 and 2. London: Hutchinson, 1919.

Pribram, Alfred Franzis. *The Secret Treaties of Austria-Hungary, 1879–1914*. 2 vols. English ed. by Archibald Cary Coolidge. Cambridge: Harvard University Press, 1920–21.

Salandra, Antonio. *Italy and the Great War*. London: Edward Arnold, 1932.

Sazonov, Serge. *Fateful Years, 1909–1916*. London: J. Cape, 1928.

Schreiner, George Abel. *Entente Diplomacy and the World*. New York: Knickerbocker Press, 1921.

Simpson, J. Y. *The Saburov Memoirs or Bismarck and Russia*. New York: MacMillan, 1929.

Stevenson, David, ed. *British Documents on Foreign Affairs—Reports and Papers from the Foreign Office Confidential Print*. Part I, *From the Mid-Nineteenth Century to the First World War. Series F, Europe, 1848–1914*. Frederick, Md.: University Publications of America, 1987.

Vitte, S. IU. *The Memoirs of Count Witte*. Translated and edited by Sidney Harcave. Vol. 3. Armonk, N.Y.: M. E. Sharpe, 1990.

William II. *The Kaiser's Letters to the Tsar*, brought from Russia by Isaac D. Levine. London: Hodder and Stoughton, 1920.

BOOKS AND MONOGRAPHS

Albertini, Luigi. *The Origins of the War of 1914*. Vol. 1. London: Oxford University Press, 1952.

Albrecht-Carrié, René. *France, Europe and the Two World Wars*. Geneva: Librairie E. Proz, 1960.

———. *Britain and France: Adaptations to a Changing Context of Power*. Garden City, N.Y.: Doubleday, 1970.

Andrew, Christopher M. *Théophile Delcassé and the Making of the Entente Cordiale: A Reappraisal of French Foreign Policy 1898–1905*. London: Macmillan, 1968.

Asprey, Robert B. *The German High Command at War: Hindenburg and Ludendorff Conduct World War I*. New York: William Morrow, 1991.

Bagdasarian, Nicholas Der. *The Austro-German Rapprochement, 1870–1879*. London: Associated University Presses, 1976.

Benedetti, Count. *Studies in Diplomacy*. New York: MacMillan, 1896.

Biersteker, Thomas J., and Cynthia Weber, eds. *State Sovereignty as Social Construct*. Cambridge: Cambridge University Press, 1996.

Birch, R. C. *Britain and Europe 1871–1939*. Oxford: Pergamon Press, 1966.

Bosworth, R. J. B. *Italy, the Least of the Great Powers: Italian Foreign Policy before the First World War*. London: Cambridge University Press, 1979.

———. *Italy and the Approach of the First World War*. London: MacMillan, 1983.

Boulding, Kenneth E. *Conflict and Defense: A General Theory*. New York: Harper, 1962.

Bueno de Mesquita, Bruce. *The War Trap*. New Haven, Conn.: Yale University Press, 1981.

Carroll, E. Malcolm. *French Public Opinion and Foreign Affairs, 1870–1914*. New York: Century, 1931.

————. *Germany and the Great Powers, 1866–1914*. New York: Prentice-Hall, 1938.

Cha, Victor D. *Alignment Despite Antagonism: The United States-Korea-Japan Security Triangle*. Stanford, Calif.: Stanford University Press, 1999.

Chiala, Luigi. *La triplice e la duplice alleanza (1881–1897)*. Torino: Roux Frassati, 1898.

Churchill, Rogers Platt. *The Anglo-Russian Convention of 1907*. Cedar Rapids, Iowa: Torch Press, 1939.

Claude, Inis L. *Power and International Relations*. New York: Random House, 1962.

Cline, Ray S. *World Power Assessment 1977: A Calculus of Strategic Drift*. Boulder, Colo.: Westview Press, 1977.

Coolidge, Archibald Cary. *Origins of the Triple Alliance*. New York: Charles Scribner's Sons, 1919.

Corti, Count Egon. *The Downfall of Three Dynasties*. Translated by L. Marie Sieveking and Ian F. D. Morrow. London: Methuen, 1934.

Coser, Lewis A. *Functions of Social Conflict*. London: Routledge and Kegan Paul, 1968.

Craig, Gordon A. *The Politics of the Prussian Army, 1640–1945*. Oxford: Clarendon Press, 1964.

————. *Europe, 1815–1914*. New York: Holt, Rinehart, and Winston, 1968.

————. *Germany, 1866–1945*. New York: Oxford University Press, 1978.

Crawford, Beverly, ed. *The Future of European Security*. Berkeley: University of California Center for German and European Studies, 1992.

Dahlin, Ebba. *French and German Public Opinion on Declared War Aims, 1914–1918*. Stanford, Calif.: Stanford University Press, 1933.

Dallin, Alexander, Merritt Abrash, Gifford D. Malone, Michael Boro Petrovich, James M. Potts, and Alfred J. Rieber. *Russian Diplomacy and Eastern Europe, 1914–1917*. New York: King's Crown Press, 1963.

David, Steven R. *Choosing Sides: Alignment and Realignment in the Third World*. Baltimore: Johns Hopkins University Press, 1991.

Deák, István. *Beyond Nationalism: A Social and Political History of the Habsburg Office Corps, 1848–1918*. New York: Oxford University Press, 1990.

de Manteyer, G. ed. *Austria's Peace Offer, 1916–1917*. London: Constable, 1921.

Deutsch, Karl W. *Political Community and the North Atlantic Area*. Princeton, N.J.: Princeton University Press, 1957.

Dockrill, Michael, and David French, eds. *Strategy and Intelligence: British Policy during the First World War*. London: Hambledon Press, 1996.

Downs, George, ed. *Collective Security Beyond the Cold War*. Ann Arbor: University of Michigan Press, 1994.

Duffield, John S. *Power Rules: The Evolution of NATO's Conventional Force Posture*. Stanford, Calif.: Stanford University Press, 1995.

Earle, Edward Mead, ed. *Makers of Modern Strategy: Military Thought from Machiavelli to Hitler*. Princeton, N.J.: Princeton University Press, 1941.

Farrar, L. L., Jr. *The Short War Illusion: German Policy, Strategy, and Domestic Affairs August–December 1914*. Santa Barbara, Calif.: Clio Press, 1973.

———. *Divide and Conquer: German Efforts to Conclude a Separate Peace, 1914–1918*. Boulder, Colo.: East European Quarterly, 1978.

Fay, Sidney Bradshaw. *The Origins of the World War*. 2nd ed. rev. New York: MacMillan, 1930.

Fischer, Fritz. *Germany's Aims in the First World War*. New York: W. W. Norton, 1967.

Fox, W. T. R., ed. *Theoretical Aspects of International Relations*. Notre Dame, Ind.: University of Notre Dame Press, 1959.

French, David. *British Strategy and War Aims, 1914–1916*. London: Allen and Unwin, 1986.

———. *The Strategy of the Lloyd George Coalition*. Oxford: Clarendon Press, 1995.

Friedman, Julian R., Christopher Bladen, and Steven Rosen. *Alliance in International Politics*. Boston: Allyn and Bacon, 1970.

Gilbert, Martin, and Arthur Banks. *First World War Atlas*. London: Weidenfeld and Nicholson, 1970.

Gochman, Charles S., and Alan Ned Sabrosky, eds. *Prisoners of War?: Nation-States in the Modern Era*. Lexington, Mass.: Lexington Books, 1990.

Goemans, Hein Erich. *War and Punishment: The Causes of War Termination and the First World War*. Princeton, N.J.: Princeton University Press, 2000.

Golovine, Lieutenant-General Nicholas N. *The Russian Army in the World War*. New Haven, Conn.: Yale University Press, 1931.

Gooch, George Peabody. *History of Modern Europe, 1878–1919*. New York: Henry Holt, 1930.

Gottlieb, Wolfram Wilhelm. *Studies in Secret Diplomacy during the First World War*. London: Allen and Unwin, 1957.

Groennings, Sven, E. W. Kelley, and Michael Leiserson, eds. *The Study of Coalition Behavior*. New York: Holt, Rinehart, and Winston, 1970.

Guinn, Paul. *British Strategy and Politics, 1914 to 1918*. Oxford: Clarendon Press, 1965.

Hardach, Gerd. *The First World War, 1914–1918*. London: Allen Lane, 1977.

Harris, David. *A Diplomatic History of the Balkan Crisis of 1875–1878*. Stanford, Calif.: Stanford University Press, 1936.

Herwig, Holger H. *The First World War: Germany and Austria-Hungary, 1914–1918*. London: Arnold, 1997.

Holsti, Ole R., P. Terrence Hopmann, and John D. Sullivan. *Unity and Disintegration in International Alliances: Comparative Case Studies*. New York: John Wiley and Sons, 1973.

Hunt, Barry, and Adrian Preston, eds. *War Aims and Strategic Policy in the Great War*. London: Croom Helm, 1977.

Ikenberry, G. John. *After Victory: Institutions, Strategic Restraint, and the Rebuilding of Order after Major Wars*. Princeton, N.J.: Princeton University Press, 2001.

Jelavich, Barbara. *The Habsburg Empire in European Affairs, 1814–1918*. Chicago: Rand McNally, 1969.

Jervis, Robert. *Perception and Misperception in International Politics*. Princeton, N.J.: Princeton University Press, 1976.

⸺. *System Effects: Complexity in Political and Social Life.* Princeton, N.J.: Princeton University Press, 1997.

Jervis, Robert, and Jack Snyder, eds. *Dominoes and Bandwagons: Strategic Beliefs and Great Power Competition in the Eurasian Rimland.* New York: Oxford University Press, 1991.

Joll, James. *The Origins of the First World War.* London: Longman, 1984.

Kann, Robert A., Béla K. Király, and Paula S. Fichtner, eds. *The Habsburg Empire in World War I.* Boulder, Colo.: East European Quarterly, 1977.

Katzenstein, Peter J., ed. *The Culture of National Security: Norms and Identity in World Politics.* New York: Columbia University Press, 1996.

Keiger, John F. V. *France and the Origins of the First World War.* London: MacMillan, 1983.

Kennan, George F. *The Decline of Bismarck's European Order: Franco-Russian Relations, 1875–1890.* Princeton, N.J.: Princeton University Press, 1979.

⸺. *The Fateful Alliance: France, Russia, and the Coming of the First World War.* New York: Pantheon Press, 1984.

Kennedy, Paul M., ed. *The War Plans of the Great Powers, 1880–1914.* Boston: Unwin Hyman, 1985.

Keohane, Robert O. *International Institutions and State Power: Essays in International Relations Theory.* Boulder, Colo.: Westview Press, 1989.

Lakatos, Imre, and Alan Musgrave, eds. *Criticism and the Growth of Knowledge.* Vol. 4. Cambridge: Cambridge University Press, 1970.

Lake, David A. *Entangling Relations: American Foreign Policy in Its Century.* Princeton, N.J.: Princeton University Press, 1999.

Langer, William L. *European Alliances and Alignments, 1871–1890.* 2nd ed. New York: Alfred A. Knopf, 1962.

⸺. *The Franco-Russian Alliance, 1890–1894.* New York: Octagon Books, 1967.

⸺. *The Diplomacy of Imperialism.* New York: Alfred A. Knopf, 1968.

Liddell Hart, Sir Basil Henry. *Strategy: The Indirect Approach.* London: Faber and Faber, 1967.

Liska, George. *Nations in Alliance: The Limits of Interdependence.* Baltimore: Johns Hopkins University Press, 1962.

MacKenzie, David. *The Serbs and Russian Pan-Slavism, 1875–1878.* Ithaca, N.Y.: Cornell University Press, 1967.

May, Arthur J. *The Hapsburg Monarchy, 1867–1914.* Cambridge: Harvard University Press, 1951.

⸺. *The Passing of the Hapsburg Monarchy 1914–1918.* 2 vols. Philadelphia: University of Pennsylvania Press, 1966.

McDonald, David MacLauren. *United Government and Foreign Policy in Russia, 1900–1914.* Cambridge: Harvard University Press, 1992.

Medlicott, W. N. *The Congress of Berlin and After.* London: Methuen, 1938.

Michon, Georges. *The Franco-Russian Alliance: 1891–1917.* New York: Howard Fertig, 1969.

Monger, George. *The End of Isolation: British Foreign Policy 1900–1907.* London: Thomas Nelson and Sons, 1963.

Neilson, Keith. *Strategy and Supply: The Anglo-Russian Alliance 1914–1917*. London: George Allen and Unwin, 1984.

———. *Britain and the Last Tsar*. Oxford: Oxford University Press, 1995.

Niou, Emerson M. S., Peter C. Ordeshook, and Gregory F. Rose. *The Balance of Power: Stability in International Systems*. Cambridge: Cambridge University Press, 1989.

Pares, Richard, and A. J. P. Taylor, eds. *Essays Presented to Sir Lewis Namier*. London: MacMillan, 1956.

Parker, Lillian, and William C. Askew, eds. *Power, Public Opinion and Diplomacy*. Durham, N.C.: Duke University Press, 1959.

Parr, John Francis. "Théophile Delcassé and the Practice of the Franco-Russian Alliance, 1898–1905." Doctoral thesis, University of Fribourg, Switzerland, 1951.

Philpott, William James. *Anglo-French Relations and Strategy on the Western Front, 1914–1918*. London: MacMillan Press, 1996.

Pribram, Alfred Franzis. *Austrian Foreign Policy, 1908–1918*. London: George Allen and Unwin, 1923.

Reiter, Dan. *Crucible of Beliefs: Learning, Alliances, and World Wars*. Ithaca, N.Y.: Cornell University Press, 1996.

Richardson, Louise. *When Allies Differ: Anglo-American Relations during the Suez and Falklands Crises*. New York: St. Martin's Press, 1996.

Risse-Kappen, Thomas. *Cooperation among Democracies: The European Influence on U.S. Foreign Policy*. Princeton, N.J.: Princeton University Press, 1995.

Ritter, Gerhard. *The Sword and the Sceptre*. Vols. 1–4. London: Allen Lane Penguin Press, 1972.

Rolo, Paul J. V. *Entente Cordiale: The Origins and Negotiation of the Anglo-French Agreements of 8 April 1904*. London: MacMillan, 1969.

Rosenberg, Arthur. *Imperial Germany: The Birth of the German Republic, 1871–1918*. 1931. Reprint, New York: Oxford University Press, 1970.

Rothwell, V. H. *British War Aims and Peace Diplomacy 1914–1918*. Oxford: Clarendon Press, 1971.

Rupp, George Hoover. *A Wavering Friendship: Russia and Austria 1876–1878*. Cambridge: Harvard University Press, 1941.

Rutherford, Ward. *The Russian Army in World War I*. London: Gordon Cremonesi, 1975.

Sabrosky, Alan Ned, ed. *Polarity and War: The Changing Structure of International Conflict*. Boulder, Colo.: Westview Press, 1985.

———, ed. *Alliances in U.S. Foreign Policy: Issues in the Quest for Collective Defense*. Boulder, Colo.: Westview Press, 1988.

Salvatorelli, Luigi. *La triplice alleanza storica diplomatica, 1877–1912*. Torino: Instituto per gli studi di politica internazionale, 1939.

Schmitt, Bernadotte E. *Triple Alliance and Triple Entente*. New York: Henry Holt, 1934.

Schweller, Randall L. *Deadly Imbalances: Tripolarity and Hitler's Strategy of World Conquest*. New York: Columbia University Press, 1998.

Seymour, Charles. *The Diplomatic Background of the War, 1870–1914*. New Haven, Conn.: Yale University Press, 1916.

Shanafelt, Gary W. *The Secret Enemy: Austria-Hungary and the German Alliance, 1914–1918*. New York: Columbia University Press, 1985.

Silberstein, Gerald E. *The Troubled Alliance: German-Austrian Relations 1914 to 1917*. Lexington: University Press of Kentucky, 1970.

Singer, J. David, ed. *The Correlates of War*. Vol. 2. New York: Free Press, 1980.

Siverson, Randolph M., and Harvey Starr. *The Diffusion of War: A Study of Opportunity and Willingness*. Ann Arbor: University of Michigan Press, 1991.

Smith, C. Jay. *The Russian Struggle for Power, 1914–1917*. New York: Philosophical Library, 1956.

Snyder, Glenn. *Alliance Politics*. Ithaca, N.Y.: Cornell University Press, 1997.

Snyder, Jack. *The Ideology of the Offensive: Military Decision Making and the Disasters of 1914*. Ithaca, N.Y.: Cornell University Press, 1984.

———. *Myths of Empire: Domestic Politics and International Ambition*. Ithaca, N.Y.: Cornell University Press, 1991.

Stevenson, David. *French War Aims against Germany, 1914–1919*. Oxford: Clarendon Press, 1982.

———. *The First World War and International Politics*. Oxford: Oxford University Press, 1988.

Stone, Norman. *The Eastern Front, 1914–1917*. New York: Charles Scribner's Sons, 1975.

Sumner, B. H. *Russia and the Balkans, 1870–1880*. London: Archon Books, 1962.

Tardieu, André. *France and the Alliances: The Struggle for the Balance of Power*. New York: MacMillan, 1908.

Taylor, A. J. P. *The Struggle for Mastery in Europe, 1848–1918*. Oxford: Clarendon Press, 1954.

———. *Bismarck: The Man and the Statesman*. New York: Alfred A. Knopf, 1955.

Tomes, James. *Balfour and Foreign Policy: The International Thought of a Conservative Statesman*. Cambridge: Cambridge University Press, 1997.

Tunstall, Graydon. *Planning for War against Russia and Serbia: Austro-Hungarian and German Military Strategies, 1871–1914*. Boulder, Colo.: Social Science Monographs, 1993.

Wade, Rex A. *The Russian Search for Peace, February–October 1917*. Stanford, Calif.: Stanford University Press, 1969.

Waites, Neville, ed. *Troubled Neighbors: Franco-British Relations in the Twentieth Century*. London: Weidenfeld and Nicolson, 1971.

Waller, Bruce. *Bismarck at the Crossroads: The Reorientation of German Foreign Policy after the Congress of Berlin, 1878–1880*. London: University of London at the Athlone Press, 1974.

Walt, Stephen. *The Origins of Alliances*. Ithaca, N.Y.: Cornell University Press, 1987.

Waltz, Kenneth N. *Theory of International Politics*. Reading, Mass.: Addison-Wesley, 1979.

Ward, Michael Don. *Research Gaps in Alliance Dynamics*. Denver: Graduate School of International Studies, University of Denver, 1982.

Weber, Frank G. *Eagles on the Crescent: Germany, Austria, and the Diplomacy of the Turkish Alliance, 1914–1918*. Ithaca, N.Y.: Cornell University Press, 1970.

White, John Albert. *Transition to Global Rivalry: Alliance Diplomacy and the Quadruple Alliance, 1895–1907.* Cambridge: Cambridge University Press, 1995.

Williamson, Samuel R., Jr. *The Politics of Grand Strategy: Britain and France Prepare for War, 1904–1914.* Cambridge: Harvard University Press, 1969.

———. *Austria-Hungary and the Origins of the First World War.* London: MacMillan, 1991.

Wilson, Keith M., ed. *British Foreign Secretaries and Foreign Policy,* London: Croom Helm: 1987.

———. *The Policy of the Entente: Essays on the Determinants of British Foreign Policy 1904–1914.* New York: Cambridge University Press, 1985.

Wolfers, Arnold. *Discord and Collaboration.* Baltimore: Johns Hopkins University Press, 1962.

Zeman, Z. A. B. *A Diplomatic History of the First World War.* London: Weidenfeld and Nicholson, 1971. (This book was also published under the title *The Gentlemen Negotiators.* New York: MacMillan, 1971.)

ARTICLES AND BOOK CHAPTERS

Abrash, Merrit. "War Aims Toward Austria Hungary: The Czechoslovak Pivot." In Alexander Dallin, Merritt Abrash, Gifford D. Malone, Michael Boro Petrovich, James M. Potts, and Alfred J. Rieber, *Russian Diplomacy and Eastern Europe, 1914–1917,* 78–123. New York: King's Crown Press, 1963.

Adler, Emanuel. "Europe's New Security Order: A Pluralistic Security Community." In Beverly Crawford, ed., *The Future of European Security,* 287–326. Berkeley: University of California Center for German and European Studies, 1992.

Altfeld, Michael F. "The Decision to Ally: A Theory and Test." *Western Political Quarterly* 37.4 (December 1984): 523–44.

Andrew, Christopher M. "The Entente Cordiale from Its Origins to 1914." In Neville Waites, ed., *Troubled Neighbors: Franco-British Relations in the Twentieth Century,* 11–39. London: Weidenfeld and Nicolson, 1971.

Askew, William C. "Austro-Italian Antagonism, 1896–1914." In Lillian Parker and William C. Askew, eds., *Power, Public Opinion and Diplomacy,* 172–221. Durham, N.C.: Duke University Press, 1959.

Axelrod, Robert, and D. Scott Bennett. "A Landscape Theory of Aggregation." *British Journal of Political Science* 23, part 2 (April 1993): 211–33.

Bennett, D. Scott. "Testing Alternative Models of Alliance Duration, 1816–1984." *American Journal of Political Science* 41.3 (July 1997): 846–78.

Betts, Richard. "Systems for Peace or Causes of War? Collective Security, Arms Control, and the New Europe." *International Security* 17.1 (summer 1992): 5–43.

Bremer, Stuart A. "National Capabilities and War Proneness." In J. David Singer, ed., *The Correlates of War: II,* 57–82. New York: Free Press, 1980.

Brody, Richard A. "Some Systemic Effects of the Spread of Nuclear Weapons Technology." *Journal of Conflict Resolution* 7.4 (December 1963): 663–753.

Chernoff, Fred. "Stability and Alliance Cohesion." *Journal of Conflict Resolution* 34.1 (March 1990): 92–101.

Christensen, Thomas J. "Perceptions and Alliances in Europe." *International Organization* 51.1 (winter 1997): 65–97.

Christensen, Thomas J., and Jack Snyder. "Chain Gangs and Passed Bucks: Predicting Alliance Patterns in Multipolarity." *International Organization* 44.2 (spring 1990): 137–68.

———. "Progressive Research on Degenerate Alliances." *American Political Science Review* 91.4 (December 1997): 919–22.

Conybeare, John A. C. "A Portfolio Diversification Model of Alliances: The Triple Alliance and Triple Entente, 1879–1914." *Journal of Conflict Resolution* 36.1 (March 1992): 53–85.

———. "Arms versus Alliances: The Capital Structure of Military Enterprise." *Journal of Conflict Resolution* 38.2 (June 1994): 215–35.

———. "The Portfolio Benefits of Free Riding in Military Alliances." *International Studies Quarterly* 38.3 (September 1994): 405–19.

Craig, Gordon A. "The World War I Alliance of the Central Powers in Retrospect: The Military Cohesion of the Alliance." *Journal of Modern History* 37.3 (September 1965): 336–44.

Deudney, Daniel H. "The Philadelphian System: Sovereignty, Arms Control, and Balance of Power in the American States-Union, circa 1787–1861." *International Organization* 49.2 (spring 1995): 191–228.

———. "Binding Sovereigns: Authorities, Structures, and Geopolitics in Philadelphian Systems." In Thomas J. Biersteker and Cynthia Weber, eds., *State Sovereignty as Social Construct*, 190–239. Cambridge: Cambridge University Press, 1996.

DeWeerd, Harvey A. "Churchill, Lloyd George, Clemenceau: The Emergence of the Civilian." In Edward Mead Earle, ed., *Makers of Modern Strategy: Military Thought from Machiavelli to Hitler*, 287–305. Princeton, N.J.: Princeton University Press, 1943.

Doyle, Michael W. "Liberalism and World Politics." *American Political Science Review* 80.4 (December 1986): 1151–69.

Duffield, John S. "International Regimes and Alliance Behavior: Explaining NATO Conventional Force Levels." *International Organization* 46.4 (autumn 1992): 818–55.

———. "NATO's Functions after the Cold War." *Political Science Quarterly* 109.5 (winter 1994–95): 763–87.

Elman, Colin, and Miriam Fendius Elman. "Lakatos and Neorealism: A Reply to Vasquez." *American Political Science Review* 91.4 (December 1997): 923–26.

———. "How Not to Be Lakatos Intolerant: Appraising Progress in IR Research." *International Studies Quarterly* 46.2 (June 2002): 231–62.

Fest, W. B. "British War Aims and German Peace Feelers during the First World War (December 1916–November 1918)." *Historical Journal* 15.2 (June 1972): 285–308.

Fischer, Fritz. "German War Aims 1914–1918 and German Policy before the War." In Barry Hunt and Adrian Preston, eds., *War Aims and Strategic Policy in the Great War*, 105–23. London: Croom Helm, 1977.

Gaubatz, Kurt Taylor. "Democratic States and Commitment in International Relations." *International Organization* 50.1 (winter 1996): 109–39.

Gauld, William A. "The 'Dreikaiserbündnis' and the Eastern Question 1871–1876." *English Historical Review* 40.158 (April 1925): 207–21.

————. "The 'Dreikaiserbündnis' and the Eastern Question, 1877–1878." *English Historical Review* 42.168 (October 1927): 560–68.

Gelpi, Christopher. "Alliances as Instruments of Intra-Allied Control." In Helga Haftendorn, Robert O. Keohane, and Celeste A. Wallander, eds., *Imperfect Unions*, 107–39. Oxford: Oxford University Press, 1999.

George, Alexander L. "Case Studies and Theory Development: The Method of Structured, Focused Comparison." In Paul Gordon Lauren, ed., *Diplomacy: New Approaches in History, Theory, and Policy*, 43–68. New York: Free Press, 1979.

Goriainov, Serge. "The End of the Alliance of the Emperors." *American Historical Review* 23.2 (January 1918): 324–44.

Grieco, Joseph M. "Understanding the Problem of International Cooperation: The Limits of Neoliberal Institutionalism and the Future of Realist Theory." In David A. Baldwin, ed., *Neorealism and Neoliberalism: The Contemporary Debate*, 301–38. New York: Columbia University Press, 1993.

————. "The Maastricht Treaty, Economic and Monetary Union and the Neo-Realist Research Programme." *Review of International Studies* 21.1 (January 1995): 21–40.

————. "State Interests and Institutional Rule Trajectories." *Security Studies* 5.3 (spring 1996): 261–306.

Haas, Ernst B. "The Balance of Power: Prescription, Concept, or Propaganda?" *World Politics* 5.4 (July 1953): 442–77.

Harknett, Richard J., and Jeffrey A. VanDenBerg. "Alignment Theory and Inter-related Threats: Jordan and the Gulf Crisis." *Security Studies* 6.3 (spring 1997): 112–53.

Hayes, Carlton Joseph Huntley. "The Fruition of Liberalism." In *A Generation of Materialism, 1871–1900*, 46–87. New York: Harper and Brothers, 1941.

Healy, Brian, and Arthur Stein. "The Balance of Power in International History." *Journal of Conflict Resolution* 17.1 (March 1973): 33–61.

Hellmann, Gunther, and Reinhard Wolf, "Neorealism, Neoliberal Institutionalism, and the Future of NATO." *Security Studies* 3.1 (autumn 1993): 3–43.

Herwig, Holger H. "Disjointed Allies: Coalition Warfare in Berlin and Vienna, 1914." *Journal of Military History* 54.3 (July 1990): 265–80.

Jervis, Robert. "Security Regimes." *International Organization* 36.2 (spring 1982): 357–78.

————. "From Balance to Concert: A Study of International Security Cooperation." In Kenneth A. Oye, ed., *Cooperation Under Anarchy*, 58–79. Princeton, N.J.: Princeton University Press, 1986.

Joffe, Josef. "'Bismarck' or 'Britain'? Toward an American Grand Strategy after Bipolarity." *International Security* 19.4 (spring 1995): 94–117.

Krebs, Ronald R. "Perverse Institutionalism: NATO and the Greco-Turkish Conflict." *International Organization* 53.2 (spring 1999): 343–77.

Lakatos, Imre. "Falsification and the Methodology of Scientific Research Programmes." In Imre Lakatos and Alan Musgrave, eds., *Criticism and the Growth of Knowledge*, 4: 91–195. Cambridge: Cambridge University Press, 1970.

Lake, David A. "Powerful Pacifists: Democratic States and War." *American Political Science Review* 86.1 (March 1992): 24–37.

————. "Beyond Anarchy: The Importance of Security Institutions." *International Security* 26.1 (summer 2001): 129–60.

Langer, William L. "The Franco-Russian Alliance (1890–1894)." *Slavonic and East European Review* 3.9 (March 1925): 554–75.

Larson, Deborah. "Bandwagon Images in American Foreign Policy." In Robert Jervis and Jack Snyder, eds., *Dominoes and Bandwagons: Strategic Beliefs and Great Power Competition in the Eurasian Rimland*, 85–111. New York: Oxford University Press, 1991.

Luvaas, Jay. "A Unique Army: The Common Experience." In Robert A. Kann, Béla K. Király, Paula S. Fichtner, eds., *The Habsburg Empire in World War I*, 87–103. Boulder, Colo.: East European Quarterly, 1977.

Malone, Gifford D. "War Aims toward Germany." In Alexander Dallin, Merritt Abrash, Gifford D. Malone, Michael Boro Petrovich, James M. Potts, and Alfred J. Rieber, *Russian Diplomacy and Eastern Europe, 1914–1917*, 124–61. New York: King's Crown Press, 1963.

McCalla, Robert B. "NATO's Persistence after the Cold War." *International Organization* 50.3 (summer 1996): 445–75.

McDonald, H. Brooke, and Richard Rosecrance, "Alliance and Structural Balance in the International System." *Journal of Conflict Resolution* 29.1 (March 1985): 57–82.

Medlicott, W. N. "Bismarck and the Three Emperors' Alliance 1881–1887." *Transactions of the Royal Historical Society*, Fourth Series, 27 (1945): 61–83.

Morgenthau, Hans J. "Alliances." In Julian R. Friedman, Christopher Bladen, and Steven Rosen, eds., *Alliance in International Politics*, 80–92. Boston: Allyn and Bacon, 1970.

Morrow, James D. "Alliances and Asymmetry: An Alternative to the Capability Aggregation Model of Alliances." *American Journal of Political Science* 35.4 (November 1991): 904–33.

————. "Arms versus Allies: Trade-offs in Search for Security." *International Organization* 47.2 (spring 1993): 207–34.

————. "Alliances, Credibility, and Peacetime Costs." *Journal of Conflict Resolution* 38.2 (June 1994): 270–97.

Mueller, Karl. "Patterns of Alliance: Alignment Balancing and Stability." *Security Studies* 5.1 (autumn 1995): 38–76.

NATO. "Defence Expenditures of NATO Countries 1975–1999." *NATO Review* 48.1 (spring 2000): D13–D16.

Neilson, Keith. "Managing the War: Britain, Russia and *Ad Hoc* Government." In Michael Dockrill and David French, eds., *Strategy and Intelligence: British Policy during the First World War*, 96–118. London: Hambledon Press, 1996.

Niou, Emerson M. S., and Peter C. Ordeshook. "Alliances in Anarchic International Systems." *International Studies Quarterly* 38.2 (June 1994): 167–91.

O'Leary, James. "Economic Relationships among the Allies: Sources of Cohesion and Tension." In Alan Ned Sabrosky, ed., *Alliances in U.S. Foreign Policy: Issues in the Quest for Collective Defense*, 41–56. Boulder, Colo.: Westview Press, 1988.

Oren, Ido. "The Indo-Pakistani Arms Competition: A Deductive and Statistical Analysis." *Journal of Conflict Resolution* 38.2 (June 1994): 185–214.

Possony, Stefan T., and Etienne Mantoux. "Du Picq and Foch: The French School."

In Edward Mead Earle, ed., *Makers of Modern Strategy: Military Thought from Machiavelli to Hitler*, 206–33. Princeton, N.J.: Princeton University Press, 1943.

Prete, Roy A. "French Military War Aims, 1914–1916." *Historical Journal* 28.4 (1985): 887–99.

Priess, David. "Balance of Threat Theory and the Genesis of the Gulf Cooperation Council: An Interpretative Case Study." *Security Studies* 5.4 (summer 1996): 143–71.

Ravenal, Earl C. "Extended Deterrence and Alliance Cohesion." In Alan Ned Sabrosky, ed., *Alliances in U.S. Foreign Policy: Issues in the Quest for Collective Defense*, 19–40. Boulder, Colo.: Westview Press, 1988.

Ray, James Lee. "Friends as Foes." In Charles S. Gochman and Alan Ned Sabrosky, eds., *Prisoners of War?: Nation-States in the Modern Era*, 73–91. Lexington, Mass.: Lexington Books, 1990.

Risse-Kappen, Thomas. "A Liberal Interpretation of the Transatlantic Security Community." In Peter J. Katzenstein, ed., *The Culture of National Security: Norms and Identity in World Politics*, 357–99. New York: Columbia University Press, 1996.

Rolo, Paul J. V. "Lansdowne." In Keith M. Wilson, ed., *British Foreign Secretaries and Foreign Policy*, 159–71. London: Croom Helm, 1987.

Rose, Gideon. "Neoclassical Realism and Theories of Foreign Policy." *World Politics* 51.1 (October 1998): 144–72.

Rosenberg, Arthur. "Social Forces under Bismarck." In *Imperial Germany: The Birth of the German Republic, 1871–1918*, 1–32. 1931; reprint, New York: Oxford University Press, 1970.

Rothenberg, Gunter E. "The Habsburg Army in the First World War: 1914–1918." In Robert A. Kann, Béla K. Király, and Paula S. Fichtner, eds., *The Habsburg Empire in World War I*, 73–86. Boulder, Colo.: East European Quarterly, 1977.

Sabrosky, Alan Ned. "Interstate Alliances: Their Reliability and the Expansion of War." In J. David Singer, ed., *The Correlates of War*. Vol. 2, 161–98. New York: Free Press, 1980.

Schroeder, Paul W. "Alliances, 1815–1945: Weapons of Power and Tools of Management." In Klaus Knorr, ed., *Historical Dimensions of National Security Problems*, 227–62. Lawrence: University Press of Kansas, 1976.

Schweller, Randall. "Bandwagoning for Profit: Bringing the Revisionist State Back In." *International Security* 19.1 (summer 1994): 72–107.

———. "New Realist Research on Alliances: Refining, Not Refuting, Waltz's Balancing Proposition." *American Political Science Review* 91.4 (December 1997): 927–30.

———. "The Concept of Alliance." Paper prepared for the Annual Meeting of the American Political Science Association, Atlanta, Georgia, September 1999.

Singer, J. David, and Melvin Small. "Formal Alliances, 1815–1939: A Quantitative Description." *Journal of Peace Research* 3.1 (1966): 1–32.

———. "Formal Alliances, 1816–1965: An Extension of the Basic Data." *Journal of Peace Research* 6.3 (1969): 257–82.

Siverson, Randolph M., and Juliann Emmons. "Birds of a Feather: Democratic Political Systems and Alliance Choices in the Twentieth Century." *Journal of Conflict Resolution* 35.2 (June 1991): 285–306.

Snyder, Glenn H. "The Security Dilemma in Alliance Politics." *World Politics* 36.4 (July 1984): 461–95.

Snyder, Jack. "Richness, Relevance, and Rigor in the Study of Soviet Foreign Policy." *International Security* 9.3 (winter 1984–85): 89–108.

Sorokin, Gerald L. "Alliance Formation and General Deterrence: A Game-Theoretic Model and the Case of Israel." *Journal of Conflict Resolution* 38.2 (June 1994): 298–325.

Stone, Norman. "Moltke and Conrad: Relations between the Austro-Hungarian and German General Staffs, 1909–1914." In Paul M. Kennedy, ed., *The War Plans of the Great Powers, 1880–1914*, 222–51. Boston: Unwin Hyman, 1985.

Taylor, A. J. P. "The War Aims of the Allies in the First World War." In Richard Pares and A. J. P. Taylor, eds., *Essays Presented to Sir Lewis Namier*, 475–505. London: MacMillan, 1956.

Vasquez, John A. "The Realist Paradigm and Degenerative versus Progressive Research Programs: An Appraisal of Neotraditional Research on Waltz's Balancing Proposition." *American Political Science Review* 91.4 (December 1997): 899–912.

Wallander, Celeste A. "Institutional Assets and Adaptability: NATO after the Cold War." *International Organization* 54.4 (autumn 2000): 705–35.

Wallander, Celeste A., and Robert O. Keohane. "Why Does NATO Persist? An Institutionalist Approach." March 1996, CFIA, Harvard University mimeo.

———. "Risk, Threat, and Security Institutions." In Helga Haftendorn, Robert O. Keohane, and Celeste A. Wallander, eds., *Imperfect Unions: Security Institutions over Time and Space*, 21–47. Oxford: Oxford University Press, 1999.

Wallander, Celeste A., Helga Haftendorn, and Robert O. Keohane. "Introduction." In Helga Haftendorn, Robert O. Keohane, and Celeste A. Wallander, eds., *Imperfect Unions: Security Institutions over Time and Space*, 1–18. Oxford: Oxford University Press, 1999.

Walt, Stephen. "Alliance Formation in Southwest Asia." In Robert Jervis and Jack Snyder, eds., *Dominoes and Bandwagons: Strategic Beliefs and Great Power Competition in the Eurasian Rimland*, 51–84. New York: Oxford University Press, 1991.

———. "Why Alliances Endure or Collapse." *Survival* 39.1 (spring 1997): 156–79.

———. "The Progressive Power of Realism." *American Political Science Review* 91.4 (December 1997): 931–35.

Waltz, Kenneth. "Evaluating Theories." *American Political Science Review* 91.4 (December 1997): 913–17.

Weber, Katja. "Hierarchy Amidst Anarchy: A Transaction Costs Approach to International Security Cooperation." *International Studies Quarterly* 41.2 (June 1997): 321–40.

Weitsman, Patricia A. "Alliance Cohesion and Coalition Warfare: The Central Powers and Triple Entente." *Security Studies* 12.3 (spring 2003).

Weitsman, Patricia A., and George E. Shambaugh. "International Systems, Domestic Structures, and Risk." *Journal of Peace Research* 39.3 (May 2002): 289–312.

Weitsman, Patricia A., and Michael D. Young. "Alliance Dynamics in the Old Europe: A Computational Model." Ohio University mimeo, 2003.

Williams, Beryl J. "The Strategic Background to the Anglo-Russian Entente of August 1907." *Historical Journal* 9.3 (1966): 360–73.

Wolfers, Arnold. "The Actors in International Politics." In W. T. R. Fox, ed., *Theoretical Aspects of International Relations*, 83–106. Notre Dame, Ind.: University of Notre Dame Press, 1959.

Zinnes, Dina A. "An Analytical Study of Balance of Power Theories." *Journal of Peace Research* 4.3 (September 1967): 270–88.

———. "Coalition Theories and the Balance of Power." In Sven Groennings, E. W. Kelley, and Michael Leiserson, eds., *The Study of Coalition Behavior*, 351–68. New York: Holt, Rinehart, and Winston, 1970.

Aehrenthal, Alois, 89
Agadir crisis, 131, 132, 134
Albania, 94, 140, 149, 201n130
Alexander II (tsar), 42, 54, 68, 76, 197n27
Alexeev, Mikhail, 160
Algeciras conference, 89, 116, 126, 134
Algeria, 87
alliance behavior: dangerous alliances, 171–
    75; during wartime, 5–7, 139–42, 150–
    54, 161–64, 166–67, 210n20, 212n73;
    peacetime and wartime compared, 168–
    70, 174. *See also* capability aggregation;
    commitment levels; peacetime alliances;
    threat levels; wartime alliances
alliance cohesion: balance of interests, 164,
    212n73, 214nn128,133; defined, 35–36,
    188n2, 192n57; during wartime, 31–33,
    37, 138, 169; external threats, 5–6, 24–
    27, 29–30, 114–17, 136; peacetime alli-
    ances, 6–7, 25, 31–33, 142–43, 150, 174,
    192n56; theories of, 5–7, 24–31, 35–36,
    188n7; and threat levels, 5–7, 24–27,
    26(tab.), 97(tab.), 114–17, 131–33,
    135(tab.), 150–53, 160–63, 166–68,
    167(tab.), 212n73, 213n86
alliance cohesion, case studies: Central
    Powers, 140, 142–51, 163, 167(tab.), 174,
    212n73; Dreikaiserbund, 47–52, 63(tab.);
    Dreikaiserbund II, 59–62, 63(tab.); Dual
    Alliance, 75, 76–78, 97(tab.), 167(tab.);
    Franco-Russian Alliance, 112, 113, 114–
    17, 135(tab.), 167(tab.); Leagues of the
    Three Emperors, 167(tab.); NATO, 174;
    Triple Alliance, 91–96, 97(tab.), 98,
    167(tab.); Triple Entente, 100, 132–34,
    135(tab.), 136, 152–62, 163, 167(tab.),
    213n86

alliance formation: colonial disputes, 105,
    119, 124, 125, 127, 132, 134; for political
    survival, 189n15; promise levels in, 35,
    47, 60, 193n67; theories of, 3–5, 17–24,
    29–31, 34–35; and threat levels, 3–5,
    18–19, 20(fig.), 22–24, 104, 117, 122,
    136, 165–66, 208n121. *See also* motiva-
    tions for alliances
alliance formation, case studies: Dreikaiser-
    bund, 40–47; Dreikaiserbund II, 53–57,
    66; Dual Alliance, 67–74, 97; Entente
    Cordiale, 116, 118, 119–24; Franco-
    Russian Alliance, 102–11, 203n21; Triple
    Alliance, 79–87, 97; Triple Entente, 96,
    99–130
alliance paradox, 2, 7, 99, 101, 136, 171,
    188n9
alliances: as conflict management tools, 80,
    96, 113, 118, 119, 135, 173; dangers of,
    7–8, 9; defined, 27, 188n1; endurance of,
    6, 13, 16–17, 26, 170–71, 188n4, 215n7;
    and ideology, 50, 52, 57, 60, 61, 95–96,
    113, 190n29; importance of, 1–3, 36;
    as security tools, 88, 90, 135; and third
    parties, 22, 191–92nn39,40,42, 208n121.
    See also power capability distribution;
    transparency
alliance theory, 11–37; balancing/balance
    of power, 4, 8, 12–15, 18, 20(fig.), 36,
    188n6; bandwagoning, 4, 12–13, 15,
    20(fig.), 30, 187n5, 189nn14,15, 190n16;
    cohesion, 5–7, 24–31, 35–36, 188n7;
    formation, 3–5, 17–24, 29–31, 34–35;
    hedging, 12–13, 20(fig.), 29–30; institu-
    tionalism, 16–17, 25–26; liberalism, 11,
    16, 25–26; military alliances, 1, 5, 8, 13;
    peacetime alliances, 31–33; power capa-

bilities, 13–14, 33–34, 189n8; purposes
of, 1–4, 7–9, 12–13, 27–29; rationalism, 15–16; realism, 11, 13–16, 98; security dilemma, 7, 188n7; studies of, 2–3,
11–13; tethering, 4, 12, 20(fig.), 21–24,
30, 187n2, 189n14; threat levels, 14–15,
20(fig.), 26(tab.), 29(tab.), 30, 33–36;
transparency, 4, 16; wartime alliances,
31–33, 37. *See also* capability aggregation; motivations for alliances
Allied Maritime Transport Council, 156
Allied Powers, 6, 26, 95
Alsace and Lorraine, 46, 51, 74, 106, 149,
158, 203n22. *See also* France
Andrássy, Julius, 67, 68, 72, 73
Anglo-Japanese Alliance, 118, 126
Anglo-Russian Convention (1907), 124–30;
as institutional alliance, 126; motives for,
124, 127, 130(tab.), 208n116; as tethering
alliance, 28, 100, 124–29, 130(tab.),
207nn95,105. *See also* Triple Entente
Antwerp, 155–56
Askew, William C., 201n130
Asquith, Herbert H., 154
Austria/Austria-Hungary: Austro-German
relations, 75, 139, 141, 145–50, 198–
99nn41,54, 212n73; Austro-Italian relations, 72–73, 80, 88–90, 92–95, 97;
Austro-Russian relations, 72–73, 102–3;
Balkan policy, 93–94, 133, 144, 201n130;
border data, 186(tab.); Franz Ferdinand
assassination, 137; Hohenlohe decrees,
94; Macedonian crisis, 88–89; military
strategy, 77, 78, 81, 84, 143–46, 199n74,
211n37; power capabilities, 45, 179–
85(tabs.), 195n54, 197n35, 200n104,
205n46, 209n134, 212–13n77; Schönbrunn Convention, 47; separate peace
offers from, 169; Treaty of Berlin, 60,
93, 133; Volhynia offensive, 145; World
War I, 140–51, 211n37
Austria/Austria-Hungary, alliance participation: Dreikaiserbund, 22, 27, 40–42,
45(tab.), 47(tab.); Dreikaiserbund II, 55,
57(tab.), 58, 59(tab.); Dual Alliance, 55,
56, 61, 62, 72–75, 74(tab.), 76(tab.), 165;
Leagues of the Three Emperors, 165;
Triple Alliance, 83–84, 87(tab.), 91(tab.),
193n67
Avarna, Guiseppe Gualtieri, Duc d', 81, 82
Axis Powers, 26

balance of interests, 164, 212n73,
214nn128,133
balance of power theory: concept of, 8, 13,
36; distribution of capabilities, 14, 188n6;
and Entente Cordiale, 119; threat levels
and, 14–15
balancing/balancing alliances: and alliance
cohesion, 26, 30, 166; commitment
levels, 29(tab.), 167; formation, 22, 30,
191n38; motivations for, 28, 29(tab.),
165, 208n121; theories of, 4, 12, 15, 18,
20(fig.)
balancing/balancing alliances, case studies:
Dreikaiserbund, 45(tab.); Dual Alliance,
71–73, 74(tab.), 98; Franco-Russian Alliance, 26, 98, 100, 101, 102, 105, 111(tab.),
114, 117, 203–4nn23,24; Leagues of the
Three Emperors, 45(tab.); Triple Alliance, 85, 87(tab.), 90; Triple Entente,
100, 130, 163, 164
Balfour, Arthur James, 121–22
Balkan League, 112
Balkans, the: annexation of Bosnia and
Herzegovina, 133; Dreikaiserbund, 41,
46, 47, 48; Dreikaiserbund II, 54, 55,
60; Dual Alliance, 72, 74, 77, 198n52;
Franco-Russian Alliance, 102, 108, 111;
Treaty of Berlin, 60, 93, 133; Triple Alli-
ance, 80, 81, 91, 93–94, 201n130; World
War I, 145, 148
Balkan Wars, 94, 112, 201–2n132
bandwagoning/bandwagoning alliances: co-
hesion, 30; commitment levels, 29(tab.);
formation, 18, 30, 190n32, 191nn34,35;
motives for, 28, 29(tab.), 166; theories
of, 4, 12–13, 15, 20(fig.), 30, 187n5,
189nn14,15, 190n16
Bavaria, 46
Beck-Rzikowsky, Frederick, 143
Belgium, 149
Berchtold, Leopold, 137
Bertie, Francis, 121, 125
Beust, Friedrich Ferdinand, 40
binding, 22–23
Bismarck, Herbert, 67–69, 95
Bismarck, Otto von: Dreikaiserbund, 43–
44, 49, 50–51; Dreikaiserbund II, 55–
57; Dual Alliance, 67, 69–75, 77, 196n3,
197–98nn27,39, 199n56; fall from power,
104–5; Reinsurance Treaty, 102–5; Triple
Alliance, 85, 86

Black Sea, 59, 155
Boer War, 116, 120
Boisdeffre, Raoul, 204–5n24
Bolshevik Party, 161. *See also* Russia
Bompard, Maurice, 125
borders, nature of, 186(tab.)
Bosnia and Herzegovina, 48–49, 55, 67, 78, 93, 131, 133–34, 144, 149
Bosporus, Straits of, 45–46, 49, 58, 60, 77–78, 156, 161
Boulanger, Georges, 201n109
Brest Litovsk, 138, 141, 145, 161
Bruck, Baron, 84
Brusilov offensive, 147
Bueno de Mesquita, Bruce, 5, 13, 188n4
Bulgaria: Dreikaiserbund, 49; Dreikaiserbund II, 55, 60–62; Dual Alliance, 72, 77, 198n47; Reinsurance Treaty, 104; World War I, 140, 145, 147, 161
Bülow, Bernhard Heinrich von, 43–44, 130
Burián, István, 147
Busch, Auguste, 85

Calais Conference, 157
Cambon, Paul, 122–23
capability aggregation: and alliance formation, 3, 8, 9, 14–18, 85, 97, 166; and cohesion, 24, 25, 167; commitment levels, 168; as threat, 172; for wartime alliances, 168. *See also* power capability distribution
Caporetto, 153
Catholicism, 51, 88, 95
Central Powers, 139–51; casualty figures (World War I), 140; cohesion, 140, 142–51, 163, 167(tab.), 174, 212n73; commitment levels, 167(tab.); Dual Alliance, 74, 76, 78, 198n52; and Franco-Russian Alliance, 203–4n24; military strategy, 143–46, 211n37; peace offers from, 149–50, 159; prominence of, 65; threat levels, 139–42, 164, 167(tab.), 169; Triple Alliance, 80, 85, 86, 90; war aims, 146–49, 158, 163, 211–12n47. *See also* Triple Alliance
Chamberlain, Joseph, 120, 125–26
Chernoff, Fred, 24
China, 172
Clemenceau, Georges, 150
cohesion. *See* alliance cohesion
Cold War, 1, 2, 11, 16, 26, 174

colonial disputes, and alliance formation, 105, 119, 124, 125, 127, 132, 134
commitment levels: alliance types, 29(tab.), 167; capability aggregation, 168; threat levels, 29(tab.), 166, 167(tab.)
Concert of Europe, 17, 39
Congress of Berlin, 47, 49–50, 54, 66–68, 80
Congress of Vienna, 79
Constantinople, 46, 49, 149, 158, 198n47
Constantinople Agreement (1915), 152
Correlates of War project, 34
Corti, Count Luigi, 49–50, 80
Crispi, Francesco, 84, 93, 95
Curzon, George Nathaniel, Marquis of, 162
Cyrenaica, 92
Czernin, Ottokar, 148, 149–50

Dardanelles, the, 46, 49, 58, 152, 156
David, Steven R., 189n15
Dawson, Douglas, 119–20
Deák, István, 210n21
Delcassé, Théophile, 122, 124–25, 126
Deudney, Daniel H., 22–23
Dogger Bank, 124
Dreikaiserbund, 39–53; as balancing alliance, 45(tab.); cohesion, 47–52; formation, 40–44; as hedging alliance, 45(tab.); and institutionalism, 17, 40–41; motives for, 45(tab.), 46–47; promise levels in, 47; role of third parties, 22; as tethering alliance, 45(tab.); threat levels, 44–46, 47(tab.); weaknesses, 52–53. *See also* Leagues of the Three Emperors
Dreikaiserbund II, 53–63; Bulgarian independence and, 55, 60–61, 62; cohesion, 59–62, 63(tab.); formation, 53–57, 66; motives for, 57(tab.), 58; power capabilities within, 41, 45, 195n54; promise levels, 60; threat levels, 57–58, 59(tab.); weaknesses, 62–63. *See also* Leagues of the Three Emperors
Dual Alliance, 66–79; as balancing alliance, 71–73, 74(tab.), 98; cohesion, 75–78, 97(tab.), 98, 166, 167(tab.); commitment levels, 167(tab.); formation, 61, 67–74, 97, 196n1; as hedging alliance, 72, 74(tab.), 98; and institutionalism, 17, 77, 79, 198n48; monarchical conservatism, 67, 75; motives for, 56, 74(tab.), 165; as

peacetime alliance, 65; power capabilities within, 197*n*35; in realist alliance theory, 98; strengths of, 75, 78–79, 198*n*41; terms of, 76; as threat, 102–3; threat levels, 74–75, 76(tab.), 97(tab.), 98, 166, 167(tab.), 168; World War I, 66, 138, 139

Dual Monarchy. *See* Austria/Austria-Hungary

East Prussia. *See* Prussia/East Prussia

Egypt, 116

England. *See* Great Britain

Entente Cordiale, 119–24; and alliance paradox, 188*n*9; formation of, 116, 118, 119–24; motives for, 28, 99, 124(tab.); as tethering alliance, 100, 121–23, 124(tab.). *See also* Triple Entente

European Coal and Steel Community, 21

external threats: behavior, 170–71, 215*n*7; cohesion, 5–6, 24–27, 26(tab.), 29–30, 114–17, 136, 150–51, 166–68, 212*n*73; commitment levels, 29(tab.), 167(tab.); formation, 12, 29–30. *See also* threat levels

external threats, case studies: Central Powers, 142, 150–51; Dreikaiserbund, 44–46; Dual Alliance, 74–75, 76(tab.); Franco-Russian Alliance, 111–13, 135(tab.); Leagues of the Three Emperors, 44–46; Triple Alliance, 80–88; Triple Entente, 100, 131–32, 135, 163, 164, 168

Falkenhayn, Erich von, 145

Fashoda crisis, 100, 116, 119, 122, 131

Fay, Sidney Bradshaw, 196*n*3, 198–99*nn*52,54, 201–2*n*132, 204*n*25

Fergusson, James, 107, 204*n*33

Foch, Ferdinand, 156

formation. *See* alliance formation

Founding Act (NATO), 23, 173

France: Anglo-French relations, 106, 119–20; border data, 186(tab.); Franco-German relations, 48, 51, 107–9, 201*n*109, 203*nn*22,23, 204*n*25; Franco-Italian relations, 84; military strategy, 112, 134, 154–57, 200*n*104; power capabilities, 45, 179–85(tabs.), 195*n*54, 197*n*35, 200*n*104, 205*n*46, 209*n*134, 212–13*n*77; Russo-Japanese War, 22; Schuman Plan, 21; as threat, 45–46, 48, 51, 74, 86–88, 90, 200*n*104, 201*n*109; threats to, 101–2;

World War I, 137, 140, 144, 149–50, 152–58

France, alliance participation: Entente Cordiale, 28, 116, 122–23, 124(tab.), 188*n*9; Franco-Russian Alliance, 17, 26, 98, 106–10, 111(tab.), 114(tab.), 122, 165, 196*nn*1,3; Military Convention, 112–18; Naval Convention, 112; Triple Entente, 118, 132(tab.), 165

Franco-Prussian War, 40, 46, 88

Franco-Russian Alliance, 101–18; and alliance theory, 171; as balancing alliance, 26, 98, 100–102, 105, 111(tab.), 114, 117, 203–4*nn*23,24; and Central Powers, 203–4*n*24; cohesion of, 112–17, 135(tab.), 166, 167(tab.); commitment levels, 167(tab.); formation of, 102–11, 196*n*3, 203*n*21; and institutionalism, 17; Military Convention, 112–13, 114; motives for, 111(tab.), 118, 165; Naval Convention, 112; power capabilities within, 205*n*46; terms of, 110, 114–17; as threat, 98, 119, 131; threat levels, 111–13, 114(tab.), 117, 135(tab.), 166, 167(tab.), 168. *See also* Triple Entente

Franz Ferdinand (archduke), 137

Franz Joseph (emperor), 42, 77, 94–95, 141

Freycinet, Charles, 105

Galicia, 140, 144, 147, 154, 156, 161

Gallipoli, 152

Gaubatz, Kurt Taylor, 215*n*7

Gelpi, Christopher, 16

Germany: Anglo-German relations, 118–23, 126, 206*n*84, 208*n*116; Austro-German relations, 75, 139, 141, 145–50, 198–99*nn*41,54, 212*n*73; Boer War, 116, 120, 126; border data, 186(tab.); Congress of Berlin, 47, 49–50, 54, 66–68, 80; Franco-German relations, 45, 48, 51, 107–9, 201*n*109, 203*nn*22,23, 204*n*25; Heligoland Treaty, 105; Kulturkampf/May Laws, 51; military strategy, 78, 104, 111–12, 131, 141, 143–46, 148, 155, 211*n*37; Mitteleuropa, 139, 147, 158; naval campaigns, 141, 148, 153, 155; "naval scare" (1908), 131; Nazi-Soviet Pact (1939), 21; power capabilities, 45, 179–85(tabs.), 195*n*54, 197*n*35, 200*n*104, 205*n*46, 209*n*134, 212–13*n*77; Reinsurance Treaty, 58, 62, 66, 77, 101, 111, 117,

196nn2,3, 198nn47,51,52; Russo-German relations, 66–69, 77, 102–5, 111, 114, 117, 127–29, 198nn47,51, 203–4n24, 208n121, 209nn122,131; Schuman Plan, 21; as threat, 112, 151–52, 164, 213n79; Treaty of Björkö, 128; Treaty of Non-aggression, 172; World War I, 139–51, 159, 161, 211n37, 211–12n47. *See also* Prussia / East Prussia

Germany, alliance participation: Dreikaiser-bund, 22, 27, 43–44, 45(tab.), 47(tab.), 48; Dreikaiserbund II, 56, 57(tab.), 58, 59(tab.), 66; Dual Alliance, 55–56, 61–62, 67–72, 74(tab.), 76(tab.), 165, 196n3; Leagues of the Three Emperors, 165; Triple Alliance, 84–86, 87(tab.), 91(tab.), 193n67

Gibralter, 124

Giers, Nicholas Karlovitch de, 41, 54–55, 104, 105–6, 203n21

Gladstone, William, 115

Goemans, Hein Erich, 211–12n47, 214n133, 215n6

Goriainov, Serge, 202n3

Great Britain: Anglo-French relations, 106, 119–20; Anglo-German relations, 118–19, 120–23, 126, 206n84, 208n116; Anglo-Italian relations, 107–9; Anglo-Japanese Alliance, 126; Anglo-Russian relations, 105–6, 120–26, 203nn16,17, 207n95,105; Boer War, 116, 120, 126; border data, 186(tab.); Heligoland Treaty, 105; Liberal party, 60, 126; military strategy, 100, 119–21, 134, 154–57, 158; "naval scare" (1908), 131; power capabilities, 179–85(tabs.), 195n54, 197n35, 200n104, 205n46, 209n134, 212–13n77; Russo-Japanese War, 22, 100; Russo-Turkish War, 48–49; as threat, 46, 98, 100, 106, 114(tab.); and Triple Alliance, 105, 108–10, 111, 118–21; World War I, 141–42, 152–58, 162

Great Britain, alliance participation: Anglo-Russian Convention, 100, 124–27, 130(tab.), 207n105; Entente Cordiale, 28, 116, 121–22, 124(tab.), 188n9; Triple Entente, 132(tab.), 165

Greece, 1, 16, 187n2

Grey, Edward, 127

Grieco, Joseph M., 22–23

Guchkov, Alexander, 160

Habsburg Empire, 41, 51, 89, 95–97, 140, 142, 147–49, 210n21

Haig, Douglas, 157

Haymerlé, Heinrich von, 55, 83, 85

hedging/hedging alliances: cohesion of, 29–30; commitment levels, 29(tab.), 167(tab.), 168; formation of, 18–21, 29, 191n37; motives for, 28, 29(tab.), 165; theories of, 12–13, 20(fig.), 29–30

hedging/hedging alliances, case studies: Dreikaiserbund, 43–44, 45(tab.); Dreikaiserbund II, 56–57; Dual Alliance, 72, 74(tab.), 98; Leagues of the Three Emperors, 45(tab.)

Heligoland Treaty, 105

Herbette, Jules, 107–10, 205n38

Herzegovina. *See* Bosnia and Herzegovina

Hindenburg Line, 142

Hindenburg, Paul von Benckendorf, 142, 145, 211n37

Hitler, Adolf, 21

Hohenborn, Wild von, 147

Hohenlohe decrees, 94

Holsti, Ole, 24

Holy Alliance (1815), 172

Hopmann, P. Terrence, 24

Hötzendorf, Franz Conrad von, 89–90, 137, 140, 142, 144–45

Humbert (king), 107

Hungary. *See* Austria/Austria-Hungary

ideology and alliance formation, 50, 52, 57, 60, 61, 190n29

Ikenberry, John, 23

India, 105, 125, 127

institutionalism: in alliance theory, 16–17, 25–27; Anglo-Russian Convention, 126; and cohesion, 25–27; Dreikaiserbund, 17, 40–41; Dual Alliance, 17, 77, 79, 198n48; and endurance, 170–71; and transparency, 27, 170; Triple Alliance, 17, 91, 92; Triple Entente, 208n121

Inter-Allied Shipping Committee, 156

Inter-Allied Supreme War Council, 156

internal threats: behavior, 170–71, 215n7; cohesion, 5–6, 25–27, 26(tab.), 29–30, 166–68; commitment levels, 29(tab.), 167(tab.); formation, 12, 29–30, 64. *See also* threat levels

internal threats, case studies: Central Powers, 142, 169; Dreikaiserbund, 46–47,

52–53, 63(tab.); Dreikaiserbund II, 57–
59, 62, 63(tab.); Dual Alliance, 75–76;
Franco-Russian Alliance, 113; Triple Alliance, 88–90, 94–95; Triple Entente, 100,
131, 135(tab.), 163, 168
irredentist movement, 41, 45, 79–81, 82,
94–95
Ismay, Hastings Lionel Ismay, Baron, 2
Italy: Anglo-Italian relations, 107–9; Austro-
Italian relations, 72–73, 80, 88–90, 92–
95, 97; border data, 186(tab.); Franco-
Italian relations, 84; irredentist movement,
41, 45, 79–81, 82, 94–95; Macedonian
crisis, 88–89; military planning, 90; power
capabilities, 45, 179–85(tabs.), 195n54,
197n35, 200n104, 205n46, 209n134; as
threat, 45; Tripoli annexation, 89–90;
World War I, 90, 95, 138, 141–42, 147,
149, 159, 211n37
Italy, Triple Alliance participation, 41–42,
79–83, 86, 87(tab.), 91(tab.), 165, 193n67
Izvolsky, Alexander, 129–30, 133, 209n131

Japan, 122, 127, 128, 129
Jervis, Robert, 188n9, 191–92nn37,39,40,42,
206n68
Joffre, Joseph, 156

Kálnoky, Gustav, 86, 92–93
Karl (emperor), 141, 148, 149–50, 169
Kerensky, Alexander, 161
Kiel Canal, 116, 206n64
Kitchener, Horatio Herbert, 156, 162
Krebs, Ronald, 16
Kulturkampf/May Laws, 51

Labouchère, Henry, 107, 204n33
Laboulaye, Antoine, 105, 108, 110
Lakatos, Imre, 13, 188n3
Lamsdorff, Vladimir, 128, 208n120
Langer, William L., 205n46
Lansdowne, William, 120, 122, 124, 126
Lascelles, Francis, 130
Launay, Edoardo de, 80, 81, 85, 86
Leagues of the Three Emperors, 39–64;
and alliance paradox, 171; cohesion, 48–
49, 166, 167(tab.); commitment levels,
167(tab.); formation, 39–42; monarchical
conservatism, 41, 50, 52, 57, 60, 61, 63;
motives for, 44–47, 45(tab.), 57(tab.),
58–60, 165; as peacetime alliances, 83;

and realism, 66; reconstitution of, 59,
65, 66, 72, 77, 101, 199n56; as tethering
alliance, 27, 41–42; threat levels, 41,
47(tab.), 59(tab.), 166, 167(tab.). *See also*
Dreikaiserbund; Dreikaiserbund II
Lewis (king of Bavaria), 71
liberalism: and alliance endurance, 170–71;
in alliance theory, 11, 16, 25–26; Triple
Alliance, 95
Liska, George, 35, 192n57
Lloyd George, David, 154–55
London Conference, 157
Loos, Battle of, 152
Lorraine. *See* Alsace and Lorraine
Ludendorff, Erich, 141–42, 145
Lutsk, 140

Macedonia, 116
Macedonian crisis, 88–89
Malacca, 124
Marne, the, 140, 159
Massowah, 86, 92
May Laws/Kulturkampf, 51
mediation, 16, 58–59
Mexico, 141
Michon, Georges, 206n64
military alliances: capability aggregation, 15;
institutionalism, 16; NATO as, 25; purposes of, 64, 136, 175; security, 19; theories of, 1, 5, 8, 13; transparency in, 19
Military Convention, 112–18
military strategy: Austria/Austria-Hungary,
77, 78, 81, 84, 143–46, 199n74, 211n37;
Central Powers, 143–46, 211n37; France,
112, 134, 154–57, 200n104; Franco-
Russian Alliance as, 118; Germany, 78,
104, 111–12, 131, 141, 143–46, 148, 155,
211n37; Great Britain, 100, 119–21, 134,
154–58; Russia, 69–70, 73, 112, 134,
151–52, 154–56; Triple Entente as, 154–
57; World War I, 143–46, 154–57,
211n37
Miliukov, Paul, 160–61
Mitteleuropa, 139, 147, 158
Mohrenheim, Arthur, Baron von, 54–55,
105
Moltke, Helmuth von ("The Elder"), 70,
78, 104, 142, 143, 198n51
Moltke, Helmuth von ("The Younger"),
144, 145
monarchical conservatism: Dual Alliance,

67, 75; Leagues of the Three Emperors, 50, 52, 57, 60, 61, 63; Triple Alliance, 95–96

Montenegro, 84, 140, 149

Morgenthau, Hans, 191n38

Morocco, 112, 113, 116, 123, 131, 133, 134

motivations for alliances: in alliance theory, 1–4, 7–9, 12–13, 27–28, 29(tab.); and commitment levels, 167(tab.), 168; during wartime, 168; NATO, 167; threat levels, 165–66

motivations for alliances, case studies: Anglo-Russian Convention (1907), 130(tab.); Dual Alliance, 74(tab.), 165; Entente Cordiale, 28, 99, 124(tab.); Franco-Russian Alliance, 111(tab.); Leagues of the Three Emperors, 45(tab.), 46, 47, 57(tab.), 58, 59–60; Triple Alliance, 87(tab.), 100, 165

NATO. *See* North Atlantic Treaty Organization

NATO-Russia Council, 23, 173

Naval Convention, 112

"naval scare" (1908), 131

Nazi-Soviet Pact (1939), 21

Neilson, Keith, 120

Nicholas II (tsar), 113, 121, 127–28, 206n64

Nicholson, Arthur, 127, 129–30, 208n116, 209n128

Niou, Emerson M. S., 203n22

Nivelle, Robert, 157

North Africa, 87–88, 91

North Atlantic Treaty Organization (NATO): cohesion, 174; commitment levels, 167; endurance of, 6, 16–17, 26, 170–73; Founding Act, 23, 173; internal threat levels, 172–73, 174; as liberal alliance, 11; membership in, 1, 6, 187n2; NATO-Russia Council, 23, 173; nature of, 25; Partnership for Peace program, 23, 27, 173; purpose of, 13, 167, 172–73; and Russia, 173–74; as tethering alliance, 22; transparency within, 27, 172–73

O'Beirne, Hugh James, 130

Obroutcheff, General, 204–5n24

O'Leary, James, 24

Ordeshook, Peter C., 203n22

Ottoman Empire, 48–49, 66, 67, 147, 155, 159

pan-Slavism, 41, 45, 48, 60, 63, 72, 74–75, 196n52

Partnership for Peace program (NATO), 23, 27

Passchendaele, 153

peace offers: during World War I, 148–50, 158, 159–62, 166; from Central Powers, 149–50, 159; to Triple Entente, 159–62

peacetime alliances, 168–70; behavior of, 174; cohesion factors, 6–7, 25, 31–33, 142–43, 150, 174, 192n56; commitment levels, 167(tab.); domestic vs. international policies, 164, 169; Dual Alliance and Triple Alliance, 65; Leagues of the Three Emperors, 83; and liberalism, 11; Triple Alliance, 83. *See also* alliances; wartime alliances

Persia, 105

Petrograd Conference, 153

Poincaré, Raymond, 149

Poland, 146–47, 161

Potsdam Agreement, 133, 210n142

power capability distribution, 179–85(tabs.); in alliance theory, 13–15, 33–34, 189n8; Austria/Austria-Hungary, 45, 179–85(tabs.), 195n54, 197n35, 200n104, 205n46, 209n134, 212–13n77; France, 45, 179–85(tabs.), 195n54, 197n35, 200n104, 205n46, 209n134, 212–13n77; Germany, 45, 179–85(tabs.), 195n54, 197n35, 200n104, 205n46, 209n134, 212–13n77; Great Britain, 179–85(tabs.), 195n54, 197n35, 200n104, 205n46, 209n134, 212–13n77; Italy, 45, 179–85(tabs.), 197n35, 200n104, 205n46, 209n134; Russia, 41, 45, 179–85(tabs.), 196n54, 197n35, 200n104, 205n46, 209n134, 212–13n77; United States, 173

Prete, Roy A., 214n131

promise levels in alliances, 35, 47, 60, 193n67

Provisional Government (Russia), 160–61

Prussia/East Prussia, 40, 142, 151, 155, 171–72; Franco-Prussian War, 40, 46, 88

Quadruple Alliance (1814), 171–72

Quintuple Alliance (1818), 172

railway construction, 61, 69

rationalism, 15–16

Ravenal, Earl, 24

realism: and alliance endurance, 170–71; alliance theory of, 11, 13–16; and cohesion, 25–26; Dual Alliance, 98; Leagues of the Three Emperors, 66

Reinsurance Treaty, 58, 62, 66, 77, 101–5, 117, 196nn2,3, 198nn47,51,52; terms of, 104, 202n3

Reuss, Prince Henry VII, 70, 73, 85, 86

revolutionary socialism, 194n28

Ribot, Alexandre, 105, 107, 110, 204–5nn24,38

Richardson, Louise, 24

Risse-Kappen, Thomas, 25

Ritter, Gerhard, 211n37

Robertson, William, 153–54

Romania, 61, 104, 141, 142, 147

Rudini, Antonio di, 80, 81, 84, 107

Runciman, Walter, 159

Russia: Anglo-Russian relations, 105–6, 120–26, 203nn16,17, 207nn95,105; Austro-Russian relations, 102–3, 133; Baltic Fleet, 124, 127; border data, 186(tab.); casualties (World War I), 152, 155; Congress of Berlin, 47, 49–50, 54, 66–68, 80; Macedonian crisis, 88–89; Military Convention, 112–18; military strategy, 69–70, 73, 112, 134, 151–52, 154–56; and NATO, 173–74; Naval Convention, 112; power capabilities, 41, 45, 179–85(tabs.), 195n54, 197n35, 200n104, 205n46, 209n134, 212–13n77; Provisional Government, 160–61; Reinsurance Treaty, 58, 62, 66, 77, 101, 111, 117, 196nn2,3, 198nn47,51,52; Russo-German relations, 66–69, 77, 102–5, 111, 114, 117, 127–29, 161, 198nn47,51, 203–4n24, 208n121, 209nn122,131; Schönbrunn Convention, 47; as threat, 74, 76; threats to, 101–2, 103; trade routes, 45–46; Treaty of Björkö, 128; Treaty of San Stefano, 49, 62, 66, 67; World War I, 152–53, 160–62, 169, 211n37. *See also* Union of Soviet Socialist Republics

Russia, alliance participation: Anglo-Russian Convention, 100, 124–31, 130(tab.), 207n105; Dreikaiserbund, 22, 37(tab.), 41–43, 45(tab.), 47(tab.), 48–49; Dreikaiserbund II, 53–55, 57(tab.), 58, 59(tab.); Franco-Russian Alliance, 17, 26, 98, 102–6, 111(tab.), 114(tab.), 165, 196nn1,3;

Leagues of the Three Emperors, 27, 165; Triple Entente, 28, 118, 132(tab.), 165

Russian Revolution (1905), 112, 127–28

Russian Revolution (1917), 106, 138, 141, 145, 153, 161–63

Russo-Japanese War, 22, 100, 113, 119, 123–26, 127, 131

Russo-Turkish War, 48–49, 66, 67

Saburov, Peter Alexandrovitch, 41, 50–51, 54, 55, 58, 68, 69–71

Salandra, Antonio, 90

Salisbury, Robert Cecil, Marquis of, 108, 120

Salvatorelli, Luigi, 81

Sangiuliano, Antonio, Marquis di, 82

Sazonov, Serge, 118

Schlieffen, Alfred von, 143–44

Schlieffen Plan, 137, 140, 144

Schmitt, Bernadotte E., 198n41

Schönbrunn Convention, 47

Schroeder, Paul, 3, 4, 16–17

Schuman Plan, 21

Schweinitz, Lothal von, 56, 68, 69

Schweller, Randall, 16, 190nn16,32, 191n35, 212n73

security, maximizing of, 14, 189nn8,15

security communities, 25

security dilemma, 7, 188n7

Serbia: and Austria, 49, 55, 67, 133; Dreikaiserbund II, 55, 61, 62; Franco-Russian Alliance, 112; Franz Ferdinand assassination, 137; and Russia, 104; Triple Alliance, 84; World War I, 140, 145, 149, 161

Seven Weeks' War, 40

Shuvalov, Paul, 56, 71–72, 102–5, 202n2

Simpson, J. Y., 194n28

Singer, J. David, 34

Sino Soviet Treaty of Friendship, Alliance, and Mutual Assistance (1950), 172

Siverson, Randolph, 34

Sixte, Prince of Bourbon-Parma, 149

Sixtus Affair, 139, 149–50

Slavic nationalism, 41, 45, 48, 60, 63, 72, 74–75, 196n52

Small, Melvin, 34

Snyder, Glenn, 15–16, 24, 189n14

socialism, 194n28

Somme, the, 141, 156

Sonnino, Sidney, 80, 199n59

Spring Rice, Cecil, 123, 125
Spuller, Eugene, 105
Stalin, Josef, 21
Starr, Harvey, 34
submarine warfare, 141
Sullivan, John D., 24
Szögyény-Marich, Ladislas, 89

Taylor, A. J. P., 198*n*51, 207*nn*95,105
tethering/tethering alliances: alliance
  paradox, 171; in alliance theory, 4, 12,
  20(fig.), 21–24, 30, 187*n*2, 189*n*14; cohesion, 5, 30, 166, 168; commitment levels,
  29(tab.), 167, 168; formation, 19, 21–24,
  30; historical examples, 171–72; motivations for, 28, 29(tab.), 165, 208*n*121;
  threat levels, 172; transparency within,
  21–23, 172–73
tethering/tethering alliances, case studies:
  Anglo-Russian Convention, 100, 105–
  6, 120–27, 129, 130(tab.), 203*nn*16,17,
  207*nn*95,105; Dreikaiserbund, 27, 40–43,
  45(tab.); Dreikaiserbund II, 54–55, 57,
  61; Entente Cordiale, 100, 121–23,
  124(tab.); Leagues of the Three Emperors, 27, 40–43, 45(tab.); Triple Alliance,
  81–86, 87(tab.), 90, 101; Triple Entente,
  100, 130, 159, 163
third parties to alliances, 22, 191–
  92*nn*39,40,42, 208*n*121
Third World Alliance, 189*n*15
threat levels: in alliance theory, 29–30, 33–
  34, 170–71; behavior of alliances, 12–13,
  20(fig.), 26(tab.), 29(tab.), 64; cohesion of
  alliances, 5–7, 24–27, 97(tab.), 114–17,
  131–33, 135(tab.), 150–53, 160–64,
  166–68, 212*n*73, 213*n*86; commitment
  levels, 29(tab.), 166, 167(tab.); curvilin-
  earity of, 4, 12, 19, 20(fig.), 64, 96–98,
  136, 166; formation of alliances, 3–5,
  18–19, 20(fig.), 22–24, 104, 117, 122,
  136, 165–66, 208*n*121; peacetime alliances, 96–97; tethering alliances, 172;
  wartime alliances, 31–33. *See also* external
  threats; internal threats
threat levels, case studies: Central Powers,
  139–42, 150–51, 164, 167(tab.), 212*n*73;
  Dreikaiserbund, 44–46, 47(tab.); Dreikaiserbund II, 57–59, 62, 63(tab.); Dual
  Alliance, 74–75, 76(tab.), 97(tab.), 98,
  167(tab.); Franco-Russian Alliance, 111–

13, 114(tab.), 117, 135(tab.), 167(tab.);
  Leagues of the Three Emperors, 41,
  47(tab.), 59(tab.), 166, 167(tab.); Triple
  Alliance, 80, 81, 87–90, 91(tab.), 94,
  97(tab.), 98, 167(tab.); Triple Entente,
  100, 131, 132(tab.), 135(tab.), 151–52,
  163, 164, 167(tab.)
Three Emperors' Leagues. *See* Leagues of
  the Three Emperors
Tirpitz, Alfred von, 131
Tittoni, Tomaso, 81, 82
trade routes, 45–46, 49, 58
transparency: in alliance theory, 4, 16, 19;
  and institutionalism, 27, 170; in NATO,
  27, 172–73; in tethering alliances, 21–23,
  172–73
Treaty of Berlin, 60, 93, 133
Treaty of Björkö, 128
Treaty of London, 147, 160, 168
Treaty of Nonaggression, 172
Treaty of Prague, 40, 46
Treaty of San Stefano, 49, 62, 66, 67
Trento and Trieste, 41, 79–80, 88, 94, 147.
  See also Italy
Triple Alliance, 79–97; and alliance paradox, 171; as balancing alliance, 85,
  87(tab.), 90; cohesion, 98, 166, 167(tab.);
  commitment levels, 167(tab.); formation
  of, 79–87, 97; and Great Britain, 105,
  108–10, 111, 118–21; and institutionalism, 17, 91, 92; irredentist movement,
  94–95; monarchical conservatism, 95–
  96; motives for, 87(tab.), 100, 165; as
  peacetime alliance, 65, 83, 96; power capabilities within, 200*n*104; promise levels,
  193*n*67; terms of, 91–93; as tethering alliance, 81–86, 87(tab.), 90, 101; as threat,
  100, 101, 105–7, 111–13, 117; threat levels, 41–42, 80–81, 87–90, 91(tab.), 94,
  97(tab.), 98, 166, 167(tab.); Triple Entente as threat to, 101; weaknesses of, 96;
  World War I, 97. *See also* Central Powers
Triple Entente, 118–35, 151–63; as balancing alliance, 100, 130, 163, 164; casualty
  figures (World War I), 152; cohesion, 7,
  100, 132–34, 135(tab.), 136, 152–62,
  163, 166, 167(tab.), 169, 213*n*86; commitment levels, 167(tab.); as conflict management alliance, 118, 119, 135; formation of, 96, 99–130; and Great Britain,
  119; and institutionalism, 17, 208*n*121;

military strategy, 154–57; motives for, 28, 58, 99, 100–101, 165; peace offers to, 159–62; power capabilities within, 162–63, 209n134; and Russian Revolution, 163; as tethering alliance, 100, 130, 163, 169, 171; as threat, 75, 78, 94, 100; threat levels, 100, 131, 132(tab.), 135(tab.), 151–52, 163, 164, 166, 167(tab.), 168; war aims, 157–59, 214n131; weaknesses of, 162; World War I, 134, 138, 148, 152–53. *See also* Anglo-Russian Convention; Entente Cordiale; Franco-Russian Alliance
Triplice. *See* Triple Alliance
Tripoli / Tripolitania, 89–90, 92
Tunis, 87–88
Tunisia, 80, 92
Turkey: Franco-Russian Alliance, 112; Macedonian crisis, 88–89; NATO membership, 1, 16, 187n2; Russo-Turkish War, 48–49, 66, 67; World War I, 145, 155, 156

U-boat campaign, 141, 148, 153
Union of Soviet Socialist Republics (USSR), 21, 172. *See also* Russia
United Kingdom. *See* Great Britain
United Nations, 17
United States, 22, 24, 141, 148, 173

Verdun, 141, 145, 153, 156, 211n37
Verdy du Vernois, Julius von, 104
Vossiche Zeitung, 82

Waddington, William Henry, 107–8, 204n33
Waldersee, Alfred, 143
Waller, Bruce, 199n56
Walt, Stephen, 3, 18, 24, 189n15, 190n32, 191nn34,35

Waltz, Kenneth N., 14–15, 188n7, 189n8
war councils, 156
wars: alliance behavior during, 5–7, 139–42, 150–54, 161–64, 166–67, 210n20, 212n73; alliance cohesion during, 31–33, 37, 138, 169. *See also* wartime alliances
Warsaw Pact, 170
wartime alliances, 168–70; behavior of, 174; cohesion of, 6–7, 31–33, 37, 142–43, 150–54, 161–62, 169, 192n56, 212n73, 213n86; commitment levels in, 167(tab.); domestic vs. international policies, 164, 169; motives for, 168; and realism, 11. *See also* alliances; peacetime alliances
Wilhelm I (kaiser), 42, 72, 76, 89, 103, 197n27
Wilhelm II (kaiser), 103–4, 121, 128, 137
Witte, Sergei, 128
World War I: alliance behavior, 6–7, 191n40; battles of, 140–41, 145, 152–53, 155–56; casualties, 140, 152, 155; Central Powers, 139–51; Dual Alliance, 66; Franco-Russian Alliance, 117; Italian strategy, 90, 95; military strategy, 143–46, 154–57, 211n37; Russian strategy, 151–52; separate peace offers, 148–50, 158–62, 166, 169; Triple Alliance, 97; Triple Entente, 134, 148, 152–53; U-boat campaign, 148; war aims, 146–49, 157–59, 163, 168–69, 211–12n47, 214n131, 215n6
World War II, 6, 11, 26

Ypres, 140

Zimmerman telegram, 141